LLEWELLYN'S
2007
Magical Almanac

Featuring

*Elizabeth Barrette, Chandra Moira Beal, Boudica,
Dallas Jennifer Cobb, Sorita D'Este, Ellen Dugan, Emely Flak,
Sybil Fogg, Lily Gardner, Elizabeth Genco, Magenta Griffith,
ilspeth, James Kambos, Corrine Kenner, Brenna Lyons,
Kristin Madden, Edain McCoy, Jennifer McDevitt,
Mickie Mueller, Muse, Sharynne NicMhacha, Olivia O'Meir,
Paniteowl, Diana Rajchel, Laurel Reufner, Cerridwen Iris
Shea, Lynn Smythe, K. D. Spitzer, and Tammy Sullivan*

Llewellyn's 2007 Magical Almanac

ISBN 0-7387-0327-3. Copyright © 2006 by Llewellyn. All rights reserved. Printed in the United States. Llewellyn is a registered trademark of Llewellyn Worldwide, Ltd.

Editor/Designer: K. M. Brielmaier

Cover Illustration: © Grizelda Holderness/Illustration LTD.

Calendar Pages Design: Andrea Neff and Michael Fallon

Calendar Pages Illustrations: © Fiona King

Interior Illustrations © Melissa Gay, pages 15, 23, 26, 47, 111, 143, 171, 239, 266, 282, 284, 339, 357; © Stephen Snider, pages 18, 93, 121, 140, 156, 163, 259, 261, 317; © David Wallace, pages 34, 80, 166, 276, 289, 312, 315; © Amy Patacchiola, pages 41, 66, 106, 124, 249, 252, 270, 329, 341, 342; © Sybill Fogg and Llewellyn Art Department, pages 59, 60, 61, 62

Clip Art Illustrations: Dover Publications

Special thanks to Amber Wolfe for the use of daily color and incense correspondences. For more detailed information, please see *Personal Alchemy* by Amber Wolfe.

You can order Llewellyn annuals and books from *New Worlds,* Llewellyn's magazine catalog. To request a free copy of the catalog, call toll-free 1-877-NEWWRLD, or visit our website at www.llewellyn.com.

Astrological calculations are performed by the Kepler 6 astrology software program, specially created for Llewellyn Publications and used with the kind permission of Cosmic Patterns Software, Inc., www.AstroSoftware.com.

Llewellyn Worldwide
Dept. 0-7387-0327-3
2143 Wooddale Drive
Woodbury, MN 55125

About the Authors

ELIZABETH BARRETTE serves as the managing editor of *PanGaia*. She has been involved with the Pagan community for more than seventeen years, and has done much networking with Pagans in her area, including coffeehouse meetings and open sabbats. Her other writing fields include speculative fiction and gender studies. She lives in central Illinois and enjoys herbal landscaping and gardening for wildlife.

CHANDRA MOIRA BEAL is a freelance writer currently living in England. Chandra is Sanskrit for "the Moon." She has written three books and published hundreds of articles, all inspired by her day-to-day life and adventures. She has been writing for Llewellyn since 1998. Chandra is also a massage therapist. To learn more, visit www.beal-net.com/laluna.

BOUDICA is reviews editor and co-owner of the *Wiccan/Pagan Times* and owner of the *Zodiac Bistro*, two online publications. She is a teacher with CroneSpeak, teaching both on and off the Internet, and a guest speaker at many festivals and gatherings. A former New Yorker, she now resides with her husband in Ohio.

DALLAS JENNIFER COBB lives in an enchanted waterfront village. She's freed up resources for what she loves: family, gardens, fitness, and fabulous food. She's forever scheming novel ways to pay the bills when she's not running country roads or wandering the beach. Her essays are in the recent Seal Press anthologies *Three Ring Circus* and *Far From Home*. Her video documentary *Disparate Places* appeared on TV Ontario's *Planet Parent*. She is a regular contributor to Llewellyn's almanacs.

SORITA D'ESTE is an author, Witch, and priestess. She is the co-author of *Circle of Fire* and *The Guises of the Morrígan* and is a regular contributor to many MBS publications. She lives and works in London.

ELLEN DUGAN, the "Garden Witch," is a psychic-clairvoyant and has been a practicing Witch for twenty years. Ellen is a master gardener and teaches classes on flower folklore and gardening at a community college. She is the author of several Llewellyn books, including *Garden Witchery, Elements of Witchcraft, 7 Days of Magic, Cottage Witchery, Autumn Equinox, The Enchanted Cat, Herb Magic for Beginners,* and *Natural Witchery.* Ellen wholeheartedly encourages folks to personalize their spellcraft and to go outside and get their hands dirty, so they can discover the wonder and magic of the natural world. Ellen and her family live in Missouri.

ELIZABETH GENCO is a systems engineer, fiddle player, tarot enthusiast, writer, and Witch—though not necessarily in that order. She divides her time between New York and Los Angeles.

EMELY FLAK is a practicing solitary Witch from Daylesford, Australia. When she is not writing, she is at her "day job" as a learning and development professional. Recently, this busy mother of two and partner of one completed training to be a civil celebrant. Much of her work is dedicated to embracing the ancient wisdom of Wicca for personal empowerment, particularly in the competitive work environment.

SYBIL FOGG has been a Wiccan practitioner for eighteen years, first as a solitary and later with her four children and partner, a group she considers her coven. She is a fiction writer, freelancer, bellydancer, and adjunct faculty member at area colleges. She holds a BA in English and an MFA in Creative Writing and is currently working on a novel of autobiographical fiction.

LILY GARDNER continues to pursue and write about her lifelong passion of folklore and mythology. She has been a practicing Witch for thirteen years. In addition to her work in folklore, she writes short stories and is working on her first mystery novel. Lily lives with her husband, her son's cat, and two spoiled Corgis in the rainy but magnificent city of Portland, Oregon.

MAGENTA GRIFFITH has been a Witch for nearly thirty years, and is a founding member of the coven Prodea, which has been celebrating rituals since 1980. She has been a member of the Covenant of the Goddess, the Covenant of Unitarian Universalist Pagans, Church of All Worlds, and several other organizations. She presents workshops and classes at a variety of festivals and gatherings around the Midwest. She spends her spare time reading, cooking, and petting her cat.

ILSPETH, a solitary eclectic Witch, learned the "old timer's" ways of working with the land from her father, who is a lifelong gardener. She strives to infuse her writing with spiritual tolerance, love, and respect.

JAMES KAMBOS is a folk artist and writer who has had a lifelong interest in folk magic traditions. He holds a degree in history and is a regular contributor to Llewellyn annuals. He lives in the beautiful hill country of southern Ohio.

CORRINE KENNER specializes in bringing metaphysical subjects down to Earth. She is the author of Llewellyn's *Tall Dark Stranger*, a handbook on using tarot cards for romance, and *Tarot Journaling*, a guide to the art of keeping a tarot diary. She wrote *The Epicurean Tarot*, the innovative "recipe card" tarot deck published by U.S. Games Systems, Inc. Corrine is also the author of *Crystals for Beginners*, an introduction to the use of crystals in everyday

life. Corrine is the vice president and communications director for Cadgraphics Incorporated, a company that specializes in creating software for fire alarm and security systems. Visit her website at www.corrinekenner.com.

BRENNA LYONS is an award-winning bestselling novelist and poet. With a BS in accounting and computer programming, it's a strange irony that she has become best known for her first love, writing. She can be reached via her site at www.brennalyons.com.

KRISTIN MADDEN is a Druid and tutor in the Order of Bards, Ovates, and Druids. Dean of the Ardantane School of Shamanic Studies, Kristin is a bestselling author of several books on parenting, shamanism, and paganism, including *The Book of Shamanic Healing* and *Dancing the Goddess Incarnate* (with Dorothy Morrison). Kristin and her work have appeared in print and on radio and television throughout North America and Europe. She travels extensively to speak and play at pagan gatherings across the United States. Kristin is also a homeschooling mom, wildlife rehabilitator, environmental educator, and raptor trainer. She and her family share their home with an ever-changing menagerie of domestic and wild animals.

EDAIN MCCOY has been in the Craft since 1981 and has been researching alternative spiritualities since her teens. Areas of special interest are Celtic, Appalachian, Curanderismo, Eclectic Wicca, Jewitchery, and Irish Witta. She is listed in the reference guides *Contemporary Authors, Who's Who Among American Women,* and *Who's Who in America.* Articles written by her have appeared in *FATE, Circle, Enlightenments,* and similar periodicals.

JENNIFER MCDEVITT has been a student of ancient beliefs for nearly a decade and enjoys the balance and harmony they bring to her life.

MICKIE MUELLER is a Pagan artist and writer. She is also a Reiki teacher and Pagan minister. Her art has appeared in publications worldwide as well as in *The Well Worn Path* by Raven Grimassi and Stephanie Taylor. Visit her website at www.mickiemuellerart.com

MUSE has been studying alternative religions, spiritual practices, and magic since an early age, and has always had a fascination with the unseen world. Among many other things, she is an avid traveler, aspiring writer, graduate student, and professional web merchandising consultant. She holds a degree in European History, and hopes to see every bit of the world her professors taught her about. Believe it or not, she still finds time to do yoga and read the latest *Harry Potter*.

SHARYNNE NICMHACHA is a Canadian writer, teacher, and bard of Scottish and Irish ancestry, a direct descendant of Clan MacLeod, long recorded in oral tradition to have connections with (and blood of) the Sidhe or Fairy Folk. She has studied Celtic languages and mythology through Harvard University, and has presented work at the University of Edinburgh, University College Cork, and the Omega Institute. Her spiritual tradition is drawn from her ancestral lineage, Celtic/Pictish Shamanism, Scottish witchcraft, Irish and Welsh wisdom texts, Celtic Re-Creationism, and the Avalonian Mysteries.

OLIVIA O'MEIR is a feminist Dianic Witch, priestess of the Goddess, and ordained reverend from the Philadelphia area. She is a craftswoman, freelance writer, tarot counselor, and Sister in the Coven of the Five Sisters. Olivia is a member of many women's spirituality groups, including the local UU Church's Womyn & Religion group, The Fellowship of Isis, and RCG-I. Her studies focus on the Goddess, geology, mythology, and Avalon.

PANITEOWL lives in the foothills of the Appalachians in northeast Pennsylvania, where she and her husband are in the process of developing a private retreat for spiritual awareness. She is co-coordinator of two annual events in Virginia known as the Gathering of the Tribes. She is founder and elder high priestess of the Mystic Wicca tradition.

DIANA RAJCHEL is a third-degree Wiccan priestess with a bent for intelligent cartoons and good food. She lives in Minneapolis, surrounded by her friends and Pagan family. Someday she hopes to learn the name of the local city spirit.

LAUREL REUFNER has been a solitary Pagan for over a decade. She is active in the local CUUPS chapter, Circle of Gaia Dreaming, and is often attracted to bright and shiny ideas. Southeastern Ohio has always been home, where she currently lives in lovely Athens County with her wonderful husband and two adorable heathens, er, daughters.

CERRIDWEN IRIS SHEA is a writer, teacher, and tarot reader who loves ice hockey and horse racing. Visit her redesigned website at: www.cerridwenscottage.com; visit her blog Kemmryk, which discusses working with tarot and oracles at: tarotkemmryk.blogspot. com. She also wrote the magical realism serial Angel Hunt.

LYNN SMYTHE is a freelance writer living in southern Florida with her husband, son, and daughter. She is the founder and manager of the online community Herb Witch. She also offers a variety of magical writing tools and supplies for sale on her website the Magical Scriptorium, located at www.magicalscriptorium.com.

K. D. SPITZER is a Witchy writer living in coastal New Hampshire. She walks a labyrinth every chance she gets, taking problems to its center and walking out with a peaceful heart. Sometimes she casts a spell in the heart of the labyrinth.

TAMMY SULLIVAN is a full time writer and solitary Witch who writes from her home in the foothills of the Great Smokey Mountains. She is the author of *Pagan Anger Magic: Positive Transformations from Negative Energies*, and *Elemental Witch*. Her work has appeared in the Llewellyn almanacs and *Circle Magazine*.

Table of Contents

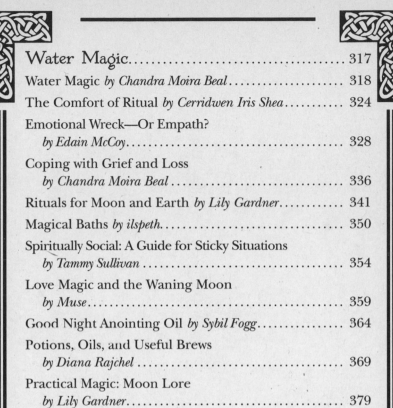

Earth Magic

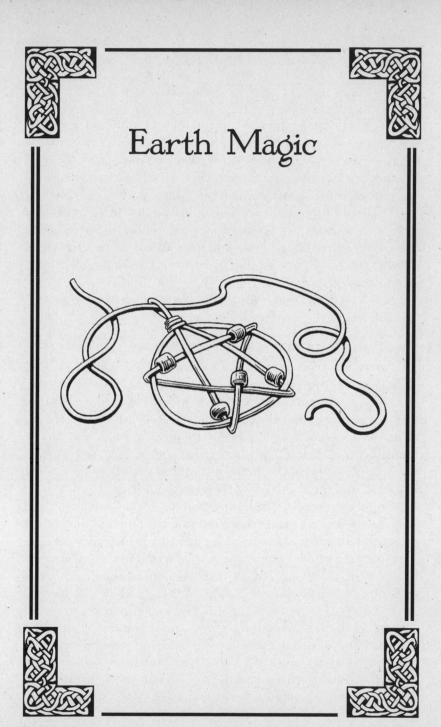

Earth Magic

by Ellen Dugan

Stones, crystals, minerals, and semi-precious and precious gems are gifts from the element of earth. What better way to tap into "earth magic" than by rediscovering their awesome powers and magical qualities? Stones, crystals, and gems are magical batteries of sorts, as they hold and focus the Earth's energies.

There are three important qualities needed for working this type of earth magic: the goal, or magical intention; the desire to create a positive change (get your affirmative emotions involved so your spell will pack a punch); and the knowledge and basic skill to be able to perform the spell.

So let's "dig in" to this topic, and celebrate the beauty, power, and mystery of the treasures of the earth.

Energies of the Stones

There are two types of energies inherent in crystals, gems, and stones: projective energies and receptive energies. Projective energies are sometimes described as electric, hot, day, physical, bright, summer, masculine, and active. Receptive energies are often described as magnetic, cold, night, spiritual, dark, winter, feminine, and inert. It is important to know that one type of energy is not superior to the other, for they each have their place in magic, and they both bring balance to our lives.

Projective stone energies are able to get in touch with the conscious mind. They are associated with the Sun and the planets Mercury and Mars. They are also linked to the masculine elements of air and fire. These stones tend to fall in the color range of red, orange, yellow, gold, clear, and sometimes black. They can be utilized to fight disease, and can attract good luck. Projective stones will bring vitality and health, and can impart courage and success to their bearers. These projective stones are powerful tools to fight off negativity, boost your physical energy levels, and grant you a strong sense of grit and determination. A few projective stones to try for these purposes are amber, banded and brown agates, carnelian, citrine, garnet, hematite, onyx, quartz crystal points, red agate, red jasper, tiger's eye, topaz, and zircon.

Receptive stones have the opposite energies. These are associated with the Moon and the planets Venus, Saturn, Jupiter, and Neptune. They are associated with the feminine elements of earth and water, and they are often cooler colors such as green, blue, purple, gray, silver, pink, and black. These receptive stones are wonderful tools for soothing and calming situations and people. They promote grounding, may assist in meditation, and can help folks search within to find the answers they seek. Receptive stones and crystals can also promote spirituality and wisdom as they encourage peace and psychic abilities. A few receptive crystals and stones to work with would be amethyst, azurite, blue and green agates, chalcedony, green jasper, lapis lazuli, malachite, moonstone, opal, peridot, rose quartz, sapphire, tourmaline (black, blue, green, pink) and turquoise.

Stones, Colors, and Magical Meanings

Just like in candle magic, crystals and stones may be grouped together by their colors. Here is a straightforward listing below for you to peruse and to work your earth magic with.

Red stones and crystals are definitely projective. Typically related to the planet Mars and the element of fire, they are forceful powers. Red stones such as carnelian promote courage and bravery, while red jasper promotes valor and banishes fatigue. Red crystals and gems also give the body a burst of energy, for both athletic prowess and sex. Red stones may be incorporated into healing rituals and spells. Try them for drawing out the heat of skin irritations or minor burns.

Orange crystals and stones are thought to be a gentler version of red stones. They are also projective and associated with the Sun, such as the orange-colored stone citrine, which can grant you a positive outlook on life. These sunny stones and crystals are perfect for shedding "some light on a subject" or for a little creative illumination. Orange stones are linked to personal power. They can boost your self-confidence and self-esteem. This is a successful color—work with it to pump up the volume on your own vitality, creativity, and energy.

Yellow gemstones and crystals are projective. These will fall under the influence of the Sun and the planet Mercury and the element of air. And what a surprise—they are worked into magics for communication, visualization, and perception. These are the stones to work with when you need to get the old brain kicked into high gear. If you need help expressing yourself, whether it's in public speaking or writing, work with yellow stones and crystals. These babies will make you more eloquent, and your thoughts will flow more freely.

Green stones, gems, and crystals reflect the colors of life, nature, and fruitfulness. Green is a receptive color and may be worked into spells for healing, gardening, grounding, good luck, and prosperity. A mystical green crystal to try is malachite. This stone encourages success, draws cash, and can even protect its bearer from danger. As you'd expect, this color stone is tied to the element of earth.

Blue gems and stones are receptive and often linked to the element of water and the planet Neptune. These crystals promote peace and soothing emotions. They can be used to promote a good night's sleep and may keep away bad dreams. A good blue stone to try is the blue lace agate, which has all of the qualities listed above. As blue is a healing color, blue stones are often incorporated into healing rituals, charms, and spells.

Purple crystals are a receptive and spiritual stone. These gems and stones correspond with Jupiter and Neptune. Purple is the color of magic, royalty, and the gods, and purple or violet gemstones such as the amethyst promote spirituality, protection,

and peace. Purple stones can alleviate tension headaches and help reduce stress and anxiety. Displaying a cluster of amethyst crystal points makes negative energy dissipate and restores harmony to your home.

Pink stones and crystals are also receptive stones and bring warm, fuzzy feelings. They are linked to the planet Venus and are used to promote love, happiness, and friendships, and can soothe frayed nerves and tempers. Stones such as the rose quartz can help encourage relaxation of both the mind and the spirit. They also can help end a spat between a feuding couple by magnifying loving feelings and relieving anger. Given as a token between friends, pink stones can gently link one magical friend to another.

White stones and crystals fall in the receptive stone category and are governed by the Moon. These stones have the magical qualities of promoting safe travel, a good night's sleep, psychic abilities, intuition, and, of course, Moon magic. White stones such as the moonstone are traditional stones used to open up psychic receptors and to encourage empathy. The moonstone is a popular magical stone and is often worked into Goddess magic and rituals.

Black stones are also receptive—and sometimes projective. As the color black absorbs light, so too will a black stone absorb negativity, despair, and anger. These ebony-colored crystals and gems are ruled by the planet Saturn. Black stones are perfect for protection work, grounding, and removing negativity. Some black stones like jet can actually help you gain influence over obnoxious or difficult people. These stones are talismans for security, self-control, and power.

The Magic and Mythology of Precious Stones

So are we finished yet? Not by a long shot. Take a good look at your jewelry. What kinds of precious stones do you already own? Here is a list of some of the more popular gems and their magical associations. Also keep in mind that if the gems are set in gold, they hold the masculine properties of the Sun—properties like confidence, determination, success, wealth, and fame.

Diamond: A projective stone that is associated with the Sun and the element of fire. The magical properties of the diamond include mysticism, security, bravery, healing, and strength. It is surprising to note that the diamond has no links to love magic or to loving emotions (it's actually supposed to help end quarrels and arguments). Also of interest: the diamond is supposed to cure sexual problems or dysfunction. Use it to encourage feelings of courage, strength, and determination.

Ruby: This is a projective stone, associated with the element of fire and the planet Mars. The powers of the ruby may be worked into spells and charms for prosperity, protection, and happiness. Rubies are among the rarest of stones. According to folklore, the ruby was used to draw prosperity to its owner, protect him from all sorts of foes, both physical and spiritual, and specifically protect him from being wounded during battle. Gem lore tells us that if your ruby suddenly goes dark it is a warning of danger. Today, jewelry that features rubies in the design is worn to bring happiness, confidence, and prosperity. And wearing rubies is thought to draw other gemstones into your possession as well.

Emerald: The emerald is a receptive stone associated with the planet Venus and the element of earth. The emerald has links to the goddess Aphrodite/Venus as well as Isis and Ceres/Demeter. An emerald may be worked into spells and rituals for promoting love, guarding against memory loss, prosperity, protection, to increase business, and to give your psychic powers a boost. This stone needs to be close to the area you are working on. In other words, if you are working for love, it needs to be worn close to the heart, so try a pendant. For prosperity, try a ring and envision the money coming to your hands. For protection, it was traditionally tied around the arm—but I think a bracelet, ring, or even a pendant worn around the neck is a much more practical alternative. Real emeralds are one of the most expensive of gems, and if you are working magic with emerald jewelry make sure it is a real stone, and not one that was created in a lab.

Sapphire: The sapphire falls in the category of a receptive stone. It corresponds to the Moon and promotes, love, peace, prosperity, intuition, and magical powers. This gorgeous blue gem has been associated with the Greek god Apollo and was used to activate the psychic centers. The sapphire also makes an excellent love stone, and would be appropriate for a wedding ring, due to the belief that a sapphire guards love and promotes faithfulness and a loving relationship between the couple. According to folklore, the most powerful magicians and sorcerers wore jewelry set with sapphires.

Pearl: The pearl is also a receptive stone and—what a surprise—is linked to the element of water and the Moon. The pearl is associated with several deities, including Aphrodite/Venus, Diana, Isis, Lakshmi, and of course Neptune/Poseidon. Pearls work well in any sort of lunar enchantments. According to Middle Eastern customs, when a woman wears pearls she is ensuring a happy marriage, which is probably why they are so popular an accessory with brides.

Opal: The opal is considered both receptive and projective at the same time (owing to the rainbow of colors found within the stone). This gemstone is linked to all of the natural elements: earth, air, fire, water, and spirit. This gem is traditionally used to encourage astral projection and psychic abilities. Wearing opal jewelry encourages your feelings of confidence, as it is supposed to make your inner beauty shine forth. Opals are also excellent for prosperity spells, and black opals are good gemstones to work with to increase your personal power.

A Charm for Enchanting Jewelry

If you'd like to enchant your gem-studded necklaces, bracelets, and rings for magical purposes, try this jewelry charm. It covers all the bases for your precious stones. No matter what sort of gem stones you call your own, this magical charm will empower them. Happy casting!

> *Sparkling diamonds do bring power and success,*
> *Add rubies for happiness and all will be blessed.*
> *Luminous pearls used for love, joy, and fertility,*
> *With emeralds, past, present, and future you will see.*
> *The opal's rainbow hue for psychic abilities,*
> *Enjoy their receptive and projective qualities.*
> *Sapphires, magical stones of deepest blue,*
> *Aid and empower all charms and spells that I do.*
> *Now spin the spell about and enchant this jewel,*
> *Make it a potent, brilliant, magical tool.*

Making a Difference

By Laurel Reufner

It's good being part of the greater community. We really do want to help make the world a better place for not only our children but also the whole of humanity. We'd like to make connections to folks in our communities. However, many of us are also on squeaky tight budgets. The following charities are some I have stumbled across and feel are good ways to get involved with a minimal financial investment. Locks of Love might even save you some money, as you won't need to get a haircut for a while.

Locks of Love was officially incorporated as a non-profit in 1997. The founder, Madonna Coffman, began Locks of Love after her young daughter developed alopecia. While in her early 20s, Mrs. Coffman had experienced what it was like to suddenly have your hair begin falling out by the handfuls when she developed alopecia after a hepatitis vaccination series. Luckily she was able to recover. She states on the website that it was difficult to lose her own hair, but watching her daughter go through the same ordeal was extremely painful. She wanted to do something to help her daughter and other children like her. Locks of Love was born.

The organization provides prosthetics made from real hair to children over the age of six who are suffering long-term or permanent hair loss. Children under the age of six and those suffering short-term hair loss, such as cancer patients, receive synthetic hairpieces. Since 1997, Locks of Love has helped spread smiles on the faces of over one thousand children in the U.S. and Canada, one ponytail at a time.

How can you help Locks of Love? Donate your hair. Hair of ten or more inches is used to create the prosthetics children receive. Since most of their clients are girls, the longer your ponytail, the better. Also, there is a listing on their website of salons willing to not only handle the collection of your hair, but to also give you a free haircut in the process.

What if you want to help now, but your hair is too short? You can still donate hair that is shorter than a ten-inch ponytail. Locks of Love will sell your donation to further finance their program. They also appreciate financial donations or donations of stamps, coins, etc. All of the hairpieces that Locks of Love provides are bought at cost and then donated to the smiling recipients. To learn more about Locks of Love and their confidence-building organization, please visit their website at www.locksoflove.org.

One of the oldest and best children's charities out there is **Project Linus**. I'm going to let the contents on the website speak for the charity, as my words would fall far short of their own. "Project Linus is a 100% volunteer non-profit organization with a two-fold mission. First, it is our mission to provide love, a sense of security, warmth and comfort to children who are seriously ill, traumatized, or otherwise in need through the gifts of new, handmade blankets and afghans, lovingly created by volunteer 'blanketeers.' Second, it is our mission to provide a rewarding and fun service opportunity for interested individuals and groups in local communities, for the benefit of children." Find out more about them at their website, www.projectlinus.org.

The **Mother Bear Project** reaches out to children suffering from HIV/AIDS in developing countries by sending them a hand-knit stuffed bear. It sounds so simple, but it's nice to have something soft and cuddly to hold on to when the world around you is so scary. This one isn't entirely free, but the cost is extremely minimal. All bears knitted for Mother Earth Bears need to be made using the same pattern, which costs $3 to purchase and appears to be altered somewhat by

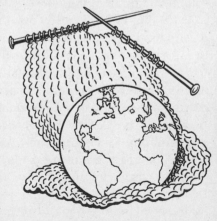

each knitter. The organization also asks that $3 shipping money be included with each bear so they can afford to ship it overseas. I'm not a knitter, but this almost tempts me to learn. Find out more at www.motherbearproject.org.

While on the subject of children, I'd like to mention **Artists Helping Children**. They started primarily as an organization creating murals for children's hospitals and such. They now offer murals to children with severe illnesses, and supply hospital children's units with art supplies and kits, cuddly stuffed animals, and handmade crocheted or knitted toys. This is an organization where even children can get involved. Check them out at www.artistshelpingchildren.org.

The **Memory Box Artist** program deals with death—specifically the death of a newborn who dies before leaving the hospital or who is stillborn. Often families have little to remind them of the life lost. Participants in the Memory Box Artist program create and decorate boxes that are distributed through hospitals to the parents of such babies, giving them something beautiful to remember their child by. If you are artsy or crafty, then I really urge you to check out their website for more information. You can find it at www.teraleigh.com/memoryboxes.

Girl Scouting isn't necessarily a charity, but they are a nonprofit organization aiming to change the world one girl at a time. If you have some free time, consider becoming a Girl Scout volunteer. Volunteering doesn't mean that you have to become a Girl Scout Troop Leader. Small bits of time here and there do add up: helping with mailings, volunteering at events or day camps, serving on a committee—they all make a difference.

Not many people know that the more than ninety-year-old ultimate girls' organization is pagan friendly. There was some debate a few years ago about doing away completely with the "serve God" part of the Girl Scout Promise. It was decided that a spiritual and religious background had long been part of Girl Scouting tradition. What they did was add a provision stating that a participant is free to acknowledge God/Goddess/Divinity as she feels moved to do so. By the time this is published, I will in all probability be gearing up for my fourth year as a Girl Scout Leader. It's an incredible thing in which to be involved. If you really want to make a difference, volunteer to be a leader in a low-income area or neighborhood. Your caring could open up a whole new world for the girls you become involved with. And guys can also become Girl Scouts, as long as they are legal adults.

While Girl Scouting isn't exactly free, there are opportunities for financial assistance. Also, you can receive financial help for your initial membership costs, especially if you are becoming a leader or co-leader for a troop. To find out more, look in your local phone book under "Girl Scouts," go to their website at www.girlscouts.org, or call (800) GSUSA 4 U [(800) 478-7248].

While there are many "click-to-donate" sites on the Internet, I've found Care2.org and The Hunger Site Network to be especially noteworthy.

The **Hunger Site Network** is one of the first legitimate click-to-donate sites. Click-to-donate sites are websites that ask commercial sponsors to donate a certain sum for every time a visitor clicks on a button on that site. The site forms a network of click-to-donate and purchase-to-donate web pages comprising the Hunger Site, the Breast Cancer Site, the Rainforest Site, the Animal Rescue Site, the Child Health Site, the Literacy Site, and the Ecology Fund.com. You can also find shopping sites: the GreaterGood.com and GearThatGives.com. You can find The Hunger Site Network at www.thehungersite.com

Care2 is an online community whose members can have an impact in the real world, make new friends, network, and sign online petitions for a wide variety of causes all at the click of a mouse. In the "Click-to-Donate" area, you can make a financial contribution from someone else's pocket to a variety of causes. The site's sponsors support breast cancer research and rainforest and primate protection. You can help sponsor an underprivileged child's food, education, and shelter. Like the big cats? There's a site for that as well. I really like Care2's site because I can keep track of how much I've contributed with my "Click-to-Donate" button. Care2 can be found at www.care2.com.

There are other click-to-donate sites out there, but these two are the ones I'm the most familiar with. Care2 has the look of a bulletin board, while The Hunger Site Network is a bit more commercial looking. Both are great sites to visit and take perhaps ten minutes of your time. Even if you spend some time visiting sponsor's sites, you can still finish your clicks in under half an hour.

Habitat for Humanity, even though it is faith-based, deserves a mention here as well. Habitat began as a small yet ambitious experiment in 1976 by Linda and Millard Fuller, who sought to put their faith into practice. At some point in 2005 they will have helped house over one million people worldwide in decent housing. And while that is all well and good, the reason I am including Habitat for Humanity, a Christian faith–based organization, in a Pagan-themed article is because the organization is Christian-rooted in the best sense of the word. They do not discriminate based on race, nationality, or religion. If you are an atheist and meet their qualifications for a home, then they will do their best to provide you with a home. There are also extra bonuses for volunteering with Habitat: not only do you feel good for helping someone own a good home, you get a great workout *and* you learn how to build that home. Furthermore, you become, through your actions, a bridge to those of other beliefs. We are a global community, and the more we learn about one another's beliefs the better we can communicate and get along.

To find out more about Habitat for Humanity, look in your local phone book or go to www.habitat.org.

So, those are the national or international organized groups that you might want to check out, but what if you want to contribute to a local organization? Well, Habitat and Girl Scouts are usually organized at the local level. Here is a quick rundown of other possible places to become involved within your local community.

Pet shelters can usually use volunteers. Check your local phone book or pet store, or call the local Humane Society officers for more information.

Become a Big Brother or Big Sister. Your time will make a difference in a child's life.

Food pantries can usually use help sorting and distributing food. Or consider organizing a food drive. More and more families need to rely upon food pantries to get through the month from paycheck to paycheck, yet donations seem to be dwindling in many areas.

Call an area school or the district's administrative offices to see if you can volunteer with them. Or try the local hospital, or a nursing or rest home. Some of those poor souls hardly ever have visitors.

If you are qualified, or want to become qualified, coach a kid's sports team.

If you don't like any of my ideas, or would just like to see what else is out there, here are some websites that would make excellent starting points:

Circle Sanctuary has a listing of Pagan groups located at www.circlesanctuary.org/liberty/pagancharitywork.html.

The International Pagan Pride group has information available at www.paganpride.org. There might be an event scheduled in your area. If not, maybe you could organize one.

If you are crafty and want to find a good place to donate your creations, start at Lion Brands Charity Connection site: www.lionbrand.com/charityConnection.html. Most of the listings are for crocheted and knitted items, but you might find what you're looking for there.

And when all else fails, pick a search engine and enter in the type of charity for which you're searching. Just, please, do something. Get involved. If we don't look out for each other, who will?

Take One Dead Chicken

by Paniteowl

There are a number of spells calling for "One Dead Chicken," and this is one of my favorites. The intent for this particular spell is to find true friendship, and perhaps even love.

Gather the woods of the fallen tree.
By oak, by ash, and soft pine three.
When the Sun is high in the noonday sky,
Light the sacred fire, and make it burn high.
Draw the sacred waters from the blessed well.
The source is our secret, you must never tell.
Gather your herbs in the dew of the morn,
*   cut with the boline, and seedless shorn.*
Dig the roots in the cool of the day.
Don't tarry, or go where the fairies play.
Clean the dead chicken of feathers and gore,
*   and place a pronouncement upon your front door.*
Scour your cauldron with salt and some renderings,
*   place it over your fire, and hear how the fat sings!*
Now place in the cauldron your chicken so tender.
Now turn it three times! This you must remember.
Now add the water you earlier toted, and
*   the following herbs, for the reasons so noted:*
Rosemary, for remembrance
Thyme, for endurance
Basil, for spirit
Sage, for the earth
Let your fire burn slowly, and tend to the coals.
Scrub the roots you have gathered,
*   cut and place them in bowls.*

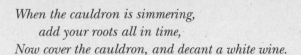

When the cauldron is simmering,
   add your roots all in time,
Now cover the cauldron, and decant a white wine.

While the cauldron simmers, prepare yourself to use the spell when it is ready. Take a sacred bath. Light scented candles and add rosewater and a drop or two of patchouli oil to your bath water. Wash your hair and rinse it with lemon juice. After your bath, anoint your body with scented creams or lotions to soothe your skin and make yourself more alluring to all who come near you. Wear an attractive outfit, and let people see you in a good light. Remember to ground and center yourself.

Now welcome your guests to your home, and serve the "spell" with a tossed salad and fresh crusty bread. A simple dessert of fresh fruit, with light syrup and a sprig of mint, would be the perfect accompaniment to this spell.

Have you guessed yet that this is simply a good chicken soup recipe? There is nothing more satisfying than a one-dish meal shared with friends. Making an effort to prepare a meal and inviting people to your home is the perfect way to nurture friendships and love. The savory scent of home cooking can do more to win friends and influence people than all the incense sticks in the world.

As you can see, the way you say something, or present something, can have a great influence on your intent. How people interpret what you say is also very important. What you think you've said is not always what others hear. Words have power. It may sound more exotic to say "light the sacred fire, and add the blessed water to the cauldron," but in reality, we're simply putting a pot of water on the stove to bring it to a boil. The fact that we're doing this to make a meal to share with others does indeed give it extra importance. Our intent is to give pleasure, and to nurture our family and friends. We use our everyday skills to provide something special. The ancient ways may seem more powerful because of the language, but the same recipes and spells of today are no less potent when we use words that are more familiar to us.

The Recipe

If you are a more modern Witch, here is the modern version for the above "receipt."

> 2 lbs. chicken (breasts and thighs)
> 4 carrots, cleaned and sliced
> 4 potatoes, peeled and cut into bite-size pieces
> 2 stalks of celery, chopped fine
> 2 onions, chopped fine
> 1 tsp. each rosemary, thyme, basil, and sage

Remove the skin from one chicken breast, and clean the chicken and rub with salt. Place the chicken skin in a skillet and heat till the juices run and the skin begins to crisp. Now add the salted chicken parts, turning them frequently to brown evenly on all sides. When they are browned, transfer the chicken pieces to a stockpot.

Add the celery and onion to the skillet and cook just until they are a bit soft, then add them to the stockpot, along with the chicken. Add enough water to cover the chicken. Cover the stockpot and use a high heat setting to bring the water to a boil. Reduce heat and let the stock simmer for approximately 1 ¼ hours. Strain the chicken and reserve the stock. Remove the skin and bones from the chicken and add the meat back into the stock, then put the mixture back into the stockpot, bringing the stock to a boil once more. Add the vegetables and spices, then reduce heat until the stock is just simmering. (Add more water at this point, just enough to cover the chicken and vegetables.) Keep the pot covered, stirring every once in a while and adding a little water as needed.

The soup is ready to serve when the vegetables are tender. Adjust your seasonings to taste. Experiment by using fresh seasonal vegetables or other spices. The most important thing is that this recipe can be started early in the day, and while the stock is simmering you can straighten your house, take care of yourself, and enjoy an evening with friends with little stress.

I must confess that the idea for the "Take One Dead Chicken" series of recipes came about many years ago during an Internet chat session. Many of us would pull our hair and grind our teeth every time someone popped into the chat rooms looking for love spells. A friend of mine finally began to give out a love spell, which started with the instructions "take one dead chicken" and from there on the recipe collection grew. So I'll raise a glass of wine to my good friend Melilot, for her impromptu "spell" which has grown to a goodly number of recipes over the years. Thanks Meli!

Magical Fasting

by Tammy Sullivan

Editor's note: As with all food plans, be sure to consult a doctor before making any changes to your diet.

Modern-day society places great importance on weight issues, both for health reasons and because of vanity. Fasting and dieting have been around since the beginning of recorded history and can be found in the oldest of religious texts. A few groups practice fasting or dieting as part of their spiritual path on a regular basis; others prefer to keep the practice confined to an annual event. Considering that both fasting and dieting came about as a means to purify the body for spiritual purposes, it makes sense to streamline both procedures into your spiritual practice.

For the purposes of this article I use the word *fasting* to describe the process of denying oneself food in general, and the word *dieting* to describe placing restrictions only on certain kinds of food.

Today, doctors achieve great notoriety for outlining methods of fasting and dieting. Each year new blockbuster books promise to be the best dieting guides ever written. But do these books deliver? For the most part, all of the meal plans are sensible and can aid the reader in weight loss, but they don't encompass the whole spectrum of body, mind, and spirit needed for true changes to occur. Once the diet stops, the weight often comes back. Mother Nature provides the best dieting guide—instinct.

A diet works much better when it is adopted into your life on a constant basis. Undergoing a fast before beginning a new diet plan can lead the body into accepting the new food intake more readily. It's like erasing a chalkboard and starting over.

Fasting For Health

The body benefits from a fast in varied ways. The body's natural detoxification patterns kick into high gear during a fast. Fasting allows the body time to rest from its normal everyday functions so that it can concentrate on purifying the body. It cleanses the circulatory system, the digestive system, and clears the sinus and lung cavities, and that's not nearly all. The rapid detoxification processes cleanse the body thoroughly, cell by cell. Fasting has even been reported to reverse the signs of aging by smoothing out wrinkles!

There are many variables to a fast. When it comes to ceremonial fasts, some are only for one day and others for several. Some allow fruit juices, others only water. When planning a personal fast, you must choose the variables for yourself. The planning stage of the fast is just as important as the fast itself. Ask yourself why you are choosing to fast. What do you hope to gain? Are you interested in performing a fast in order to cleanse the spirit or the body?

Many people choose to combine their fasts with colonic irrigation or, to put it simply, using enemas. Because of the high rate of saturated fats in the typical adult's diet, combining the two is often the only way to completely cleanse the digestive system. If choosing to make use of colonic cleansing, be advised that the most optimum period for its use is within the first three days of your fast.

Fasting For Spirit

Originally, fasting and dieting were thought to help one achieve a higher state of consciousness—to transcend the mundane world. It follows reason to think that if the body is pure and the mind focused, the spirit will be pure as well, and capable of reaching even the loftiest of heights.

Pagans have traditionally fasted at the Autumnal and Vernal equinoxes in an effort to promote the Earth's fertility. Likewise, some Native American tribes fasted to atone for their wrongs. Hoping to please the Earth by doing so, it was believed that fasting would assure a bountiful harvest. It was further believed that the fast would help them to avert natural disaster. When viewed in this manner, fasting was considered a petition to a higher source, or in other words, a spell.

Many religions also have dietary restrictions. Muslims must not consume pork, Hindus may not consume beef, Buddhists avoid meat in general for the most part, and Jews avoid shellfish and pork, among other things. These restrictions are imposed in an effort to keep the body "pure." The particular foods involved are generally thought of as either unclean (not fit for human consumption) or sacred by the participants.

Fasting Safely

Fasting may be an old and distinguished component of one's spiritual path, but that's no reason not to do it safely. Before beginning *any* new diet or fast it is best to consult with your doctor, particularly if you are on medication. If you have a history of eating disorders or are diabetic, do not even attempt it. Also, there is no reason to deny yourself the daily-required vitamins and minerals—just take a pill version of them.

I do not recommend extending any fast for longer then ten days. Gandhi, Jesus, and Buddha were all said to have fasted for

forty days, but for most of us it would not be practical or safe. After ten to fifteen days the body begins to use cells from muscles and organs and converts them into energy. You won't be burning fat; you will be burning vital tissues.

Before beginning your fast, cut down on your daily intake of food to prepare your system. If undergoing a water-only fast, prepare your body by making the first day a fruit- and vegetable-juice day. Also, limit your sugar and caffeine intake.

During the fast, keep physical activity to a normal level. If you are currently planning a water-only fast, it's best to limit physical activity as much as possible. As your body cleanses itself it may not smell very "clean." Bad breath and excessive sweating are the body's way of throwing off toxins. Fresh lemon juice is a wonderful addition to any fast, as it provides extra cleansing power. During a fast the tongue may become coated with a white substance. Lemon juice squirted in a glass of water helps to relieve this affliction. Do not chew gum—the act of chewing stimulates the body's natural digestive processes.

When this smelly stage begins, be sure to pay special attention to your dreams. While your body is purging all of the harmful material, your mind will be as well. It is normal to have nightmares during this part of the fasting procedure. While nightmares may be scary, in this case they are a very good thing because they are moving the negative thoughts out, making room for a more positive outlook.

You can also expect to experience discomfort. Hunger pangs, headaches, and dizzy spells occur in most instances when the body is deprived of fuel. From this stage, it is simply a matter of focusing the mind away from the body and concentrating on the spirit. Meditation should be a part of every fast. It is especially important during the uncomfortable period. It provides relief from all those little aches and pains and allows you to focus on your goal.

When the physical discomfort begins to wane, you may find that stress has melted away, the creative process has kicked into high gear and you find yourself in a state of peace. You may also feel a bit out of sorts or "stoned." If it is at all possible to increase your meditation time it would be most beneficial during this period.

Creating a special altar for the fast also helps to reinforce the goal. Use a soothing color theme such as seafoam, lavender, or aqua. Select a tranquil scented candle and only burn it when you are meditating in front of the altar. Try to visit the altar daily during the fasting period.

I do not recommend undertaking any strenuous magical work while on a fast, unless the fast is a necessary addition to a particular spell. In other words, add fasting to magic, but not magic to fasting. Fasting is considered to be magical on its own. Combining it with body-taxing activities, such as dancing, is not only unnecessary but also wasteful. Your body would be using its energy to fuel the dancing instead of cleaning all the toxic materials from your system.

When breaking your fast, break it slow and easy. You may be tempted to feast on everything you see, but only consume small amounts. Gradually build yourself back up to the level of a sensible diet. Fresh fruit is the easiest for the body to digest. Therefore, it is the most sensible choice of food for the first day after fasting.

During the fast you probably will become aware that you are the one in control of your life. Sure, it sounds like something we all should know anyway, but with today's hectic lifestyle and high-pressure jobs it is much easier to forget than you might think. Because a fasting period brings the fact that it is you who is in charge back into the forefront of the mind, it is the best time to break bad habits. The chalkboard is blank—fill it wisely.

Power Objects and Ritual Tools

by Kristin Madden

When Harry Potter first went to Hogwarts, in the wonderful series by J. K. Rowling, he had a long list of books and tools he needed to take with him in order to practice his "magic." Many modern Pagans feel much the same way, particularly when they are new to their paths. They want to be sure they have all that they need to do it right. And more than that, most Pagans just love to work with beautiful garb and tools.

The truth is that we don't really need any of these things to practice magic. It has been said that magic is the practice of effecting change in one's life. While this is certainly true and we all do small magics each day, real magic effects change through the use of ritual action. This may be something as simple as a mantra or visualization done each morning, or it may be as elaborate as a ceremonial magic ritual. For most of us, it is something in between. The energy that goes into the magic flows through you. You are the main tool and you provide the desire, intent, and belief that make it manifest.

But power objects and ritual tools are most definitely not irrelevant. They hold, magnify, and direct power for us. For many people, the power of magic is increased with the addition of ritual tools, and access to the energy of spirit allies is much easier when focusing on power objects. Our relationships with these tools and their uses are not interchangeable, however. As you will find, they are complementary but often very different magical assistants.

Power Objects

Do you ever pick up special rocks, feathers, or shells? Do you have a special necklace or ring that you wear just for ritual? Can an array of crystals be found around your house, office, or in your pockets? If so, you already have some personal power objects.

Power objects are items that hold strong energy for you. A power object may evoke a connection with spirit allies, bring healing, act as a focal point, or heighten your own magical abilities. These may be objects whose energy is apparent to all that come in contact with them—perhaps soil from Stonehenge or water blessed by the Dalai Lama. On the other hand, they may be items that resonate with you alone. Your grandmother's wedding ring may hold power for you, or a lock of your child's hair.

Power objects are often believed to be gifts from the gods or spirit allies. While walking in the woods, you may come across a feather or unusually shaped stone that seems to call to you. Your attention is drawn to it again and again or you might know instantly when you see it that it is there just for you. You may find yourself in a store, just wandering on a lunch hour or shopping for a friend. Before you know it, a crystal speaks to you in some way and you just know that you can't leave the store without taking it home.

For whatever reason, these objects have a reason for being in your life. The reason is likely to be incredibly personal, something specific to you and you alone. For some people, the meaning is rather general. A bear fetish or turkey feather reminds you of all that these spirit animals have been to you and provides an instant connection to their energy. For others, a power object is very specific. A horse hair represents freedom from an abusive relationship, or a blue topaz holds the ability to voice one's needs and opinions. Attuning to your power object will not only help you understand the power and meaning it has for you, but will also assist you in accessing that power.

Attuning to Power Objects

Attuning to an object creates a resonance between the two of you. In a way, it sets up short cuts or a speed-dial relationship between you, allowing you to use this power more quickly and easily while increasing the ease with which your spirit allies can communicate with you. Before doing the actual attunement, it is a good idea to release any unwanted energies from the object. A crystal may be a true gift from the gods, but it is unlikely that you want or need residual energies from previous owners or other people that may have handled it. So purify this object by smudging with sacred herbs, holding it under running water while visualizing unwanted energies breaking up and being washed away, burying it in soil for seven days, or leaving it out under the Sun and Moon for a full day and night.

To begin the attunement ritual, create sacred space in your usual manner. Smudge the area, cast a circle, light your candles, or chant your power song. Invite in your spirit guides and guardians and ask for their blessings.

Take some time to center your energy. Breathe deeply into your muscles—particularly into any areas of tension—and feel them relax. Count yourself down from ten to one, consciously relaxing more with each descending number. Relax the focus of your eyes and become aware of your connection to all things. Now call upon your spirit allies or patron deities, whether you know them or not. Let them know that you are here to open yourself to them and that you seek communion with them.

Pick up your power object and hold it in both hands. Visualize pure white energy filling this object, breaking up and releasing any remaining unwanted energies. Then sit with it for a moment and allow your energies to begin to mesh. Feel how this object feels. Feel how it makes you feel.

Now imagine that this object before you is as big as a house. Walk around and take a good look at it from all sides. What do you notice?

Visualize a door on one side. Place an offering at the door and introduce yourself. State your reason for coming and ask permission to enter. If you feel that permission is not given, try again later or ask if you need to do something else before entering.

When permission is granted, enter through the doorway. Take note of the colors, light, temperature, and anything that you see inside the object. If someone meets you at any point, greet that being with respect and be open to any messages he, she, or it might have for you. Express your reasons for exploring this object and ask for guidance into a deeper attunement with the power this object holds for you. Then wander through the object, going where you feel led and stopping at any place you find attractive in some way.

When you feel you have gained all that you can in this meditation, or when you feel it is time to leave, return to the doorway. Give thanks to the object, your spirit allies, and any beings you encountered here. If you wish, ask for continued guidance in how best to work with this object.

Count yourself back up from one to ten into ordinary consciousness. If specific guidance was given or requests were made for housing or use of this object, be sure to follow through on those in a respectful manner.

Keep in mind that this meditation can do more than simply attune you to this object. Repeated use of the meditation can introduce you to previously unknown spirit allies that may be associated with this object. It can also allow you access to your own lost power and provide a forum for you to regain some of it. Although quite simple, this little attunement exercise can be surprisingly powerful.

Ritual Tools

While many power objects find a home on the ritual altar and are used in ceremony, they are not necessarily the same as ritual tools. Ritual tools arc objects that have very specific uses in a ceremonial setting. The smudge fan is used to

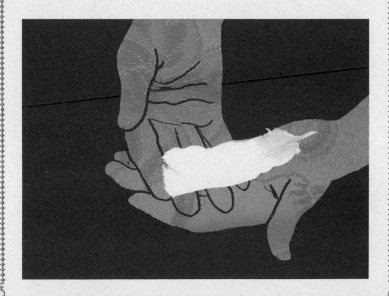

purify space. Smudge and incense begin to induce a sacred state of mind. The ritual sword may be used to cast the circle and cut openings in it for participants that need to leave or re-enter. These tools may be gifts from your spirit allies, but they have a purpose other than connecting you to Deity and holding power for you individually.

Ritual tools bring great mystery and powerful belief to a ceremony. Simply by using them, you may be transported into a magical state of consciousness. The belief in their power alone can spur you into more effective magic and deeper trance states. This can be particularly true in the early stages of your practice, but continued use can increase their power exponentially. The more you work with these tools, the more conditioned you become to the states of consciousness that you experience through using them. In this way, they can be invaluable catalysts to the creation of magic.

Because of the important role these tools play in the creation of ceremony and the intimate nature of your psychic relationship with them, it is vitally important that ritual tools be properly cleansed and ritually consecrated and accepted by the deities of your path.

Dedication Rite

This is a fairly simple ritual for the consecration and dedication of your ritual tools. Use it as a basic guideline for the creation of a rite that is uniquely suited to you and your path. Trust your intuition and feel free to adapt this to meet your needs. You will need: the altar of your choosing, set with symbols of your spirit allies and deities; smudge or incense; pure water that has been left in sunlight and moonlight for twenty-four hours; sea salt; essential oil of myrrh, frankincense, lemongrass, or rosemary.

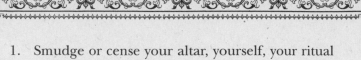

1. Smudge or cense your altar, yourself, your ritual space, and your new tool. Visualize any unwanted energies breaking up and releasing from your tool. Say, "By fire and air do I cleanse and consecrate this space."

2. Add a pinch of salt to the water, then sprinkle your altar, yourself, your ritual space, and your new tool. Say, "By water and earth do I cleanse and consecrate this space."

3. Call upon your spirit guides, patron deities, and any other beings you wish to have present. Invite them to share in this ritual and ask for their guidance and protection. State the purpose of this rite: that you have come before these honored spirits to present your new tool for their blessings. Tell them that you dedicate this tool to the highest good and ask that only the most beneficial energies might flow through the tool and through you when you use it.

4. Holding the tool in both hands, feel your energy filling it and forming a connection between you, so you might use it to its greatest benefit.

5. Replace the tool on the altar and pick up the essential oil. Offer the oil to those invoked and ask again for their blessings. Anoint yourself with the oil, inviting into yourself the qualities you want to bring to your path. Then anoint the tool, blessing it with the intent for which it's designed. Sit with your tool for a few moments to allow any spirit messages to come through.

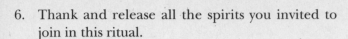

6. Thank and release all the spirits you invited to join in this ritual.

7. Close sacred space and keep your tool in a safe and special place.

It has been said that ritual tools and other magical equipment must be crafted by the user to be truly effective. It is true that making your own working tools imbues them with a rare focus and attunes them to your energy like nothing else. The process of crafting your own tools involves you, from start to finish, in the journey from idea all the way through manifestation. It's an experience that is not to be missed. However, sometimes our tools are already out there somewhere, and will find the way to us when we are ready to receive them. Some people find tools that connect instantly and directly to their hearts and souls at garage sales or metaphysical stores. Others receive the ideal tool from their spirit allies in a vision and then enlist the aid of magical craftspeople. The tools they now work with have been accepted by their gods and are a physical manifestation of the tools they were given in these powerful visions.

Whether you find your magical objects on the seashore or in a yard sale, power objects and ritual tools can be significant partners and potent conduits for your spiritual development. These unique items bring great mystery and allure to ritual, magic, and meditation, thereby increasing the energy of those very sacred times. As gifts from the spirits, we are all blessed to receive such treasures, whether they come to us in simple or elaborate forms.

Household Magic

by Diana Rajchel

Don't expect, after a spell or ten, for your environment to stay static. Nope—a conjured force, even one conjured only within the scope of your mind's eye, still has an effect. I won't break down the particle physics for you because I can't distinguish an electron from a proton, but in utterly unscientific speech, I can tell you this: when you do some magic, you stir the stuff that makes the dust. After some magic, over time, the floors, ceilings, and corners get dirty. Magical dirt differs from plain old dust dirt in that the magical dust bunnies will, over time, develop minds of their own rather than simply menacing you from the depths beneath your bed. Over time, as you practice more and more magic, your home environment will eventually slag you.

In severe cases of energy overuse and neglect, some people have reported poltergeist-like activity. This phenomenon is simply the result of unintelligent energies finding an occupation in the absence of magical direction. If you raise energy without a purpose, the energy will make its own purpose. Sometimes, depending on how the energy was initially raised, it develops a sentience, which can result in anything from minor temperature variations to a night-hag phenomena (paralysis when just awaking). Since not all energy can be grounded out easily, some residue is unavoidable. Having the residue behave in a way you don't like, however, is easily preventable. Aside from keeping your energy levels high to normal, you have the additional motivation of preventing any accidents of energetic work that might spook yourself or other household members.

A practiced Witch will perform a house blessing as soon as she moves into a new home. This rite is optimally performed before any furniture or belongings cross the threshold, but a cleansing and blessing will still work even with furniture underfoot.

Many Witches repeat this once a year after the initial blessing, although I've found that cleansing works better when repeated more frequently. This may be because I prefer to live in urban, high-traffic neighborhoods. Rural and suburban homes have less human traffic and may have less need for a routine cleansing and re-sealing process.

What we think about regularly influences our atmosphere. Total focus while cleansing is ideal; however, it takes years to develop that level of meditative skill. Even the best of us have our thoughts sometimes stray during a working, and where our thoughts go the magic will follow. Because of this, cleansing the home once or twice a month helps eliminate the ricochet effect of a spell having an unintended—or undesired—consequence. You can also control what lives in your home with you—particularly what may be of your own inadvertent creation. Your home will always have something living with you; you are never alone, but for the mighty amoeba. Yes paranoiac, you are surrounded all the time. And that's a good thing: it keeps you humble, or at least amusingly twitchy. It also asserts your connection, molecule by molecule, to the rest of the world on all levels. You can't help being surrounded. But you can help what surrounds you, and that's where cleansing and house blessing comes in handy.

For any house (apartment, tent, dugout, dwelling) cleansing, apply the following principles:

1. Clutter = bad

2. Fire extinguishers and house insurance = good

3. Clear out the astral and physical first

4. After clearing out, *then* you cleanse

5. After cleansing, shield

6. After shielding, anchor

7. After anchoring, offer

8. After offering, invite in your guests (and residents) and let them know the rules by verbalizing them clearly. Sometimes, you may have to add consequences to your arrangement.

My typical house cleansing follows this process:

First, I clear the clutter. I am a less than stellar housekeeper, so for me a clutter cleaning means taking clothing off the floor and books off the furniture. Once I have anything on the floor that might trip me moved out of the way, including any animal household members, I grab my broom and begin the process of cleansing *everything*.

The broom, or besom as some call it, is a ritual implement intended to sweep out stagnant and negative energies. I found my most recent besom in a Halloween costume shop, sold as a "real Witches' broom." If it wasn't before, it is now. Starting at the most frequently used entrance to my home, I take the broom and begin to sweep, brushing particularly at corners, the ceiling, and behind walls. I also take the opportunity to disrupt any cobwebs in my way. Be very thorough on a first time cleansing: open the oven and microwave, sweep cupboards and closets, even brush over drains and electrical outlets (do the drains *after* the electrical outlets). Sometimes a rhyme or chant helps the magical flow of this process, such as "Out, about, I turn all out—what dawdles here, I turn out!"

Once the cleansing has been completed, the household should feel like it has more breathing room. The effect is temporary. A swept-through area left unattended fills again all too quickly. Nature abhors a vacuum. A shielding or warding must fill this void, or the void may be filled by something you don't want. You will get everything you swept out back, and often the sweep-outs bring their friends. Some people enjoy their homes being hot-spots of chaotic energy. I don't.
It has a detrimental (i.e., draining) effect on the inhabitants that pay the rent or mortgage, and most find it preferable to fill up the space with pre-selected energies and inhabitants that leave them their normal mental function.

I build protective energy in layers. I build the first layer by smudging my living space. I choose white sage because it suits the land I live on best; the ancestral spirits come from a culture that used sage, and respond best if I honor the traditions surrounding the plant. In order to smudge a home, I carry a lighter, a ceramic pot to catch the ashes, and the sage bundle. Sage frequently goes out when initially lit, so I carry the lighter to re-ignite it. I proceed through my home, waving the sage while holding the ceramic pot beneath it, catching all ashes. Generally a brush through in the corners and over the primary traffic areas establishes a strong, purified area. I visualize the sage spreading into every corner of the home, pushing through floors and ceilings, creating a glowing wall. Just so you're aware, sage has qualities that will cause you to sweat, and sweat profusely—and while a purge may be good for you and your skin, you might want to open some windows while you smudge.

A sweep and a smudge will hold for a bit, but if you're like me you'll want some assurance that your work will stick for awhile. This is where shielding comes in. I prefer blessed water for my anchor. I mix a pinch of sea salt in with a cup of water, and I say a prayer that the salt and water be pure, and carry the blessings of water and earth.

It's acceptable to mix these ingredients in the bowl and then simply flick the water into corners, over doorways, and on windows. I store this material in a plastic spray-bottle (pray 'n' spray) and spritz each room, door, and window in all the designated cleansing areas. The blessed water cleanses any residual energy that sweeping or smudging might have missed, and, through the salt crystals in the water, give the sage something to anchor itself to. This strengthens the shield over the home by adding some reinforcements in the form of the salt crystals.

Being of a religious bent, I always complete my house cleansing and warding with an offering to the gods of home and hearth. These beings are many, and cross many cultures. Because I incline towards the Hellenic mythos, I honor Hestia, but she is by no means the limits of domestic life. Other priests and priestesses I know opt for singular dedicated pantheons, often with strong arguments towards never playing mix 'n' match with gods.

In every pantheon I'm aware of, there is a feminine divinity that oversees the home. The Celtic Brigid is a popular domestic goddess frequently called upon, as is the Egyptian Hathor. Always do some research before asking for the blessing of any divinity, because what that divinity views as a blessing may not fit with your intentions. For instance, if you ask for the blessing of Pan, he may well bless you with some very literal fertility. Unplanned pregnancies are most certainly a double-edged sword of curse and blessing. Even something as seemingly innocuous as a house blessing can trigger deeper consequences whenever the gods are involved. Hit the library and read books with actual stories of the gods so you know what you're getting into before you open up the line and ask. These stories reveal plenty about the character of a given god or goddess, and give strong clues of how to best approach them.

But you're not quite finished with house blessings and protections yet. You will likely need to ward once in awhile, but it is not a task that needs repetition on a regular basis so long as your home is kept clean and stable. Warding puts a block on your home—a sort of sealant that doesn't allow any energies to pass in or out. This can create a new level of stagnation that can lead to an additionally unhealthy environment for living. Just like an organic being, the space you live in needs to be allowed to "breathe." A home shield allows for some traffic through the home—the shield simply filters out specific types of traffic you declare undesirable. Small amounts of astral traffic through the home are good things: if you call for assistance from the elements, or from local spirits, they can go through the shield because you invited them. Wards, however, tend to slow down the process because nothing gets through until you take the ward down.

Warding is best used in situations where there is a quantifiable physical threat to the safety of yourself or your home. Such instances include nearby thefts or robberies, a predatory criminal in your area, or a person directing threats clearly and unequivocally to you. Warding in no way replaces the need to call 911 should you wind up in a truly dangerous situation; however, it helps in delaying or preventing that need. Warding also helps in the extremely rare instances of hauntings or poltergeist activity.

In order to ward, you need to perform the basic house cleansing and blessing. Follow this with a self-purification; this may be a simple or complex action. I prefer simplicity in all things, so my purification follows this procedure: I lay out fresh clothes for myself, and after making sure the bathroom is clean, I draw myself a bath and add basic purifiers like sea salt and hyssop. The hyssop can be closed in a muslin bag or a tea bag to prevent the hassle of having to fish it out of the drain afterwards. While in the bath, I pray to be cleansed of negativity, ill intention, and harmful relationships. As I pray, I submerge my head two or three times. Once I feel sufficiently purified, I drain the tub and dress in the clean clothing or robes I laid out for myself.

While dressed in clean clothing, I take some olive oil with a few drops of lemongrass essential oil mixed into it, or some specially blessed water, and walk to each door and window. At each entry to my home, I draw a simple pentagram or an equal-armed cross—both are well known protective symbols. As I draw the symbol, I visualize it glowing until the light takes over the whole of my home. I make sure to ward all possible entrances: doors, windows, drains, outlets—even my cable modem. Any excess energies may no longer enter. While it's still possible to perform spells and rituals, the wards will have a deadening effect until they wear off. Any influence you invite through will feel muted through the filter of your wards.

If you're extra concerned for your safety, after warding your home you can do a simple protection spell for yourself. You can create a talisman such as a cross or pentacle, or follow a simple candle spell for protection, such as that found in Ray Buckland's *Practical Candle Magic.* Think of these actions as additional backup to the normal precautions of locking your doors at night and making sure your cell phone has its emergency contacts clearly labeled.

These routine rituals establish your home as a sacred place. As most Witches are their own priests and priestesses, their homes become their temples. Any temple requires routine cleansing and acknowledgement of its sacredness to be a fit temple. House cleansing, and sometimes warding, imprints that reminder both on yourself and on the traffic patterns of your home. This way you can ensure your home continues as both sacred place and sanctuary, where just entering fills you with peace and healing. Cleanse and bless regularly, and this feeling builds in strength over time.

Kitchen Witchery

by Ellen Dugan

Indeed, is there not something holy about a great kitchen?
—Angela Carter

Aaaaack! Did you say "Kitchen Witch"? *Dear Gods, no.* Not that. *Anything* but kitchen witchery. (I can just hear you all now, dropping your athames in horror.) There is sort of a reverse type of discrimination here in regards to this magical tradition—and it is beyond ridiculous. When you say the words "Kitchen Witch," many magical practitioners get all in a huff.

"Well, I mean, really," the grand high pooh-bah Lady Crystal-Morgana-Golden-Hawk-Coyote mutters as she flips her flowing midnight cape behind her, narrowing her elaborately outlined eyes in displeasure. Her hubcap-sized pentagram shivers against her breast as she attempts to control her moral outrage. Why, her Witchy Supremeness is in a state of shock at having to even *discuss* this most upsetting of all possible magical subjects.

There are those who think a Kitchen Witch is somehow a Witch of lesser stature. I imagine they see a Kitchen Witch as some little housewife type of Witch who keeps a very low profile and does fluffy bunny magic with the most mundane of objects. I have met quite a few Lady-Crystal-what's-her-name types over the years. (I bet you have too.) And they couldn't be farther from the truth about the Kitchen Witch and the tradition of being a hearth and home practitioner.

Truthfully, there are a lot more of those suburban types of Witches out there than you'd think. Witchcraft

isn't only flourishing in the rural areas or in the cities. It's thriving wonderfully out in the 'burbs, too. So if you are a home-based Witch who happens to be a soccer mom, or dad, good for you! Help break a few stereotypes of what folks imagine a real "Witch" is like. Actually, a Kitchen Witch is a mysterious and most adaptable creature. They are whispered to be domestic goddesses or gods: they live their magical lives quietly, raise their families, and have charming homes, successful jobs, and, believe it or not, health insurance. I have even heard a few terrifying rumors of Kitchen Witches that drive minivans.

Well, that explains it. Those Kitchen Witches are simply regular folks who practice the Craft in a matter-of-fact, discreet, and practical way. Being a real Witch doesn't require a lot of drama and intrigue. Sometimes the most magical thing you can do is just to go about your life making a difference quietly, just because you can.

The Magical Kitchen

The kitchen is a place filled with the aroma of food and the bustling sounds of family, life, and love. Traditionally, the kitchen held a place of honor in the home. According to custom, most of the work of the wise woman took place at the hearth. By the light of the flickering flames, food was prepared, medicines were brewed, and spells were cast. In the old days the hearth was the center of the home because it supplied light and warmth and was the place for food preparation. Today, unless you have a fireplace or wood stove, your hearth area is actually your kitchen stove. It's not too surprising that an entire tradition of magical practitioners sprang from this most enchanting of rooms.

The kitchen is a room full of magic and creative energies, and it has an incredible potential for magic. Remember, the hearth flame is actually a living symbol of the spirit of the family. There are even several hearth gods and goddesses, including the Greco-Roman goddesses Hestia and Vesta and the Celtic goddess Brigit. These ladies were important deities of their time, since the maintenance of the hearth, raising a family and, yes, cooking were considered among the most revered of tasks.

Kitchen magic is unique in that it can be applied to any magical path or tradition. When you work magic in the kitchen, you have a chance to be creative with the natural items you have on hand, plus you have the chance to put your own spin on things.

A Few Enchanting Ideas for the Kitchen

Try clearing out a cabinet that's out of reach from young children. Then stock a few tools of the magical trade in there so you have supplies on hand for your down-to-earth magic. Make sure that if you have magical herbs in the kitchen you label them and keep them stored in a spot well away from culinary herbs and seasoning. (Better safe than sorry.)

Add a few tea-light candleholders on the counter and keep a supply of tea-light candles on hand. These are great for affordable spell candles—they burn for approximately four hours, and those white unscented candles are practical and an all-purpose color. You can add a pinch of dried herbs to the bottom of the cup, or add a drop of essential oil to the candle to customize it for any magical purpose you can dream up.

Having supplies close at hand saves time. There is nothing more frustrating than wasting twenty minutes hunting down various pieces of equipment. Keep a few things handy in the kitchen and you can focus more on your spellwork and not where in the world your supplies have run off to.

To add some more positive magical energy to the kitchen, try hanging a prism in a sunny window. This is a great idea to add the power of color to the room. All the colors of the rainbow appear when sunlight refracts through a crystal prism, sending those dancing lights across the walls. Also, hanging prisms in the windows is an old Feng Shui technique that helps to break up any negative energy hanging around. According to Feng Shui practices, the crystal prisms should be round or oval in shape (spiky edges cause unbalanced chi energy). Pick up a prism or two and hang them in the windows on some heavy fishing line. When the sun hits the prisms, give them a little spin and watch the rainbows dance across your kitchen walls and floor.

Another practical idea is to display a rope of braided and dried garlic. Braided garlic can be hung in the kitchen to encourage protection and promote well being and contentment for the entire family. Garlic also encourages a happy, healthy home environment. Garlic is one of the best protective herbs, and when it is hung over doorways in your kitchen it will fight negativity, absorb evil, and ward off spiteful people, psychic vampires, and roaming ghosts.

Work the following Kitchen Witch spell at any time or Moon phase. This kitchen spell is light-hearted and encourages you to laugh—because a touch of humor is a potent magic indeed.

Kitchen Witch Braided Garlic Charm

Directions: Hang the braided garlic up in your magical kitchen, enchanting it for all the good things that were listed above.

I enchant this charming braid of garlic so fine,
Keep negativity out of my home at all times.
Psychic vampires, roaming ghouls, and ghosts beware,
You will never find refuge in this Witch's lair!

You can also display a Kitchen Witch doll. These charming and cute dolls are often found at fall arts-and-crafts festivals. They may be rag dolls made of cloth, or they can be cornhusk dollies. Typically, the rag-doll variation is decked out in Halloween finery and holding a broom. The little cornhusk dollies are more plain, but they are still fun to tuck onto a shelf. These are charming Witch figures and a fun addition to any magical kitchen.

The legend behind these dolls is that if one is displayed in a kitchen, then the food will never spoil and dinner will always turn out well. The doll is a modern interpretation of the ancient grain dolly that was created to bless the harvest. According to agricultural tradition, after the harvest a few sheaves of grain were twisted and shaped into the semblance of a doll. This grain dolly was kept on prominent display until the following year's harvest. The spirit of the grain was thought to stay with the farmer's family and watch over the crops for the following year.

Hurray for the Kitchen Witch!

As a Kitchen Witch is a practical and down-to-earth magical practitioner, he or she may practice the Craft by inspiring and helping those in need, offering guidance and comfort. The Kitchen Witch works with the most elemental and natural magical supplies: an enchanted tumbled stone, a simple tea-light candle, an empowered herb from the pantry, or a few blossoms from the magical garden. They use the simplest of supplies and accessories because they are very practical magicians.

A Kitchen Witch knows it's not the drama of your outfit or the size of your pentragram that makes you an adept practitioner. It's all about what you do with what you have. Kitchen Witches can turn the simplest of items, such as a pot of homemade soup or a little cup of chamomile tea, into magic spells with ease and efficiency. For example, a Kitchen Witch could brew that chamomile tea with intention, so the drink would soothe and relax the recipient. She may hold her hands over the cup, empower the brew, and recite a short spontaneous charm:

> *I now enchant this cup of chamomile tea,*
> *May it bring comfort and peace swiftly to thee.*

She then confidently offers it up with a smile, secure in the knowledge that it will indeed ease the stress and tension of the situation. The soup could easily be enchanted to bring about health and protection. Just the Kitchen Witch's magical intention and a quick shuffling of the words is all that's required:

> *I now enchant this pot of homemade soup.*
> *May it protect and give your health a boost.*

See? Quick, practical, and easy. The Kitchen Witch creates a cozy sanctuary in her home, following her own unique and powerful spiritual path every day of the year. For within her residence, be it apartment, mobile home, condo, or house, her magic flows powerfully out to create positive change. Whether at the fireside, kitchen stove, or counter, this simple Witchery shines compassionately out from a Kitchen Witch's very soul. Her magic is real and incredibly strong, because it comes from her own personal power base: the home and the heart.

Sacred Pendants

by Sybil Fogg

People wear talismans or magical charms for reasons beyond simple luck. Pendants can be created to harness any influence you feel is missing from your life, such as love, money, or protection. Sometimes people wear pendants as a means to commune with nature spirits or loved ones who have passed on. You can create a charm during a spell and then wear it for a full Moon cycle to bring the magic to fruition, and then bury it, burn it, or release it into running water as a way of giving thanks. Some of the most potent magical pendants can be found right in nature; others are filled with the personal power of the creator's intent as he or she labors to make an original piece of jewelry. No matter how the pendant is procured, it should be charged beneath a Full Moon and a bright Sun and be consecrated in a ritual designed to infuse the piece with a purpose.

Sometimes, the most puissant pendants are found on nature hikes or walks on the beach. Sea glass can become intriguing pieces of jewelry when you drill a small hole through them or wrap them in wire and attach a chain. They are already throbbing with water magic, mermaid lore, and the ambitions of the sea goddess and/or god. If a specimen is found that appears to be free of blemishes, it was probably meant for you to find, and you should spend time with the item to discern what the gods might be asking of you. Once you have come to a conclusion, give thanks to Thetis or Aphrodite or Poseidon himself for bringing the talisman into your life. This process is best done at the seaside, when the glass is discovered. You could even toss something of yourself into the ocean, whether it be a piece of jewelry you were wearing when you found the glass or a stone or coin that you happen to be carrying.

A coworker of mine wears a stone with a natural hole in it that she found in the woods. The magic that follows her through her day is that of dryads, the Green Man, Pan, and Artemis. These correspondences would also work for pine cones, sticks, and leaves (for a very short-lived pendant, unless they are crumbled and kept in a vial). As you walk, scour the forest floor. It is important to keep an eye out so that you won't miss anything that might be placed intentionally in your path. Natural pendants can also be charged with intent: my youngest daughter wears an acorn to protect her from thunderstorms. It is important to remember that although a natural "found" pendant is charged by whomever wished for you to own it, you should still devise a ritual to at the very least thank the nature spirits that left the gift.

For those who want something that carries an individual mark, there are some simple pendants that can be made in an afternoon. With wire and pliers, you can fashion small spirals to bring something into your reality or banish an unwanted emotion, situation, or person from your life; a pentacle for protection; a triple Moon for Goddess magic; or any type of small figure. Keep in mind that the final appearance of these pendants will be somewhat crude. Don't get caught up in trying to make them look as though they were factory made because wire will break if you continue to fuss with it. They won't look machine-made because they are handmade, and as such each will be original, as well as filled with much more potent magic. For this venture, you'll need:

Wire. Craft wire can be found in any hardware store in basic colors. If you desire a more extensive choice, it is best to take a trip to a craft store. Any gauge wire will do, as the width depends entirely on the skill of the artist and the size you wish your pendant to be. The higher the gauge, the smaller the diameter of the wire. For example, if I were making a simple spiral or triple Moon, I would choose to go with a smaller-number gauge to avoid having a flimsy piece when finished. If I were going to wrap a gemstone or something found on a beach walk or nature hike, I would want a thinner and therefore higher-number gauge, so that the stone's natural beauty would show through.

Pliers. Needle-nose pliers work best to shape the wire and create the loop where the chain or cord will be threaded.

Safety goggles. Wire has a sharp point and can easily spring back and hit you in the face when you are working with it. It's always wise to wear safety goggles when doing any kind of craft project that involves sharp and/or bouncy materials.

Gloves. Wear gloves because wire is sharp.

Wire cutters. Use them to cut the wire when finished.

Hammer. A copper head does best for flattening jewelry without leaving dents, but any metal hammer will do if copper is unavailable.

Accessories. Gems, coins, family heirlooms—anything that pertains to the spell being cast or the meaning of the pendant.

Chain or **satin cord** to serve as the necklace.

Circles and Small Figures

Circles are the easiest shape to create. Wrap the wire around the nose of the pliers to create a hanger, and then drop the wire down and form the circle. Variations of the circle include forming a crescent Moon shape inside the circle for a goal that you want to start at the New Moon and achieve by the Full Moon.

Circles are also the basis for small figures. Create these for love magic or to draw on the energies of someone who has passed on. (Remember, a love spell should never be directed at a specific person; abide by the Wiccan Rede.) These pendants are perfect to give to your significant other when fabric from clothing, pieces of hair, or anything else that belonged to you is woven in during the twisting process. If this figure is to help you connect with the energies of someone you've loved who has passed on, use articles from them in the piece.

1. Start by making a hanger and circle.

2. Thread a long wire through the circle's bottom, twisting it around itself to form the neck of the figure.

3. Bend the wire and use the pliers to pinch it, then bring it out to the side to create an arm.

4. Twist the wire back along itself. Use the pliers to bend the wire and bring it out to the opposite side to form the other arm.

5. Twist the wire back along itself and then drop the wire down to form the torso.

6. Repeat the process for the arms to forge the legs, twist the wire back around the torso, and cut off any excess with the wire cutters.

7. Place the pendant on a small anvil or workbench and use the hammer to flatten it. Thread a satin cord or chain through the hanger.

Simple Spirals

Spirals are almost as easy as circles. First decide whether your intention is to bring something into your life or whether you are going to banish a negative aspect. You will want to curl the spiral in the appropriate direction: deosil (clockwise) for attracting and widdershins (counterclockwise) for dispelling.

1. Using the needle-nose pliers, begin by wrapping the wire around the nose of the pliers. Continue to curl the wire around the tip of the pliers until you achieve the desired size.

2. At the end of the spiral, loosen the wire a bit and make a small loop through which to thread the chain or cord.

3. Finally, place the piece on an anvil or work bench and hammer it flat. Thread satin cord or a chain through the hanger.

Pentacles

Pentacles are a little trickier than spirals. They tend to look crudely handmade no matter the skill of the artist. I find them more attractive because of the imperfections. Adding colored beads is the perfect way to weave in correspondences for specific spell work. Pentacles work well for magic that will be achieved within a Moon cycle. When you're done, you can  leave it on the altar, bury it, or toss it into running water for an offering. If you are going to add beads, do so after each one-inch section is formed, right before making the bends in the wire.

1. For this project, it's best to begin at the top and loop the wire around the nose of the pliers to make an opening for a chain or cord. Then drop the wire down about one or two centimeters. This is the neck of your pendant.

2. Next, using the pliers (or your fingers if you are nimble), pull the wire to a 30° angle from vertical to create a diagonal line approximately one inch long. Then bend the wire back on itself and bring it up at another 30° angle in the opposite direction for another one-inch section.

3. Bend the wire back on itself again and bring it straight across horizontally for one inch. Make another bend in the wire and bring it down at another 30° angle for another inch. Finally, bend the wire back on itself one more time, then bring it up to the starting point. Now you should have a five-pointed star.

4. At this point form the circle around the pentacle by weaving the wire through the points of the pentacle and using the pliers to crimp each point together after you pass the wire through. Bring the wire back to the top, wrap it around the neck a few times, and cut it with the wire cutters. Lay the pentacle on an anvil or workbench and hammer it flat. Thread the satin cord or chain through the hanger.

Goddess and God

The most difficult pendant to fashion is the triple Moon shape. Create the hanger and then drop the wire down one or two centimeters to form the neck.

1. Compress the wire with the pliers and then bring the wire in a curve to form the top-right quarter of the Full Moon.

2. Pinch the wire at this point, and curve the wire in the other direction to create the bottom horn of the waning crescent. Use the pliers to pinch the wire again to form a point, and bring the wire back to make the inner edge of the crescent Moon. Pinch the wire one more time at the top point of the crescent, and bring it down, completing the crescent Moon.

3. Pinch the wire and create the lower half of the Full Moon.

4. Using the pliers, flatten the wire again and form the top quarter of the opposite crescent. Pinch the wire at the point of the horn and form the inner curve of the waxing crescent, and then pinch again and bring the wire up to create the bottom quarter of the waxing Moon. You now have the maiden or waxing crescent Moon and are almost finished.

5. Fold the wire yet again and form the final quarter of the full moon. Wrap the wire around the neck of the pendant and cut the excess with the wire cutters. Hammer the pendant flat and step back to admire your triple Moon.

Not as hard, but still requiring some skill, is the symbol of the horned God.

1. I find it easiest to fashion the horns first, working up to the points and then crimping the wire with the pliers.

2. Now, fashion the neck and hanger and coil wire back down the neck.

3. Form the entire circle, twisting wire around the neck and then cutting off the excess with the cutters. Flatten the pendant with the hammer.

Consecrating Your Pendant

Once you have finished creating your piece, remember to leave it on an outside altar, or in a window if you don't have access to a yard or balcony, for a full day and night to be charged with both Sun and Moon energy.

Check the calendar and pick the right time, day of the week, cycle of the Moon, and Moon sign corresponding to the spell you are casting. Pick candles in colors that will strengthen your magic: reds and pinks for love, blues and silvers for Goddess magic, greens and yellows for the God, black to banish and white to attract, and so on. Do the same for incense. Write down the words of your intention.

When it is time to cast your spell, set up your altar as you normally would, but use the candles and incense that you have chosen. Call the four quarters, cast your circle, and invoke the Goddess and God in the manner to which you are accustomed. Do a ritual that works with your cause and fits with your path.

Pass the pendant through water, earth, air, and fire to fill it with each element (unless your intention is to have an amulet specific to a particular element). Then charge it accordingly. Speak your words; draw down the Moon and/or Sun. Dance, sing, sweep—do whatever you feel necessary to raise a cone of power and release your intention. Place the pendant around your neck and experience a moment of silence and meditation.

Thank the God and Goddess and the elements. Blow out your candles and close the circle. Now your pendant is ready. Use it wisely.

Knitting Witchcraft

by Olivia O'Meir

Knitting a sweater is a tremendous act of faith.
—Bernadette Murphy

Modern Witches are some of the craftiest people around. But like everyone else, we are also busy people, trying to make time for ritual, study, meditation, work, family, and crafts. Sometimes it seems like an impossible task, but there is a way to do it. The path is found by balancing and mixing the magical and the mundane. That is why paths like Kitchen Witchcraft are so popular—they allow the Witch to practice magic and fulfill a mundane need at the same time, such as eating or bathing. Witches can also add a bit of magic when making crafts. Every craft project bursts with opportunities to make magic. One of the witchiest crafts is knitting: many spells can be weaved using two knitting needles and a ball of yarn.

Spirituality

Knitting is a spiritual craft that gives us many gifts. We gain patience and perseverance while learning to make the stitches. We learn the value of free will and making mistakes. Our mistakes are those things that we truly own: we have the power to fix them, live with them, and even embrace them. As Witches, we strive to practice tolerance and compassion in our lives, and working with different yarns reminds us of the treasures found in our own diverse world and that everyone has something valuable to teach and learn. Also, Witches can use their knitting skills to volunteer and help others. There are a number of charities that need donations of knitted blankets, linens, and clothing. In this way, knitting provides an outlet to give joy and comfort to others.

Witches attempt to live in balance and harmony with the elements and nature, and we can create knitted pieces inspired by each element, Moon phase, or season. Each project's symbolism and power can be increased by using corresponding yarn colors and beads. Every time you wear the finished project, you'll be connected to the energies it represents.

Knitting also helps to teach us that we can find the magic in the mundane, if we change our viewpoint. It provides Witches with a way to use our creative and logical sides at the same time, which is especially important to strengthening the magical mind. Knitting also teaches us how to make goals and follow through on plans. A knitting project starts with just one stitch, and the project is created one stitch after another. Our lives are made like this, one step at a time. After finishing a piece, it is magic to see a finished creation and to know that not long ago, it was just a strand of yarn.

Meditation and Mindfulness

Witches can also use knitting as part of their everyday meditation practices. When using knitting for meditation practice, I recommend working on a simple project made with a basic knit stitch. As you get more experienced, you can do more complex projects. I find the simpler the project, the better the meditation, as there are no worries about making mistakes. You can use any size needles, although medium sizes such as 8 or 9 seem to work best. I do not recommend using fancy yarns to work with—they can be tricky to use and too distracting for meditation.

Try to take about twenty minutes for each meditation session. If that is too long or too short, adjust the length of time to your schedule, comfort, and skill level. Work in a quiet, safe environment and make yourself comfortable there. I try to enhance the atmosphere by listening to relaxing music and lighting candles and incense. Take one deep breath and begin. I use the stitches as a way of timing my breathing. Take one breath for each stitch, breathing in and out slowly. While working, let any thoughts that enter your mind float by. Do not pay much attention to them. Just focus on breathing and making each stitch. During the meditation, my advice is to relax and do what feels comfortable.

Try working the act of knitting into your guided meditations and visualizations. For example, if you want to commune with the Goddess, knitting can help. When meditating, try to see her knitting with you, sharing her wisdom and advice. Or, use a knitting meditation to help solve a problem. Imagine you are working on a knitting project and this project will help with your problem or

set you on the right path. Let go of any preconceived ideas you have about the project, but pay attention to it. The yarn, the stitch, or the project itself may hold the key to the solution.

Also, you can use knitting to relax

any time you feel anxious, tense, or stressed out. Just grab the needles and start knitting. Concentrating on breathing and making each stitch helps stop and release frantic, worried thoughts.

Knitting Deity

As I mentioned above, we can use knitting to connect to the divine—especially creative or inspirational deities. Witches can commune with them or invoke their aid and blessing for a project. Deities associate with knitting include the Fates, Arachne, Spider Woman, Ariadne, Athena, and Hephaestus. This is by no means a complete list, however. There are many deities in other pantheons that can help with knitting and crafts.

The Fates

The Fates embody the Triple Goddess. They are viewed as the Maiden, Mother, and Crone. The Fates spin the threads of our lives, measure them out, and cut them at their ends. These goddesses are so powerful that even other gods and goddesses are subject to their rule. Call on them when you need guidance, confidence, and self-knowledge. If you are stuck on a project, invoke their wisdom to know when to keep trying and when to give up on a project. Ask for their blessing when making gifts for loved ones or for charity.

Arachne

Arachne was an expert weaver who gained great renown. Her pride in her work was such that she challenged the goddess Athena to a weaving competition. Arachne's talent was formidable, but did not exceed the goddess's skills, and for her presumption in challenging a goddess, Athena turned Arachne into a spider. Call on Arachne when the truth is needed or when you need to face the shadow side of yourself.

Spider Woman

Another spider-related deity is the Spider Woman of Native American tradition. She is the creatrix of the world. She spins it into creation each morning and undoes the web each night. Spider Woman can be called on for inspiration and for when you begin a new project.

Ariadne

The Minoan Moon goddess Ariadne gave Theseus the yarn ball that kept him from getting lost in the Minotaur's labyrinth. Call on her when you are confused about which path to take or need to reflect on the past. Invoke Ariadne when deciding when and how to proceed on a project or new idea.

Athena

Athena was the goddess of wisdom and the patron of arts and crafts. Her only equal in yarn work and weaving was Arachne. In their contest, Athena created a weaving piece that showed all the wonderful things that the gods and goddesses gave humankind. She is exact and precise. Call on her for skill and detail. Athena also rules inspiration and blesses the planning and beginning of a project.

Hephaestus

Hephaestus is the god of blacksmithing and crafts. He is best known for metal working and weapons, but Hephaestus is multi-talented. He wove the magic net that caught his wife Aphrodite and her lover Ares in a compromising position. It was woven with strong fibers and held with tight knots, and it was so well made they could not escape. Men can invoke Hepha-estus's aid and skill in their projects.

Spellcraft

Knitting can also be used in spellcraft and magic. Since knitting is a repetitive exercise, it has the potential to allow the crafter to change her consciousness. This change in consciousness can aid in magic by putting us in the right state of mind to cast spells. Just picking up the needles can help shift your mind toward magical workings.

Knitting magic is connected to knot magic: they both involve weaving and moving yarn. Knot magic has always been popular. The ancient Greeks and Romans used it often to ward off negativity. It was also used for finding lost objects or to manifest a goal or wish. Ancient knot shapes became a part of sacred Celtic artwork. Knots are considered sacred in the Chinese Buddhist tradition too. It is believed that when enlightened masters meditate, their intestines take the form of the Mystic Knot. In modern witch-craft, the Witches' Ladder is made of nine knots on a bit of cord. Each knot has a feather tied in it. It can be used for any goal, including healing, prosperity, and love. A charm or chant is said while each knot is being tied, reinforcing its purpose. Any type of string or yarn can be used in this spell, and knitting Witches can use this technique with left over bits of yarn.

Witches can also put energy and intent into their knitting projects. In this magic, use yarn color and tex-ture to your advantage. Use red in a sweater for a boost of energy. Blue used in a blanket can help you fall asleep. Pink is for projects of love and affection—work pink into a project for a lover or friend. Black can be protective and is great for a purse or bag. It will match any outfit and protect your valuables at the same time. Adding a bit of energy and magic can make a beautiful, handmade gift even more special. Witches can empower any project, so use your imagination. There are many ways to knit and charge your own magical tools, like altar cloths, sachets, and robes.

I have included two practical knitting spells. I tried to keep them open-ended so that any Witchy knitter, regardless of experience and skill level, can use them. Adapt these spells to any scarf- or bag-knitting pattern you desire.

Raising Confidence Scarf Spell

Scarves are the perfect projects: they can be as easy or complicated as you like. For beginners, I recommend using a simple knit stitch. The scarf will knit up quickly if you use large needles and make it narrow. For this spell scarf, use bright colors like red or purple, or metallics like gold and silver. There are a lot of cheap, stylish, and fun yarns now available at most chain craft stores. When casting on the first row of stitches, chant: "I bind on one, my spell's begun." With each knit stitch, chant: "My confidence rise and reach the skies." Allow the stitch and chant to create its own rhythm. When completing the cast-off stitching, say: "Now I'm done, the spell is sealed." With the final stitch, say: "So mote it be!" Next, stop and look at your beautiful scarf. Admire and feel proud of it. Lift your head high, put on your scarf, and face the world glowing with beauty and confidence.

Protective Knit Bag Spell

As you learn more stitches and patterns, you can move from making simple scarves to making bags.

While making a bag, you want to empower it to protect your valuables. It doesn't matter what stitches you use, but some appropriate colors would be black, green, brown, or any "earthy" color. As you cast on the first stitches, say: "As I bind on one, my spell's begun." This starts the magic. With each body stitch: "Protection is bound all around." When binding the final row: "Now I'm done, this spell is sealed." With the last stitch, say: "So mote it be!" Strengthen the spell by placing protective symbols on the bag, like an eye, five-petal flower, star, or Sun. The symbols can be placed inside or outside the bag. They can be embroidered, beaded, or attached as a charm. Also, you can create a small pouch for protection herbs or crystals and attach it to the inside of the bag. You can use protection herbs such as sandalwood, rue, sea salt, black salt, dragon's blood, or fennel. Apache tear, obsidian, smoky quartz, or clear quartz make good protective crystals.

Knitting is a wonderful and Witchy craft. It can be relaxing, challenging, and empowering. You can use it for meditation, working powerful magic, and connecting to nature, deity, and the ancestors. However, the greatest lesson knitting teaches us is how to blend and balance the mundane and magical every day.

Fulgurite:
Crystallized Lightning

by Corrine Kenner

Think back to the last thunderstorm you experienced. Maybe you were in bed, when the distant rumble of thunder stirred you from your slumber. Maybe you watched from your living room, as lightning filled the sky and lit up your yard. Maybe you even took a chance and opened a window or a door, so a rush of negative ions could clear away the tired, stale air of your everyday existence.

Of all of nature's phenomena, there is nothing so awe-inspiring as a thunderstorm. The low vibration of moving clouds, the clash of thunder, the blowing wind . . . during a thunderstorm, the air is literally filled with spine-tingling electricity. A thunderstorm puts on a show like no other—and when lightning strikes, we are allowed to witness a natural phenomenon that both inspires and enlightens.

Thousands of years ago, the ancient Greeks were as spellbound by lightning as we are today. They believed that Zeus, the king of the gods, used lightning as a weapon of war. His Roman counterpart, Jupiter, was said to carry three thunderbolts; in *A Dictionary of Symbols*, J. E. Circlot said the three bolts symbolized chance, destiny, and providence, three forces that mold the future.

Lightning and thunder have been associated with gods in every culture. In Scandinavia, the Vikings believed lightning occurred whenever Thor struck an anvil with his hammer. Buddha was once depicted carrying a thunderbolt, and Native Americans told stories of the Thunderbird—a giant, winged spirit that carried lightning in its beak, and created thunder through the powerful beating of its enormous wings. Other native people have said that lightning was a visible manifestation of Father Sky impregnating Mother Earth.

In fact, lightning has symbolized divine intervention in every culture. In *An Illustrated Encyclopedia of Traditional Symbols*, J. C. Cooper wrote, "Thunder is the voice of the sky gods, with the thunderbolt as their weapon, the destroyer of serpents and spiritual enemies; divine anger; it is also an attribute of monarchs and magicians."

Even today, we use lightning as a metaphor for communication from the gods, along with inspiration and enlightenment. We speak of being struck by a bolt from the blue, or being hit by a flash of inspiration. And lightning—perhaps as a result of all those late-night thunderstorms—is a symbol of awakening.

You can find a potent symbol of that awakening in fulgurite, an otherwise unassuming little crystal that many people overlook.

That's because fulgurite is literally a piece of crystallized lightning.

Most fulgurite is sand fulgurite, which is formed when lightning strikes a sandy beach and superheated sand is instantly transformed into tubes of melted glass. When you hold a piece of fulgurite in the palm of your hand, you hold a sliver of the atmosphere. Fulgurite is a tangible reminder of the power in the air around us. Fulgurite can energize your creative process, reinvigorate your moods, and recharge the atmosphere in your home or office. In short, fulgurite can help you harness the power of a thunderstorm, for inspiration, enlightenment, or awakening. Fulgurite also makes a thoughtful gift—especially for creative people like artists and writers, who may be seeking a flash of illumination and insight.

Fulgurite is a fascinating crystal. While it's not classically beautiful like the amethyst, ruby, or rose quartz, it is as mesmerizing as lightning itself. In fact, fulgurite embodies a mystical power that could even surpass the more traditional stones in your collection, because fulgurite represents the physical union of earth, air, fire, and water, all combined in a flash.

You can find fulgurite in many gem and mineral shops, or through rock and mineral dealers, or even in school-supply stores. (Fulgurite is often sold as a study aid for science students.) If you're looking for bargain fulgurite, the least expensive specimens seem to be sold through eBay, where you can expect to pay as little as a dollar for a small sample of the crystal.

Of course, if you happen to live near the seashore—especially in an area that has many lightning strikes, like the Gulf Coast of Florida—you can find fulgurite yourself, simply by combing the beach after a thunderstorm.

Thunderstorms are the driving force behind all types of severe weather. They are the engine that keeps our atmosphere in motion, mixing and stirring the cauldron of life on Earth. Thunderstorms produce rain, hail, flash floods, tornadoes, and hurricanes. Thunderstorms are raw, unbridled displays of primal energy: they can both destroy life, and help to preserve it. Their violent destructive power—and their corresponding gifts to the natural world—are legendary.

And most of that power is based in lightning.

A lightning strike is a sudden, massive discharge of energy that moves from a cloud to the ground. In the ancient world, there was practically no distinction between lightning and thunder—and to this day, even from a distance, we can be struck by the sound of a raging thunderstorm. Lightning causes thunder because it superheats a column of air, which in turn causes a change in pressure and sends a shock wave out into the atmosphere.

And while thunderstorms can be frightful and dramatic, they also symbolize renewal and refreshment. Thunderstorms can be a welcome relief from summer heat waves, especially when they roll quickly through, breaking the intensity of an oppressive heat wave and clearing the air for a crisp, fresh morning. Thunderstorms break any period of drought. They recharge the Earth, literally, by generating negative ions, and they refresh and re-energize both people and plants.

Thunderstorms, in short, are magical, whether we think of them in terms of ancient gods waging war in the heavens, or moving bands of high and low pressure, battling for supremacy in the Doppler images on our television screens.

The word "fulgurite" comes from the Latin *fulgur*, which means "lightning." In medieval times, church bells were inscribed with the words *fulgaro franco*—"I break the lightning." According to Dr. Martin Uman, a lightning expert from the University of Florida, those inscriptions were a valiant attempt to divert lightning away from buildings and people, and safeguard the community. Unfortunately, those church bells were also positioned to be on the receiving end of more lightning strikes than they averted. Those who designed them were simply overpowered by a natural force that occurs far more often than most of us realize.

Dr. Uman's colleague, Vladimir A. Rakof, reports that lightning flashes somewhere on Earth about one hundred times a second. Only about a third of those lightning flashes actually strike the ground, however. Most lightning occurs within a cloud, or between clouds, or stays above the Earth.

When lightning flashes, most of its energy is discharged in the form of heat, light, and radio waves. The small fraction of power that's left over, however, is enough to kill, start fires, and create major electrical disturbances.

According to meteorologists, the temperature of any lightning strike ranges from 15,000 to 60,000 degrees Fahrenheit—and at its hottest, lightning can reach a temperature that's five times hotter than the surface of the Sun.

Which is why lightning can easily turn sand into glass. Sand melts at about 3,000 degrees Fahrenheit. When lightning strikes a beach—assuming that conditions are right and the lightning lingers just long enough—it vaporizes the grains of sand that are directly in its path. That leaves a hole in the sand. At the same time, the sand around that wormhole melts, which creates a glassy tube. Sometimes that tube has a few bubbles in it, the result of trapped moisture vapor, exploding outward. Some sand, only partially melted, clings to the outside of the tube.

A less common form of fulgurite, rock fulgurite, is formed when lightning strikes rock, particularly on mountaintops, and leaves a brownish-green glaze in its place. Some people also compare the smooth, glassy interior of sand fulgurite to tektite, the glass that results when a meteorite strikes the Earth's surface.

Sand fulgurite is branched and forked, just like the lightning that creates it. Because most lightning shoots straight down, most fulgurite specimens run straight down, too, branching off in several directions and growing narrower as they descend. Once it has formed, fulgurite cools quickly.

Most fulgurite specimens are fairly small, because they're fragile and they break easily. Fulgurite is essentially glass, so it takes great skill to recover large samples. Scientists can sometimes unearth museum-size specimens by excavating them like dinosaur bones; the largest piece of fulgurite on record was found in Florida in 1996, and its two branches totaled thirty-three feet.

Beachcombers can find smaller specimens—an inch or two in length—on the surface of the beach. Fulgurite isn't a well-known crystal, and it can be easy to overlook. On a sandy beach, fulgurite is the same color as the rest of the sand—whether that sand happens to be tan, gray, black, or white. To a practiced eye, however, fulgurite is recognizable: the hollow, glass-lined tubes look a lot like small twigs and tree branches. The exterior is usually rough, and it is often covered with loose grains of sand. The inside is hollow, with smooth and glassy sides. Most of the specimens you'll find for sale range in size from a quarter of an inch to three inches in length.

Once you get a piece of fulgurite, study it carefully. You can easily cradle it in your hand—fulgurite weighs next to nothing—or balance it on your fingertips.

Let fulgurite remind you of everything you know about lightning, as well as the transforming power of spirit and energy in our physical lives. Fulgurite will probably remind you of storms, but its sandy makeup might also remind you of long, moonlit walks on the beach, or playful days on the shore, or watery cruises across oceans and seas.

Examine the rough exterior, along with the grains of sand that symbolize time, eternity, and community. Try to peer through the hollow glass tube that runs through the center of each specimen, and imagine your own life, right now, as a moment frozen in time. In every piece of fulgurite, the sands of time have been preserved . . . perhaps not for eternity, but for as long as you can safeguard them.

And you will want to keep your fulgurite in a safe place. Don't get it wet, or try to polish it, or rub it excessively with your fingers, because the external coating of sand will come off without much effort, leaving your fulgurite even more susceptible to damage.

You might even want to imagine yourself as Zeus, the Greek god, hurling thunderbolts through time and space in an attempt to control those around him and manifest a world more to his liking. Just be aware that if you really throw your fulgurite, you'll probably break it. In which case, you may have to wait for another thunderstorm to blow a new piece of fulgurite into your life.

The Well-Organized Witch

by Magenta Griffith

Can't find your athame and robes when it's time to leave for your coven meeting? Do you have trouble finding that apartment-seeking spell when you need a new place to live? Being a Witch isn't just about magic—it's also about being able to work effectively and efficiently. Yes, witchcraft requires work, and many organizational and efficiency skills can be applied to the Craft.

Where do you do your magical work? Few people have a whole room to devote to magic, but many can find a closet. A crate or small chest of storage drawers can be the altar, covered by a length of cloth (a night-table works well, too). Fabric stores often have cloth remnants that are inexpensive and large enough to cover a small altar. Or you can use a length of cloth sold as a sarong. If you use a closet, you can hang your robes and other magical clothes at one end of the closet. If there is a shelf, you can use it for books or supplies. The drawers of the altar/chest can be used for smaller supplies like incense.

If you don't even have a spare closet, find some space in your bedroom that you can use as an altar. If you cannot leave altar equipment out when you aren't using it, put it all in the same drawer. If you can, take every item off the altar in the same order each time, and put it away covered by your altar cloth. You might want to wrap wands and athames in protective cloths—silk scarves or handkerchiefs work well. Some items can remain out: a chalice may be an ordinary glass you can put in the cupboard or a goblet you keep on your dresser because it's beautiful; a candle or two can be useful if the power goes out, or add atmosphere to your bedroom.

If you have more space, a larger chest of drawers or bureau is an excellent altar. Drawers are useful for storing supplies, such as incense, candles, extra altar cloths, robes that won't wrinkle, Tarot decks, and out-of-season altar decorations. After all, that jack-o'-lantern candleholder has to go somewhere when it isn't Samhain, and so does that long black robe.

Robes need to be stored neatly, either hung up on a hanger or folded and put in a drawer. They need to be washed frequently to keep them physically clean and to purify the energy that will cling to them after a ritual. (I'd advise against putting them in your regular laundry.) Having more than one set of robes makes it easier to have clean ones available when you need them.

Your supplies need to be organized so that you can find everything, and anything perishable needs to stored properly. Incense can lose its scent, as can essential oils. Candles can warp and melt, as well as rub wax on other items. Robes need to be kept clean; if you have robes you use only on certain occasions, you may need to store them specially.

Incense needs to be stored in an airtight container. A tall jar may work, and so might a cylindrical plastic container made for storing spaghetti. Put different scents in separate plastic bags inside the larger container, or all the fragrances will start to blend after a while. You probably don't want frangipani-scented frankincense, or copal that smells of rose. A word of caution: some incense ingredients can eat through plastic. Cinnamon, for example, will ruin a plastic container, and eat through rubber bands and plastic bags quickly. Check your storage containers every few weeks to be sure nothing like this is happening. Almost nothing will eat through glass, but glass is breakable.

Candles need to be kept in a cool, dry place. If you put them in the freezer for several hours before you burn them, they will last longer and drip less. Unless you have a lot of freezer space, most of your candle supply can be kept in the basement, or at the bottom of a closet. Check frequently to see if they are stay-ing in their proper shape, especially in summer.

If you keep salt on your altar, it should probably be in an airtight, moisture-proof jar or container, unless you live in a very dry climate. Have a small salt dish for ritual purposes, and keep the rest dry.

Keep the herbs you use for magic separate from cooking herbs. Store herbs in a tightly closed jar; most commercial spice jars are too small and made for decorative use. Unless you use herbs rarely, you need to keep them in a convenient place. Small squat jars, wider than they are tall, with tightly fitting lids, work best for all sorts of herbs. Many cooking herbs have magical uses, but you may want a separate supply if you use them for both purposes on a regular basis.

Whether you keep your Book of Shadows on paper or on computer, it helps to have it organized. If you prefer paper, consider a three-ring binder, divided into sections such as "Rituals Performed," "Dreams," "Tarot Readings," etc. Whatever you need to keep track of, have a section for it. If you prefer a bound book, consider reserving the last few pages as an index. Number your pages, make a list of page numbers in the back, and write a word or two about each entry in pencil. Later, you can go back and rewrite the index if you need to.

If you use a "Disk of Shadows," be sure to keep multiple back-ups. Again, a folder for each different sort of record helps keep things easier to find, and so does a consistent naming format. For example, rituals could be in a separate folder, and within it, the files could be named "Samhain 2002," "Beltane 2005," and so on. If you are concerned about other people reading your "book," you can devise a file-naming system that isn't so obvious. A file named "r-103102" might mean the same as "Ritual for Samhain 2002." Set up a schedule for doing back-ups, such as every Wednesday or every New Moon.

If you ever have occasion to practice away from home, you might want to assemble a Traveling Witch Kit. Choose a container that can also serve as a small altar—a lunch box works well, or a wooden box with a tight lid. Stock it with incense and an incense burner, a candle in its holder, a collapsible or unbreakable cup for water (and a bottle of water if you have room), salt in a waterproof container, a small cloth to put on the box as an altar cloth, and possibly a small goddess and/or god statue or other images. You might also have a miniature Tarot deck, a feather, a few crystals or other stones that have some significance to you, and anything else you might want to use to do magic on the go.

If you regularly go to coven or other group rituals, you probably want to be prepared to take food and drink along. It's good to have three or four recipes to bring that everyone likes, or foods you can keep on hand. Some people bring a gallon of cider or a pan of brownies. It's very useful to have a regular food or drink to bring, so you don't have to think about it. Be sure to mark coven meetings and other rituals on your calendar as soon as you can (if necessary, just write "busy" on that evening). That way, you won't double-book yourself.

Some covens like to get together a few times a year for a "business meeting" to plan activities. Everyone brings a calendar, making sure at least one person has a guide that shows holidays and the Moon's phases. Schedule your Sabbats as far ahead as people feel comfortable making plans.

Keeping your books on magic and Witchcraft in alphabetical order by author's last name will save you a lot of work in the long run. When you only have three books, it seems silly, but when you have thirty, it makes more sense. When you have three hundred, it becomes absolutely necessary if you want to find a given book without extended searching. If you have a lot of books, you might even want to arrange them by subject as well, and alphabetical within that. Some people prefer alphabetical by title, which is fine if you can remember the title. If you have trouble remembering the author, arrange by subject instead. But have some sort of system as early as possible.

There are a number of good websites online that deal with keeping your life tidy and organized. Many of them have hints you can apply to being a well-organized Witch. My favorites are www.flylady.net and lifeorganizers.com.

Magic happens spontaneously, but being reasonably well organized makes it easier to be spontaneous, so you can let the magic happen.

Magical Herbs
For Protection and Purification

by James Kambos

Herbs have been used as ingredients in protection and purification magic since before biblical times. In the ancient world, herbal healing, protection magic, and purification rites were considered to be highly respected talents, usually entrusted to the local wise ones. Most likely it was the ancient Egyptians who developed herbal protection magic into an art. For example, we know that they used the scent of myrrh to purify their temples.

As ancient empires rose and fell, herbal protection magic and lore began to spread. From the land of ancient Egypt, this magical herbal knowledge was absorbed and enhanced by the Greeks. Next, the Romans were responsible for keeping these herbal secrets alive.

As Christianity grew, however, the lore of the old herbalists became somewhat distorted. The plants and herbs known since antiquity for their healing and protective qualities were naturally linked to Paganism. Unfortunately, any herbal protective folk magic, or herbal healing charms associated with Paganism, were mistakenly thought to be evil. This being the case, herbal magic was either practiced in secrecy or avoided completely.

Eventually, thanks to the brave efforts of magical people such as early Witches, Gypsies, and herbal healers, much of this herbal wisdom did survive and was passed down through the ages. The herbal spells and charms used for protecting and healing became a magical legacy, willed from one generation to the next. In many instances this knowledge became a closely-guarded family secret.

I was raised in such a family, and my interest in herbal magic began at an early age. My family came to America from a Greek island just off the Turkish Coast. My grandmother, Katina, brought with her a knowledge of herbs and plants which she used in herbal protection spells. Like many Greek people of her era, my grandmother was an Orthodox Christian, but at the same time, she blended the ancient magical herbal knowledge of her heritage with her Christian faith. The tradition of utilizing the magical healing qualities of herbs in protective magic was taught to her by her mother, then passed on to my mother, and eventually to me.

As a child I learned that ordinary kitchen ingredients such as garlic, olive oil, basil, cloves, and almonds could be magically changed and used to ward off evil, increase fertility, or bring general good fortune.

Herbs For Protection and Purification

Without realizing it, many of us already practice herbal protection magic. When you hang mistletoe in your home at Yule for instance, you are actually encouraging love and protection to surround your living space. And by placing flowers outside your front door on May Day (Beltane), you are invoking fertility magic. Another example is the use of bittersweet in autumn decorations. Originally, bittersweet was hung about the home for protection, and was used in love charms.

What follows is a collection of magical herbal lore, traditions, spells, advice, and long-forgotten practices which focus on the use of plant materials to achieve protection, healing, purification, and general well-being.

I've divided the information into these categories: Home and Garden, Love and Friendship, Spiritual Protection, and Ritual Purification and Cleansing.

The magical herbal lore provided here is only a small sample of the herbal knowledge possessed by our ancestors. It is intended to help create interest in this fascinating area of herbalism, and to remind all of us how herbs can help bring positive changes into our lives.

Protective Herbal Magic In The Home

Herbal magic began in the home and garden. It was here the herbalists first raised the plants destined to be used in folk magic. Herbs not grown in the garden were gathered in the nearby woodland. Since life centuries ago centered around the home and hearth, the home became the focal point for herbal healing and magic.

If there is one room in the house to begin your practice of herbal magic it would be the kitchen. You'll be surprised to find that many of the ordinary foods and seasonings you already have in your kitchen cupboard are loaded with magical power.

One of the most important herbs to have on hand for protection is basil. Here are a few ways to use it to protect your home.

A Basil Blessing

Wash three stems of basil and tie them together. This will be your "wand." Face east while holding the basil in your power hand, and gently shake it as you move clockwise around your kitchen. As you do so, speak this charm:

> *Bless the pantry and every pot.*
> *Bless the oven that cooks my food and keeps it hot.*
> *Bless each appliance, cupboard, and drawer.*
> *Bless this kitchen, forever more.*

Hang the basil to dry, and use as needed in recipes to bless your food. When the basil is used, repeat the blessing if you wish.

An alternative basil blessing would be to simply sprinkle some dried basil in a corner of each room. To prevent negativity from entering the home, sprinkle basil on the porch and on the threshold of any exterior door. Or, you can do what my grandmother always did—keep a pot of basil growing on your porch or patio. Touch it frequently to release its healing and calming scent.

Another good all-around protective herb to have in the spice cabinet is clove. Ground or whole, clove sprinkled in the pantry will deter ants and at the same time attract abundance. Cloves are ruled by Jupiter, which means they are highly effective at repelling any hostile energy away from the home and from all who reside there. The clove spell that follows is very old and has been used in my family for four generations. Use it to protect the home or break a hex.

Nine Cloves Spell For Protection

Assemble the following: A white candle, ¼ cup water, ½ teaspoon olive oil, one small bowl, and nine whole cloves. Mix the water and olive oil in the bowl; light the candle, visualizing your home surrounded by a circle of white light. Pick up one clove at a time and hold it by the stem end so the bud end is directly above the tip of the candle's flame. It will ignite instantly. Immediately drop the burning clove into the water/oil mixture to extinguish it. Repeat with remaining cloves. The smoke and scent released by the smoldering cloves will repel any evil and purify your living space. When done, pour the clove and water mixture onto the earth of your garden or wooded area. Let the earth absorb and purify any negativity.

Soothing Lavender

To promote soothing vibrations throughout the home, especially in the bedroom and bath, lavender is my herb of choice. A lavender wand, which you can purchase from an herbal craft store, is ideal to place on a night table by the bed. In the bath, lavender scented soaps and bubblebaths will ease tension, and dried lavender will also repel moths when placed among linens.

Herbs To Protect The Front Door

According to folk tradition, the front door is where the resident household spirit dwells. To keep your friendly spirit around, or to attract one, hang any of the following herbs, according to their season, on your front door. Or keep them on your porch.

Bittersweet: Use to promote healing and for protection.

Corn: Indian corn attracts luck and encourages fertility.

Fern: A potted fern, or hanging fern, is known for its protective qualities when placed by the front door. Ferns are also a favorite of the Fairy Folk.

Goldenrod: Hang dried goldenrod along with bittersweet to attract prosperity and good health.

Pine: At Yule and Christmas, pine wreaths serve to remind us about the eternal cycle of the seasons. The ancients believed pine represented the life-force. Combined with pine cones, it will also represent fertility.

Garlic And Protective Herbal Magic

Of all the herbs used in protective herbal magic in the home, garlic may be the most powerful. Hung in the kitchen, by the front door, or placed in the bedroom, garlic will protect against almost any hostile energy.

When garlic is combined with any of the seasonal herbs for the front door that I described above, its power is even greater. Crush a clove of garlic and place it in olive oil during a waxing Moon, then use this mixture to bless and anoint any new appliance or machinery. To guard the home from evil, slice a clove of garlic into three pieces. Combine with salt and sprinkle on your doorstep.

Protective Herbal Magic In The Garden

Many of the old-fashioned flowers and herbs found blooming in the gardens of our grandparents were not planted just because of their beauty or food value; they were also planted because of their ability to draw protective energy to the home and garden. Here is a list of only a few herbs and plants prized for their protective and healing qualities. The plants I've selected are hardy, common, and easy to find at most local nurseries.

Alyssum: This small plant blooms with honey-scented blue and white flowers. It is usually used as an edging plant, and can create a calming effect and guard against tension.

Chrysanthemum: Highly regarded in Japan, this autumn-blooming flower is a good all-around protective herb. It protects against all evil.

Dill: Hung near the front door or grown in the garden, dill guards against jealousy and any negative magic. Let a few plants go to seed so that they will attract beneficial insects to the garden.

Hyacinth: Sweet smelling and attractive, hyacinths help relieve depression and encourage love. Brought into the home, they will protect any area.

Hydrangea: To break a hex, scatter pieces of the bark around the outside of the home or garden.

Ivy: Grown near the home, ivy guards against envy and bad luck. Scatter a few leaves around your property as needed for protection.

Lilac: Lilac was originally planted to protect a property from all evil. The blue and white varieties are the most powerful. Bringing the freshly cut flowers indoors has a purifying effect and can remove unwanted spirits.

Lily: Lilies (not daylilies, which are actually *hemerocallis*), are excellent for protecting the garden against the evil eye. White varieties are thought to be the most powerful.

Lovage: This flavorful herb, if planted near the home, attracts positive vibrations to you.

Morning Glory: Blue morning glories draw happiness to the garden. They bloom from mid-summer to hard frost.

Mugwort: This member of the artemisia family is one of the most powerful purifying, healing, and protective herbs. Be cautious when planting in the garden, because it can become weedy. To protect the home, sprinkle a bit of dried mugwort in a pail of clean water, then wipe thresholds to protect and cleanse. Hang a bunch of dried mugwort above a garden gate or along fences to repel any evil.

Primrose: Despite their diminutive size, primroses bring powerful herbal magic to the garden. The red and blue varieties especially offer general protection from many forms of adversity.

Rose: No magical herb garden is complete without at least one rose. Roses, the symbol of love, also attract good fortune and have a calming effect.

Rosemary: This Sun-ruled herb is one of the most ancient of all the protective herbs. It is said to deter robbers if hung near the entryway. Place sprigs of rosemary near the foundation of a house, or sprinkle around the perimeter of the garden to protect from harm.

Valerian: Known since medieval times, valerian purifies and protects. It has a calming influence.

Yarrow: Common yarrow may have yellow, pink, red, or white flowers. All are believed to protect property or individuals when carried. The aromatic foliage cleanses any space.

Zinnia: The zinnia is the star of the late summer garden. Zinnias were honored by the ancient Aztecs. Use their clear, bold colors to draw happiness to the garden border.

An Herbal Witch Bottle Spell

Now, let's utilize some of the protective herbs I've described in an actual spell. The spell I've chosen to share with you uses a very old form of herbal protection magic known as a "Witch bottle."

A Witch bottle can be any bottle, jar, or earthenware vessel used for a magical purpose. These magical bottles have been used for centuries. To prepare a Witch bottle, the magician fills the bottle or jar with herbs and other materials suitable for the magical goal while concentrating on the result of the wish. The number of herbs placed in the bottle are usually odd in number—three, five, or seven are common. Frequently some type of liquid is added, then the bottle is sealed and hidden. By doing this, the magic is left undisturbed to do its work. The bottle may be buried on your property, hidden in a basement, or sealed into a secret opening in a building's foundation.

For your herbal protection Witch bottle you'll need a clean small jar with a screw-top lid, such as an empty mustard jar. Then obtain at least three protective herbs from the list. Next, add some rose petals or a rose thorn. Place all the herbs in the bottle, and pour a cleansing liquid, such as vinegar or lemon juice, over the herbs—just enough to cover them. Cap the bottle and shake. Bury the jar where it won't be disturbed. As you place the bottle into the earth, say, "Bottle fulfill my need [you may state the specific need at this time]. Herbs of protection, do your deed." Cover with soil and walk away.

If the earth is ever disturbed and the jar is damaged, repeat the spell if you wish. The bottle will serve to protect you and your property for as long as you want. I have a Witch bottle buried on my property that has remained in the same location for twenty years.

You may be surprised to learn that there are about two hundred plants and trees classified as protective herbs for the home and garden. Naturally, I don't have enough space here to write about all of them; however, the information I've provided thus far will give you a good idea of how to begin using herbs for protection magic in and around the home.

Herbs To Protect Love and Friendship

Probably the next most popular reason to use herbs is to promote love and friendship. This area of herbal folk magic can also be the most tricky. Remember, no form of protective love magic should be performed unless both parties involved want a relationship, otherwise you'll be manipulating another person's free will.

Herbalists, both ancient and modern, have frequently been called upon to use their knowledge to promote fidelity, devotion, affection, protection, and healing in love and friendship.

Violet Love Charm For Loyalty

Violets inspire loyalty. To ensure loyalty, try this Appalachian love charm. Follow the instructions below:

To ensure your love remains true;
Pick six violets, all must be blue.
Put them in water you have blessed;
Place them where your lover's head shall rest.

After you do these things, take three ribbons—pink, yellow, and white—and wait until the darkness of night. Tie them around the branch of a tree and say:

We are now bound, so mote it be.

Return A Lover Home Safely Spell

In the center of a piece of red fabric place the following: a bit of dried crushed mint, three bittersweet berries, and a crushed almond. Tie up the bundle with a piece of pink ribbon about three feet long. Lay the bundle on a table; holding the ribbon, pull the bundle toward you, saying:

Mint, bittersweet, and almond dust
My lover is coming safely home.
Come to me; this is a must.

Finish by placing the bundle beneath your lover's pillow.

Maintain A Friendship Spell

This spell is especially effective if you have a long-distance friendship. You'll need a votive candle scented with a spicy fragrance such as cinnamon or allspice, preferably orange in color. You'll also need half a teaspoon or so each of lemon balm, pennyroyal, and crushed bay leaf. On the candle, scratch your friends' initials. Light the candle and think about all the good times you've had with your friend. Crumble together the three herbs in a small dish. Let the candle burn out. End by taking the herbs outdoors and sprinkling them in the direction of wherever your friend lives.

Herbal Purification and Cleansing

Herbs have been used to purify and cleanse the sacred space found in temples, shrines and other religious sites since the human race first believed in a divine power. I developed the following rite after watching the morning mist rise above the river near my home on summer mornings. Use this ritual to cleanse your magical area, or use it to cleanse new magical tools as I do.

In a heat-proof dish, combine one part each of dried lavender, wormwood, and sage. Ignite the herbs and let them smolder a while. As the smoke curls about you, hold the tool you wish to bless and say:

Smoke rise, let me be wise
This [name of item] is cleansed
I will use it only for the good of all.

Your magical tool is ready to use. Inhale the scent of the herbs; think of the ways you'll use your new magical tool, and use it wisely.

Labyrinths

by K. D. Spitzer

Ancient labyrinths are often found at the entrance to sacred sites and at the crossing of the subtle Earth energies beneath. They have been dated back 4000 to 4500 years and have been found around the world and across cultures and religious traditions. Their origins are lost in the mists of time. A universal symbol, the circle/spiral design has been wrought as jewelry or worn as embroidery to protect the wearer against the evil eye or, especially, limned over doorways to protect the whole household.

Across the ages, labyrinths have been walked with solemnity for problem solving, healing, fertility, magic, meditation, and transformation. They have been run with joyous hearts and danced in ecstasy. They have launched many shamanic journeys. In coastal areas of Scandinavian countries, they have been walked by fisherman on the way to their boats in the hope that the evil trolls following them will get lost in the labyrinth; the fishermen can then get underway for the day with good weather and, most importantly, safely return home with a full cargo of fish.

There is a difference between a labyrinth and a maze. A maze can have many false turnings and dead ends—or even have several routes to the exit. It is a left-brain activity, requiring decisions and choices to walk back out. A labyrinth has one way in and the same way out. It's passive and receptive, and its physicality frees up the mind and spirit for insights, creativity, and intuition.

The labyrinth pattern has been found in ancient petroglyphs, but is also a recognizable pattern in baskets made by early Native Americans. The classic seven-circuit labyrinth of western tradition is believed to spring from Knossos, Crete, which was the home of the mythological Minotaur and the cult of Dionysius. While the labyrinth, which was part of the whole Minoan palace/temple complex on the island, was destroyed several times, the design of this famous labyrinth has survived on coins and pottery.

The name *labyrinth* itself was found in ancient Greek writings, but probably derives from the Near East and the Lydian word *labrys*, which means "double-headed axe." This tool was not only a symbol for royalty, but represented the authority and power of the Goddess. Even today, this two-sided battle axe is an inspiring symbol of the power source of ancient matriarchies. It has been adopted by Witches everywhere.

The Romans took their square pattern to the far corners of their empire, although it appears that the labyrinths in the British Isles predate this. These engineering Romans must have loved the geometry very much, as sixty mosaics incorporating labyrinths of varying sizes have been identified around the Roman world.

Ancient labyrinths have been found in such diverse places as India, Egypt, Cornwall, and Arizona. They have been laid out with stones, carved into rocks, or cut into the soil as turf mazes. One seven-circuit labyrinth was found in Sicily in the ceiling of an excavation and dates to 3500 BC.

The medieval Christian church adopted the labyrinth as a symbol of faith; to walk it was to tread the path to God. Using a pattern of eleven circuits, but always divided by four quadrants, it was laid into the floors of the great Gothic stone cathedrals of France. The builders, designers, and masons used their understanding of sacred architecture to lay out the labyrinths. Often placed near the baptismal font, it served as a metaphor for this life's journey.

This design is commonly referred to as *Chartres-style*, after the labyrinth in the cathedral at Chartres, France. Dividing this mandala into quadrants reveals the equal-armed cross at the heart of the design, which is a symbol that predates Christianity. Also, attached to the outer ring of the Chartres labyrinth are 112 small rays that poke outward. These are called *lunations* and there are

twenty-eight and a half in each quadrant, representing the lunar month. It is a calendar of sorts, and can be used to date Easter each year, which is a Moon-based holy day.

There has always been a hint of mystery attached to these labyrinths, as they were dusted with associations of the Knights Templar and the Temple of Solomon. These romantic rumors probably arose when the Knights were first organized to protect travelers to the holy city of Christ's death, which was the center of the world.

When travel to Jerusalem became dangerous for pilgrims during the time of the Crusades, and then became less fashionable as interest fell off and the price became prohibitive (your money *and* your life, so to speak), walking the labyrinth (repentantly, on one's knees) became a metaphor for the pilgrim's journey. It was called *Chemin du Jerusalem*, or the Road to Jerusalem. For some it was the Road to Paradise and the Kingdom of Heaven.

First, these pious Christians would make their pilgrimage to Canterbury or Chartres or other centers, usually facing great hardship and privation. Awestruck with the soaring power of the great cathedral, they would begin the next phase of their journey.

With a radius of 40 feet, the path at Chartres is about 285 yards long, but if you are shuffling along on your knees, it takes about an hour to do. Medieval pilgrims could walk about 3 miles in an hour, so, in a bit of wishful rationalization, they considered they had walked 3 miles, emerging purified. Seeing others taking this path reinforced the idea of spiritual commitment and that all people are on the life journey together.

Labyrinths were not only walked with solemnity, but children played upon them during services. Indeed, in the cathedrals at Reims and St. Omer, they were taken up because the kids were too noisy.

Sig Lonegren and the American Dowsers Society have discovered that many ancient labyrinths are sited above the crossing of underground water (yin) and straight ley lines (yang). They have done much work at old sites and have made it easy to establish new ones by following the same form. Modern labyrinths are laid out using twin dowsing rods to locate the center and mouth, and then using a compass to orient its direction. There is a seed pattern to facilitate construction once the location of the key elements have been identified.

Today, there are portable canvas labyrinths that are easily stored and just as quickly unrolled and ready for walking. Temporary ones are laid out with powdered lime, herbs, flowers, paint, tape, hay, or ribbons, or are cut into tall grasses with mowers. More permanent ones are being installed at private homes or in public churchyards and hospitals.

Since the renaissance of labyrinth construction and their perambulation, many diverse claims are being made for them by Christians, New Agers, self-described shamans, and the whole field of psychoanalytical thinkspeak. Regardless of all that, know one thing for sure: It requires shifting the use of the brain from the left side to the right side and back again with every 180-degree turn. The ultimate effect of this is a balancing and centering, thus creating a feeling of wholeness. It is a way to find the center of yourself.

A labyrinth is not only sacred space or a meditation space, but magical space. There are no dead ends or false trails—just one way in and one way out. It's about the journey; you don't need a map and you can't get lost. Perhaps on some occasions the labyrinth will just be a nice walk or a mind-quieting meditation; you might receive a mundane but enlightening insight, but not necessarily. You don't need to expect a life-altering experience. It is enough to follow your path.

There is no right or wrong way to formally walk a labyrinth, but when walking with a group, it is courteous to wait until the person before you has moved to the next circuit. Everyone gets time in the center alone. Some walk to the labyrinth heart with their palms toward the ground, releasing unwanted baggage; after a meditation they return with palms turned to the heavens to receive the messages and blessings of the universe. You may want to leave a gift behind—a flower, stone, shell, or crystal, or even a plant if you're at an outdoor labyrinth.

Simple Magic
for the Modern Witch

by Mickie Mueller

In ancient times the local village witch made her own soap, baked her own bread—in fact, she made everything from scratch. She would never purchase these items from the grocery store or drug store, because there was no such thing. Making such things was an arduous, time-consuming process, so if ancient people could find a way to save steps, they did.

Modern Witches tend to be a pretty practical bunch too, when it comes right down to it. We are busy folks, with jobs, kids, and house payments, but the spirit of our time-saving ancestors has been passed down to us, and we have a treasure trove of potential magical items available at our very fingertips, if we just know where to look.

You don't have to drive for miles to Ye Olde Magic Shoppe to get your every need, nor do you have to harvest your own wheat for Sabbat cakes or stand over a cauldron all day stirring that magical brew. You can make magic with lots of items you can get easily from the corner store or around the house. You just need to be a little inventive, and work smarter, not harder. After all, learning magic teaches us that it's not what you have that is most important, but what you do with what you have, and the magical intention you put into it that makes everything work. Brothers and sisters, it's time to move into the modern age, and bring our magic to a new level. I'm sure that most of you, like myself, are very busy these days, so I will share with you some great ideas for quick magic that is as effective as it is simple.

Easy Magical Bubble Bath

Here is a wonderful and easy recipe for a wash that will keep negative influences at bay. When the going gets tough, I whip up a bottle of this great wash and use it daily until things calm down.

You'll need a bottle of your favorite bubble bath or shower wash. Pour out about ¼ cup (you can save it to add back to the bottle after you've used it a few times if you wish). Place the following herbs in a tied cloth bundle or a tea ball, and steep in about ¼ cup of hot water for half an hour: a pinch each of powdered frankincense, vervain, basil, rosemary, and sea salt; a very small pinch of rue (test your skin for sensitivity first); 1 bay leaf.

Pour the infusion into the bottle of bubble bath and shake. Raise energy and charge the bottle with your intention that it remove all negativity from you and protect you from negative influences.

Use it every time you take a bath. You can use it in the shower on a washcloth or bath puff—just make sure you get it all over you: face, feet, ears, everywhere. If you don't want to use it in your hair in the shower, just wave the washcloth through your aura, above your head. You have now destroyed the negative influences clinging to you as well as creating a barrier for future negative influences.

Mercury to the Rescue

I've got two words for you: Mercury retrograde. We all know what that means: problems with communication, difficulties in transportation—what a mess! During the last Mercury retrograde my car broke down—twice! So what the heck is Mercury retrograde? We see it on the magical calendars, so we know *when* it is, but if you are not an astrologer or astronomer, you may not know *what* it is. Mercury retrograde is when the planet Mercury seems to be traveling backwards through the zodiac. It's not really going backwards, but the orbit of the Earth in relation to the planet Mercury creates the illusion that it is.

As magic workers, we would really like to be able to do something to avoid the glitches, breakdowns, and delayed communications associated with this astronomical event. What to do? We can't break out a spell to move the planets, and we are constrained to working within the cycles. So how about making friends with the god Mercury? Boost that positive Mercury energy in your life while it is running backward astronomically, and even things up a bit. It might not completely negate Mercury retrograde's influence, but this little amulet bag spell can really ease the pain quite a bit.

First, acquire a Mercury dime. Mercury dimes are silver coins from 1940, and while the image on the dime isn't really Mercury, everyone thought it was, so that's what people called it. These dimes contain Mercury energy because of their popular association with the messenger god. If you can't find one on your own, you can pick one up from a coin dealer for fewer than two bucks. Once you get it home, cleanse it the way you would a crystal to rid it of the energies of those who handled it before you.

You'll also need a purple or orange votive candle, an orange square of cotton cloth, purple ribbon or string to tie the cloth, a few dandelion seeds or petals, caraway seeds, celery seeds, and a few purple chrysanthemum petals.

Light the votive candle in a votive cup, and place the Mercury dime and the other items in the middle of the square of cloth, and bundle it up in your hand. Repeat this chant to charge it:

> *Mercury, messenger of the gods,*
> *Don't let your path put me at odds,*
> *Please help me pass this time with ease,*
> *As I do will, so mote it be.*

Repeat this several times until you feel energy has been raised, and then channel that energy into the bag. Tie it closed with the ribbon, making three knots and repeating the chant one more time as you tie the knots. Leave it by the candle until it burns out. Carry the amulet bag with you during Mercury retrograde, and every time it goes back into retrograde, recharge the bag.

Curiously Strong Spells

Here are a few wonderfully simple spells using those lovely little mints in the neat little tins that we know as Altoids. These mints come in an excellent variety of flavors and most contain large amounts of natural herb oils. Another ingredient in every flavor is gum arabic, used for spirituality and purification, and to destroy negativity, which is useful in any spell.

The idea here is that you empower the entire tin of mints to your purpose, and then by eating them later you absorb the magic into your very cells.

Obtain a tin of candy mints of the flavor corresponding with your purpose: peppermint to create prosperity; ginger to boost energy, success, and power; spearmint to sharpen mental powers.

Then empower the tin of candy with your intent. Light a tealight in its metal cup and place on top of the tin. Here are some charms you can use to charge your tin of mints, or feel free to make your own.

Peppermint, grant to me success.
Bring to me the very best.
Heat up my power with your spice.
Bring me riches and all that's nice.

Ginger, boost my energy,
Grant to me vitality,
Keep my will brave and strong,
And help it last the whole day long.

Spearmint, keep my mind alert,
Upon my goals and on my work.
File my thoughts within my brain,
That I may recall with ease again.

Let the candle burn out. Whenever you need an extra magical boost, like before a job interview, big meeting, or important event, break out your little tin of magic mints and eat a few. A word of warning: you really shouldn't share these mints with others at random—remember, it really isn't ethical to offer magic to someone without his or her knowledge.

A Spell You Can Take to the Bank

Here is another great mint spell. The next time you are at the bank, pick up a mint if they offer them in a jar or dish at the counter. Many banks offer mints; if yours doesn't, find one that does and grab a couple of brochures and a mint. In some Feng

Shui traditions, water that comes from a successful business carries the essence of prosperity. Any magic user worth her salt knows that mint is a great herb for bringing prosperity. (Not to mention that money is made in a "mint" or if you do well on a big investment they may say that you "made a mint.") So, using these connections, you can see how the humble little red-and-white mint you acquire from a bank can carry a great amount of power if you use it in a spell. You can, of course, just charge the mint and eat it! Here is a charm.

Mint from money,
Money from mint,
This candy brings
Prosperous energy lent

Nothing Says Lovin' Like Something From the Coven

When I have my circle over, I always end up running around the house like mad trying to get everything in order. It just won't do to have our ritual while tripping over Tonka trucks and miniature versions of the entire cast of Lord of the Rings. I really want to have something special when our group gets together, but I'm usually pressed for time. So I came up with a compromise that falls somewhere between homemade Sabbat cakes, and a box of Oreos. These lovely little floral Sabbat cakes are made with a cake mix, edible flowers, and lots of magic!

    1 yellow cake mix
    1 tablespoon lavender buds

1 tablespoon dried rose petals,
   crunched up to the size of
   confetti
½ teaspoon marigold petals,
   prepared like the rose petals
1 tablespoon poppy seeds
1 tablespoon honey

Bake according to the directions on the box, using water blessed under the Full Moon if you have it. If you don't, no big deal. As you stir in the rest of the ingredients, try this charm:

> *Lavender, bring us happiness and peace,*
> *Petals of rose bring the bright lady's blessing.*
> *Golden honey the gift of the bees,*
> *Marigold's gift, intuition unfleeting.*
> *Poppy seeds and bad luck's put asunder,*
> *I bless this feast by Lord and Lady,*
> *With these Sabbat cakes, may we never hunger,*
> *And now as I will it, so mote it be.*

You have several options for baking. I have a really neat star-shaped tube pan that I use. You can also put the batter into a jellyroll pan and use star and moon cookie cutters when the cake cools. You can make mini-cupcakes, or you can just put the batter in a 9 x 12 pan and cut it into squares. They make a really nice presentation, as easy as making a box cake mix, and taste just magical!

The Subtle Art of Magic for the Workplace

by Mickie Mueller

It's Monday morning and you grab a cup of coffee as you hit the timeclock. A million mundane thoughts begin to swarm into your mind about deadlines, company cutbacks, or that big inspection you have to get ready for. It all makes you wonder, as you clock in for work—do you really have to clock out the Witch? As magical practitioners, we walk between the worlds, therefore that answer would be a resounding "No!"

Now, most companies have policies regarding diversity. They're all for it—just ask them. However, if you showed up at work in your ritual robe with a bundle of white candles and smoldering smudge stick ready to clear up some of that negativity lurking around the checkout counter, you would probably be pushing the envelope on how much diversity is really acceptable. Having been a working Witch for many years, I have some suggestions on ways to subtly use your magical talents to keep your workday running smoothly.

Remove Negativity Without Creating a Stir

Negative energy has a way of lurking around the workplace due to difficult customers and co-workers alike. Since negativity tends to build upon itself, it is wise to neutralize it before it gets out of hand. If you try the following little trick, pay extra attention throughout the day and see if the place feels nicer and tempers cool.

Purchase an ammonia-free glass cleaner with a vinegar base, and pour out just a bit. If you can't find a vinegar-based product, just add a little white vinegar to regular glass cleaner. At home, place the following herbs in a hot cup of water: basil, lavender, sage, and just a pinch of sea salt. Feel free to substitute your favorite cleansing and protection herbs. Allow the mixture to steep for at least five minutes, strain through a coffee filter, and pour a small amount into the glass cleaner. (Really strain it well: any little chunks of herbs will clog up your sprayer.) Holding the bottle in both hands, raise energy by repeating the following chant and sending it into the bottle:

Herbs and vinegar do your best
A cleansing mixture I request.
Destroying negative energy
As I spray and as I clean.

When you arrive at work the next day, clean your work area with your enchanted cleaner as you repeat the chant in your head to reaffirm your purpose. Your boss will think you are quite industrious. Keep your magical spray at work and use it any time, or when you feel the place is bogged down with negativity.

If negativity has already gotten the better of you, here are a couple of ideas to magically blow off some steam. If you work in an office, it's time to shred some documents. As you hold the papers in your hands, shove all your angry, hurt, or frustrated feelings into the documents. As you drop them one by one into the paper shredder, feel all that psychic sludge destroyed with the sheets of paper. If you work in an environment with a box crusher, volunteer to take the boxes back to crush. As you place each box in the crusher, lightly blow your anger or bad feelings into the boxes. Visualize them as clear glass bubbles. Then hit the button and let the big machine crush those bad feelings to oblivion. Do you work in a restaurant? Easy! Just throw all your daily angst into a dish of left-over food and toss it right down the garbage disposal, followed by a slice of lemon and some salt. There are probably other ways you can come up with at your place of business to create the same result.

Computers, Machines, and Gadgets. We Love 'Em, We Hate 'Em

Most of us have to deal with some kind of machinery at work, be it a cash register, computer, pricing gun, or possessed coffee maker. When these workplace gadgets are functioning, they make our lives easier—but when they get fussy, they can make our workday very difficult. I currently work with a lot of problematic machinery, and I like to jokingly blame it on gremlins.

Sometimes equipment just seems to go haywire for no apparent reason, and while magic won't keep you from having to regularly care for equipment and call in the technician sometimes, you can keep problems to a minimum by sending positive energy into the machinery you work with. When we think about equipment, it is important to remember that everything is filled with energy, and that goes for both living and inanimate objects. Therefore, what you need to do to keep your mechanical devices going is basically noncellular healing.

Depending on your work environment, you may be able to bring a pretty crystal to work to set near your computer. If you can, it works great. Quartz crystals boost energy and raise positive vibrations. You can cleanse the crystal first at home by holding it under running water and visualizing all the negativity being washed away. My favorite method is to leave it outside in a rainstorm. Then you can magically charge it to boost your computer. Here is a simple chant you can use to charge your crystal, and you can also use it to boost the crystal at work if something seems to be going awry:

> *Shining stone, bright and clear,*
> *Support machinery that lies near.*
> *Protect and heal each circuit too,*
> *And keep them running smooth and true.*

If you're not in a situation where you can place a crystal near your workspace, try a penny. Copper is a magical metal that helps boost energy flow. But don't just grab one out of your pocket—it needs to be prepared first. A penny has gone through many hands and will need serious cleansing. Run it under cold running water in the same manner as for a crystal, then bury it in some earth or a dish of salt for one month. If you choose to bury it in dirt, place a marker over it so you don't forget where you left it.

Now you can magically charge your penny. Anoint the penny with sandalwood or olive oil, and place it under a white candle. A tea light works great. You can use this chant:

Bright copper, metal of the Earth,
Boost my machinery for all it's worth.
Good metal by all the elements cast,
Keep it all running and make it last.

Then place the penny in an inconspicuous place near or even under the computer or other equipment.

Another subtle method is the use of a magical symbol or rune. Good choices for symbols for healing your office equipment would be an equal armed cross, the "ansur" rune for communication, the "eolh" rune for protection, the infinity symbol, or any healing symbol you like. You can draw the symbol or symbols of your choice on the sticky side of a piece of opaque tape or sticker and then stick it to the problematic piece of equipment in a place you can easily reach, but that won't be obvious. Silently use this chant:

Magic symbols, powers stick,
Brightest blessings do the trick.

Place your hand over the tape to add to the charge any time you feel the need.

Personnel Communications

Sometimes interactions with those at work can become difficult due to stress, or even personality clashes. You may experience difficult co-workers, clients, or customers, but before you try to set that pricing gun to "stun" let's discuss some ways to keep personal relationships at work from getting out of hand.

First let's start with something that nearly everyone has experienced. Have you ever had a day at work when it seems like everyone is acting erratic, crabby, or just plain weird? Then suddenly a co-worker says, "What's up with everyone today, is there a Full Moon or something?" Little do they know that you are all too aware of the Moon's phase, and sometimes on those days it is indeed full.

You usually won't notice that it is the kind of day where everyone is a little "off" until you have gotten well into the day. The minute that you realize, "Man, everyone is so crabby today," it is time to act. Make any excuse to head for the front door, and as you walk toward it, chant the word "balance" in your head over and over. The walking will raise energy, so feel it build in the center of your chest. When you reach the door, touch it and release the energy as you repeat "balance" once more in your head, followed by "So mote it be." Most people who walk through that door will feel that balancing energy and be less likely to fall under the influence of whatever is causing personality anomalies. You can also do a similar kind of spell by raising the "balance" energy and sending it as you do a page over the loudspeakers. Most people within the sound of your voice will feel a soothing effect, and things should calm down a bit.

You will notice that I said "most people." That is because this is not manipulative magic. Most people really don't want to be crabby and unbalanced, so they will benefit from their own wish to take the opportunity to find balance. There are a few people who are so attached to their anger that they are not willing to give it up. That is their choice, but to try to force the issue would be manipulative and unethical. When dealing with others it is very important to remember to act ethically.

Perhaps you have been in a situation at work where you feel that your voice is not being heard. You have a great idea, or want to discuss a raise or promotion, but you feel that your words just aren't getting through. Before you go to work that day, spend a few minutes on this simple meditation. Lay down on your back and place a blue stone of your choice at the base of your throat. Close your eyes and visualize a beam of bright, warm light coming down from the sky and shining down into your throat chakra. Your throat chakra is the energy vortex that enhances communication and expression. Feel it filling with energy, becoming stronger. When you feel the energy in your throat chakra is glowing and strong, you are done. Carry the stone in your pocket when you go to work, and let the communication begin.

Don't Take It Home with You

OK, you had a rough day at work, despite your efforts to keep things running smoothly—hey, it happens.

You have a lot on your mind and all you want to do is go home and relax. But everything you had to deal with is still on your mind. There is no reason to take it home with you—what's done is done.

So find a place to pull the car over safely for about five minutes (a well-lit gas station works fine). Lock the doors and relax. Visualize a red balloon on a string before you. As you inhale slowly through your nose, exhale through your mouth and "blow" all that anxiety into the balloon. See it getting larger and larger as you fill it with everything that bothered you that day. When everything you wish to rid yourself of has gone into the balloon, imagine a lovely pair of scissors in your hand, decorative and magical. Reach out with your hand and cut the string with the scissors as you say "snip" and see it float away. It passes through the atmosphere and into space as the gravity of the Sun catches it and pulls it in. All your anxiety is incinerated in the blazing Sun and will be turned into neutral energy. Now take a deep breath, go home, relax, and recharge. Tomorrow is another day.

When you get to work the next day, take your inner Witch with you. When you form a true relationship with your magical self, you can take that part of yourself everywhere with you. Remember that the kind of magic that is most effective at work is subtle. Intention is very important, and this kind of magic helps to train your mind to work without all the bells and whistles. The magic is always in you.

Air Magic

Air Magic

by Jennifer McDevitt

Inhale. Exhale. Every day, your body is moving with the power of the air around you. The very breath of our inspiration, the air is full of magical potential. So much a part of our daily lives that we can often take it for granted, it is important to remember that this element sustains and nourishes the mind, which is our most powerful magical tool.

As elusive as the wind, impossible to pin down, the power of air magic is nevertheless universal in its ability to soothe and to clear the mind and to awaken thoughts that bring us closer to our own inner abilities. It stands for thought, action, inspiration, and wonder. The boundless energy that comes from performing an air-magic spell sings in the blood and refreshes us for a new day.

Many powerful deities are linked to the element of air. Among them is Mercury, Roman god of messengers and speakers. The winged feet of Mercury symbolize the powerful sweep of air magic. With him come the undertones of the new spring, the dawning of a new day. The element of air is connected to the east, after all, and in the east lies the magnificent sunrise.

From an early age Mercury was linked to the powers of the sky. In his infancy, it is said, he constructed the lyre, or harp—a nod to the creative powers of air magic. But from him we also get the term mercurial, meaning temperamental and unpredictable. Sadly, many people traditionally linked to air and air magic can be moody and hot-headed at times, as unexpected as a hurricane or a torrential gale.

Yet Mercury for his part was a much-loved god. His wit and gift for trickery made him a favorite among thieves and poets; his diligence, speed, and ability to garner wealth made him exalted by the merchant classes. Great things flow down through the power of the air, when used appropriately. Wicked Mercury was often a torment to those mortals he considered intellectually beneath him, yet was also constantly interfering on the behalf of men, serving as a messenger between the gods, guiding souls after they departed the mortal world, and producing musical instruments which, when used by Apollo, the god of music and the Sun, gave mankind great gifts of lyrical beauty.

Mercury was celebrated throughout the world in many different forms. To the Germans he was Wodan. To the Greeks he was also known as Hermes or Alipes (the one with winged feet). To the pre-Roman Etruscans he was Turms, guide of the deceased to the underworld, and messenger of the gods. To the Egyptians he was known as messenger of the gods, Thoth, and as such he was the origin of the deity Hermes Trismegistus, or "Thrice-great Hermes." This title, extolling his virtues three times over, comes from the belief that Hermes (or Mercury) wrote astrological texts for the Greek people, as well as being responsible for the volatile but irresistible occult art of alchemy. He was also believed to be the Egyptian god who invented hieroglyphics (the traditional air-inspired gift of communication), as well as calendar-keeping. He also judged the souls of the deceased, using the intellect inherent as an air deity to provide justice for those who wished to travel to the world beyond. To the Sumerians he was Gud, a god favoring welcome rains, agricultural fertility, and harvest abundance. To the Assyrians he was known as Nabu. His role was that of a herald, proclaiming news to the peoples of the Earth. Instead of being the messenger of the gods, he was the secretary of the heavens. His task was to keep track of the words spoken by the gods. This also made him the Assyrian god of knowledge and wisdom, and the recorder of fate and destiny for people for the year ahead. The traits of the air element show up here again in mental organization, and as a bringer of new and inspirational messages.

Mercury was celebrated during the festival of Mercuralia, which occurred on May 15. This is an excellent day to perform air magic spells—to try to bring about new events, to gift yourself with words and with intellect, and to will change to blow into your life as the winged feet of the messenger god himself. Wednesday is Mercury's day: in French, Wednesday is *mercredi*, coming from the Latin *Mercurii dies*, or Mercury's day. Our English word Wednesday is derived from *Wodan's day*, named for Mercury's Norse counterpart, Wodan. This makes Wednesday an excellent day of the week for air-magic spells.

Like Mercury, the element of air is a messenger of greater things. It rules the mind, and brings with it knowledge, inspiration, and the power to think in abstract detail. What one of us has not stared at the sky and seen strange shapes moving above us in the clouds? This is the power of air magic: to see beyond, to open our minds to the possibilities that lie hidden within us. It is also the element of justice. It is only when we are focused that we can truly decide what is right, and make sure that we "harm none," as the law requires us. Air is the element of the astrological signs Libra, Gemini, and Aquarius— signs well known for their creativity, intellect, wit, and charm. It is the very breath of speech and communication itself.

However, the power of air does have its downside, as does all magic. We must be careful that we use it in good balance. Just as it brings wisdom, it can also bring chaos. Just as a tor-

nado can emerge from the calmest breeze, so too can misuse of the element bring about a mind that is too easily distracted, too full of questions that cannot be answered. It can leave the soul unsettled, and it can harden our heart to feeling. No one can live solely within the power of the mind. We must remember to use all elements equally and in balance, or else we risk the dangers inherent in them.

There are diverse spells that call for the use of the element air. Occasions where the gift of speech and communication are required are often the most prevalent for the use of this type of spell. Whether it is a meeting with an employer, a presentation that needs to be given, or simply a desire to express one's innermost feelings in the most eloquent way, the use of air magic can certainly aid you in discovering your gift of speech.

Air is also beneficial in spells that seek to open the mind to new possibilities. A student studying for an exam or trying to produce a piece of written work could call on the element of air to guide her to a better understanding of what she wants to say. It serves as the gift of inspiration. Just as opening a window and letting in a cool breeze can air out even the darkest, dullest room, so too can a touch of air magic release the cobwebs from the mind and set thoughts in order.

A gentler use for air magic can be found in meditation. Simply by focusing on our breath we are able to transcend the weight of our bodies and open our spirits, listen to our souls, and achieve a better understanding of ourselves. Indeed, air magic can lend itself to almost any need at any time.

During air spells, it is important that the magical tools and ingredients take root within the powers of the element. The color of air is yellow. Its direction is east. Its magical tools are the athame, sword, and censer. Most interesting is its association with the athame (or dagger) and the sword. Masculine symbols to be sure, they are also sharp and deadly. One imagines, when using these tools during an air spell, that we are cutting through ignorance and making our minds as honed and sharp as the blades. To invoke the element of air in a pentagram, you must make sure that you move toward the left, or the east. To banish, the movement is opposite, to the west. Be sure that you have closed your mind and banished the magic. No one wants to walk around with his mind trapped in abstract thought.

There are many examples of air-magic spells. A simple spell that has proven effective when dealing with difficult or stressful situations involves the power and tumultuous nature of the north wind.

Choose a day that promises a strong gale coming from the north, or at least a breeze powerful enough to carry away something as heavy as a piece of paper. That requirement is crucial, as it becomes the crux of the spell. Wearing the colors of the east—yellows, and even the reds of a new sunrise—will assist you in focusing your mind on the task, which is to release yourself of care and bring about a new beginning.

Normally, spells involve the casting of a circle. However, in this case, a circle would prove to be a hindrance. The goal of a magical circle is to offer both focus and protection for the spell at hand. Nothing is meant to break through its barriers of spirit. However, this spell requires that those boundaries be down so that harmful energies can be cast from you into the gale.

The steps for this spell are simple enough. On scraps of paper, write down those thoughts or feelings that you feel are holding you back from your creative potential. Perhaps they are concerns that are troubling your mind, or situations in your life that are preventing you from seeing clearly. Remember always that the focus of an air spell is to open one's mind to communication and new possibilities.

Once the scraps of paper have been produced, carry them to a secluded area outside where you can meet the full force of the north wind as it blows about you. Facing north, cast the papers into the wind, saying, "Powers of the north, bring about a change. Take from me my sorrows that I may begin anew." Be sure that your mind is open and you focus on those papers being carried away by the wind; with them go your troubles. Then, turn to the east. Say, "Dawn of a new day, let me begin anew. From henceforth, I shall walk in the light of the new Sun." You may then close your ceremony as you wish. I like to go home and write down ideas on how I can start to improve myself, now that I have cast off my sorrows to the wind.

A variation on this spell is to pick a warmer day—preferably a Wednesday, which is the key day for air magic. This is an opportunity to bring to fruition thoughts and plans that have been sitting in your mind for too long, and desire the freedom to take wing and fly.

Again, on pieces of paper, write down the issues that are whirling in your mind. However, this time, the papers will carry those thoughts and desires you want to see succeed. As before, carry these papers to a secluded area and wait for a breeze. Face the east, and scatter your hopes to the wind, saying, "East wind, open my mind. Carry my hopes and dreams to new horizons. Let my spirit take flight, let my soul grow wings. Bring about these changes and let my mind travel with the Sun as he rises." Again, the closure of the ceremony should be personal and relevant to you, the caster.

The wonder and the energy of air magic is not to be taken lightly. There is always the risk of being swept away, or distancing one's self from the feeling heart. Wind may bring about change, but it also blows cold, and too much focus on the high peaks of the mind can freeze the spirit and leave it unable to touch the other elements which are so dear to the use of magic. Above all, like breath itself, air magic is best when allowed to flow through you, refreshing you, sweeping the dust from your mind and opening your thoughts to newer and greater possibilities.

Incantations and Power Songs

by Kristin Madden

Om. *Awen. Freya. Shakti. Hathor. Rhiannon. Isis. Astarte. Diana.* If you have ever chanted or intoned any of these words, you must have noticed the effect they had on you and on those around you. By simply experiencing their resonance, your awareness was changed in some way. The truth is that words and other sounds have power. Prayer, invocation, incantation, chants, and songs have been used throughout time for communicating with the gods, speeding healing, creating protection, and touching the heart and soul of all those who hear it.

We've all heard the childhood song about sticks and stones breaking bones but words not hurting. Is that really true? Haven't we all been harmed by words—or more accurately by the intent behind certain words? Of course we have. And we've also been comforted, empowered, and even healed by the intent behind other words. "Merry meet," "bless you," "I love you"—these are some powerful and wonderful words.

For millennia, vocal sound has been recognized for its powerful effect on human consciousness. Screams, grunts, and humming contain no words, yet they are capable of expressing a wide range of needs and feelings. Simple intonations of seed sounds have been used throughout the world to induce trance and project the will. Much like the drum or rattle, vocal sound has long been used as an auditory driver, entraining body, mind, and spirit into a healthy, otherworldly state of awareness. From this level of consciousness, we can more effectively direct our intent through vocal sound, and other means, to connect with the divine and create healing.

The use of incantation and power songs can be found in the myths and histories of every culture on Earth. Stories abound of ancient druids that could stop battles, lay curses, and cast a variety of spells, all through the use of vocal sound. In modern movies we see primitive shamans chanting and singing over the ill and injured. And who hasn't heard a fantasy witch say "boil boil, toil, and trouble" over her bubbling and smoking cauldron? These images come to us from our own heritage. Their timelessness reminds us of the great power that may be found in an exploration of the truth behind the stories.

Incantations

Shamans and sorcerers, witches and druids, healers and magicians—all of these people have used incantations to invoke the spirits and to channel and bind specific energies. The basic premise of incantation is that through the specific combination of words and other sounds, a deity is invoked and access to power is granted. In a way, it may be seen as a verbal spell, though incantations are often used in conjunction with other forms of spell work.

Incantations frequently take the form of toning or monotonous chanting. Within the chant, there are usually certain words that you will use to carry the force of your intent. These may be names of deities or action words. Sometimes incantations use words that are seemingly made up or sounds that are not words at all, but they carry a whole range of metaphoric symbolism that activates magical intent. These words should be intoned, much like one might chant a mantra like *Om*.

Intonation is created through more than the mouth. It is vibrated through the throat and head. Its resonance is felt throughout the body. This technique vibrates the physical body and the energy field in much the same way a tuning fork vibrates all over when it is struck. This energy is magnified and radiates outward from the individual. By using this intonation within a specific incantation, that vibration is radiated toward a very specific intent.

Intonation is generally preceded by a deep breath. As you exhale, you send the intent of this incantation out with the intonation. You will feel your throat, then your body, and then the energy of the area begin to vibrate with this sound. As you project the tone, you project the thought and emotion. The use of breath is important when creating incantations. Many cultures believe that the will or goal is carried on the breath. Therefore, it is just as important to blow the thought out into the multiverse or onto the specific object as it is to vibrate your words.

There is no definite rule regarding the creation of effective incantations. You must find what works best for you through practice and experimentation. At least in the beginning, it is generally best to keep it simple and short. Repetitive, and often rhyming, phrases help you to remember what you need to chant and reinforce the will behind the words.

Power Songs

Basically a form of incantation, power songs have been used in shamanic cultures since time out of mind. Often the melodies were traditional and the words were specific to the shaman. Power songs are often slow and monotonous, much like shamanic drumming, and they are frequently used to induce trance states. Power songs are also used for healing, to commune with spirit guides, and to raise the energy of sacred sites.

Power songs are used to open the self to spirit guidance and to infuse oneself with the energy needed for the situation at hand. The personality and its associated limitations slip away as the power song begins the process of funneling this energy through the singer. You will find people using power songs before doing healing work, at the beginning of any ritual, when doing protection work, and even at the beginning of a new day or before going to an important meeting.

Once you have invoked and merged with your power song, you may call it up whenever you have need. In some cultures, it is believed that the song and the singer are one, each reflecting the essence of the other in a very spiritual way. As such, your song may change over time as you do, but it will forever be a part of you.

Seeking Your Power Song

Some people have a wonderful ability to channel spirit guidance as they write. They can sit down with a piece of paper or at a computer and their power songs just flow through them onto the pages. But to seek your power song in nature creates a unique and very kinesthetic experience that is not to be missed. And it makes the process so much easier for many people.

1. Find a place in nature where you feel safe and are unlikely to be disturbed. Wander around, getting a feel for this place.

2. Make an offering of thanks, and perhaps sacred herbs or water, to the spirits of this place and to the Creator. Ask for their blessings and protection in this work that you are about to do.

3. Invite your personal deities or spirit guides to join you in this work and guide your inspiration.

4. Enter a light trance by your usual method. If you prefer, you may count yourself down from ten to one, stopping periodically to take a deep breath and remind yourself to go deeper.

5. While in your meditative trance state, go deep within your self. Find who you are at your core, beyond your identity and the roles you play in this world. Feel yourself embodying the true you as you are filled with the energy of the multiverse. You are open to healing energy and to communication with spirit guides.

6. Begin to hum or make noises that seem appropriate. Continue doing this until you feel comfortable and your creativity is ready to let more of you flow into a song.

7. Sing from this place of vitality, honesty, and power. Allow all you feel and all that you are to flow into your song. Allow your spirit guides to add their voices to your song. Take note of any changes in your energy or body as the song becomes part of your being.

8. When you feel you have experienced what you set out to do, or that your song is complete for now, give thanks to all those that walk with you, guide you, and enliven you. Sit in silence for a moment and take note of how you feel. Then return to normal consciousness.

You may wish to write this song down, along with a full account of everything you experienced. Practice singing your song whenever you are alone to allow the energy and feel of the song to become second nature to you. An excellent way to begin your day is to greet the east and honor the other directions

as you sing your power song in a morning ritual. Notice if the song changes depending on your state of mind or life situations.

Then begin to really use your power song for magic and ritual. Sing it before casting a circle or at the beginning of a spell or healing session. Be aware of any changes in your experience of ritual when you use your song. Also become more aware of the times when you feel called to sing your song. Some people find that they instinctively call it to mind in times of stress or fear.

Anchoring This Power

You can "anchor" the power that your song brings to you for use in just these types of immediate-need situations. A physical anchor is a specific posture or movement that you associate with the frame of mind necessary to access your song, and using it can speed up the time it takes to reach your power. Anchors can be found in many modern methods, and they find their origins in the *mudras* and magical postures or hand positions that have existed for millennia.

The easiest way to create this physical anchor is simply to use it whenever you perform your preferred method of clearing and grounding. Through continued use, this anchor will become associated with that state of consciousness.

To consciously create a physical anchor for yourself, you will need to decide what your anchor position will be. This should be something that is not too obvious but also is not something you do all the time—perhaps touching your left ring-finger to your right elbow or holding your pinky and thumb together.

1. Create sacred space. To anchor a power song, you may want to return to the area where you first sought your song.

2. Invoke your spirit guides, the Creator, and any other spirits or deities you feel are appropriate. Ask for their blessings on the work you are about to do.

3. Enter trance in your usual manner. You may want to count yourself down from ten to one, twice. It may help for you to visualize yourself descending one step with each number.

4. Become aware of your breathing. Observe it for a few moments. If you still feel any areas of tension, direct the breath to these areas until they relax.

5. Now, begin to increase the duration of your exhalation until you have attained a 1:2 ratio between inhalation and exhalation. If you find you are gasping for breath on the inhalation, reduce the length of the exhalation. This should flow naturally without creating stress. Stay with the breath until you feel your trance deepen.

6. Place your hands or body in the form you have decided will be your physical anchor. Take a deep breath and sing your power song. Feel the physical sensation, the skin against skin, the pressure, whatever it is that this posture feels like in combination with the effects of your song

7. Once you have completed your song and have a strong feeling of its power flowing through you, tense the anchor position. Say to yourself and to those you have invoked that taking this position will automatically create these conditions in your energy field. State with intent that you will automatically assume this position without conscious thought whenever you have need of these conditions. State that this physical posture anchors these conditions in your physical body. Repeat this process twice.

8. Thank all those that you invoked for their presence and blessings and release the sacred space in your preferred manner. If you counted yourself down from ten to one, count back up from one to ten, using imagery you used in the beginning of this exercise.

It is important to continue using this anchor when you sing your power song to solidify the link between the two. Once you feel the effects of the song become automatic when you engage the anchor position, you no longer need to use them together.

Freeing your creativity can open your access to spirit guidance, healing, and power. As you reactivate your heart and throat, your creativity will be enhanced. The energy in your body and your life will flow more freely, bringing you insights and abundance. You may be surprised at the magic you observe in your own life, simply through reconnecting with your manifestation of divine inspiration.

No Smoking

by Boudica

Sacred space. It is the space where we reside. It is a place where we sit and meditate. It is our "cube" at work; it is our backyard. It is a place where we invite Deity. It is our home, our hotel room, our tent, our circle, or a park. It is the place where we find comfort, where we shut out the mundane. It is the place we make secure. It is where we come home to at the end of the day or at the end of a journey.

In other words, sacred space is all around us. However, when I say, "We are going to clear our sacred space," I bet you all reach for the smudge stick and a lighter.

There are folks, like myself, who do not take too kindly to smoke. For those who have allergies, or are ex-smokers, or wish to avoid secondhand smoke, the whole smudging ritual is awkward. Most circles you go to, they smudge you before you enter a circle. Many folks will use smudge sticks and incense to purify their houses, their cars, and their tools.

While this is an accepted practice, what about those who are allergic to sage? Yes, there are folks who are allergic to the stuff. Ever notice the gal who immediately starts to cough when the smudging stick is lit? The kids who walk into a room after it's been smudged and start coughing? Did you think that was just because of the smoke? Well, it could be. And it could also be the sage. And if it is either, why do you continue to use the smudging stick?

For most folks, it's the smell, it's the accepted practice, and it's how they were taught. Smoke purifies. Well, yes, it does. It can also send someone home sick or to the hospital. And with folks constantly worrying about the effects of smoke on themselves and their kids, maybe we should start looking at alternatives. Some folks are going to frown at this. Nothing quite smells so good as scented smoke, does it? Be it sage, frankincense, or your favorite incense, the smell of scented smoke is wonderfully calming and a clearing trigger to the human mind.

But smoke is not the only way to spread scent around. Let's look at some alternatives to "smoking."

Aromatherapy does not rely on smoke to get the scent around. It relies on oils delivered in a number of ways to fill the air, and yourself, with calming, relaxing scent. The same can be done with the ritual scents we are familiar with and that put our minds into the "sacred space" feeling.

The most popular way is to use scented candles. I am not talking about your ritual candles, but rather the addition of candles to the circle to provide a scent that denotes sacred space. You can either make your own or purchase the good varieties of scented candles.

Another popular method is to use an oil diffuser. These are small candle-heated or electric warmers that heat water. You add oil to the warm water, and the diffuser gently heats the oil and diffuses it into the air. However, I would not recommend a diffuser if you are the sort of person who "lights and leaves." The water and oil mixture will evaporate—usually in less time than the tea light will take to burn. You will end up with a cracked plate and a possible fire hazard. I have seen electric diffusers that automatically shut off, and you may want to check those out.

The one-piece ceramic diffusers are my choice. Electric or tea-light versions are all good, and with the tea-light versions, look for a large space for the tea light inside the diffuser. This prevents the ceramic from getting too hot on the sides, yet does a very good job at warming the water on top and allowing the oil to spread its scent. Remember, you don't have to boil the oil/water mixture, just get it warm. Look for plenty of holes in the ceramic holder for the heat to dissipate through, and check that it's elevated a bit above the surface it sits on. You don't want the heat from the tea light transferring down to the ceramic bottom of the diffuser and then heating up the counter or surface underneath, possibly charring or damaging it. If it's not raised, be sure to place the diffuser on a ceramic tile.

Oils can seem expensive. Essential oils can sell for six or more dollars per bottle, depending on size, quality, and the oil itself. I've seen some priced at fifty dollars a bottle, or higher. But how much do we actually use? How about that smudge stick you use? Is that the big chunky five-dollar-each variety? How many uses do you get out of that? You light it, you smudge, and you place it in a fireproof tray, where it continues to burn till it goes out. How much is left? Do you use it again? Or was it one of the smaller three-dollar ones that you use once and throw away?

How many drops in the diffuser? You would use about five drops total. For some of the stronger scents, three drops per diffuser will do. I think if you add up the costs of both methods, you will find that it will be just about the same, or maybe just a little less for the oil diffuser, depending on how heavily you apply the oils.

What about the cleansing issue? Smoke clears the space. It also cleanses the individuals coming into the circle. Let's take a look at that as well.

One traditional practice is to anoint members with scented oils. Look at a variety of old myths and legends, and you will read about washing with scented water, placing oils on a person's forehead, or sprinkling someone with scented water to cleanse and bless them. Some of these traditions are still used today.

There are many ways to produce the scented water, from allowing water to sit with flower petals in it overnight to adding some oil for scent. Allow the water to come to room temperature.

You can put water in a bowl with flowers and petals, and the members come in, dip their fingers in the water, and flick the water on themselves. I've seen high priestesses take a small handmade broom and flick the water on the members as they enter the circle before a ritual, and the high priest draw a small pentacle on the foreheads of the members with a finger that had been dipped in the same oil. There are many variations. Find one that works for you.

Finally, there is the actual cleansing and grounding of sacred space. From clearing a circle to a house cleansing, the trusty "sage smudge" can be dropped from the list in favor of a favorite mixture that is applied dry and then "swept away" in twenty-four hours.

Most hotel rooms would not appreciate your setting off the smoke alarm with incense or sage smudge sticks. I have a favorite "herbal cleansing mixture" that I take with me. The housekeeping unit will be sweeping and cleaning after I leave, so placing the mixture on the bed, floor, or furniture does no harm here.

The base of the mixture is equal parts salt, pine needles, rosemary, and sage leaves. The combination is obvious: salt to ground; pine, rosemary, and sage to cleanse. The pine needles, rosemary, and sage leaves are cut and crushed up fine. I prefer kosher salt because it is a larger grain, but sea salt ground fine can be used just as well. Remember, you are going to vacuum this up after twenty-four hours, so it will not remain anywhere to do any harm to carpet or furniture.

If you are leaving a house, you may want to add cedar to ground your energy and leave a clean space behind. For a hotel room, add cedar or lavender to ground energy and suppress vibrations from previous tenants. For a bedroom, add rose petals. For circle, you can add magical herbs like meadowsweet for love or love spells, calendula for clairvoyance, lily of the valley flowers to attract the Fey, mugwort for divination and clairvoyance, or any combination of herbs that you feel will enhance the activity you have planned.

At my office, I always keep those little packets of salt you get at the fast-food joints in my desk drawer. Anytime I feel the office has gotten to be too much, I sprinkle the salt around my "cube" area. Works every time!

Anything can be cleansed without the use of smoke. Give some of these ideas a try the next time you have a cleansing or ritual.

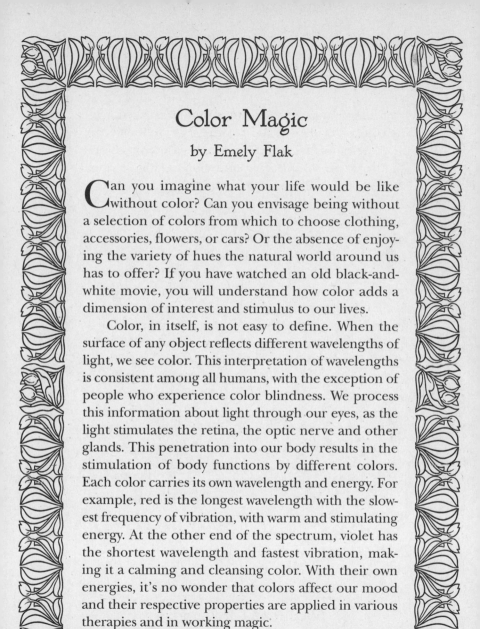

Color Magic

by Emely Flak

Can you imagine what your life would be like without color? Can you envisage being without a selection of colors from which to choose clothing, accessories, flowers, or cars? Or the absence of enjoying the variety of hues the natural world around us has to offer? If you have watched an old black-and-white movie, you will understand how color adds a dimension of interest and stimulus to our lives.

Color, in itself, is not easy to define. When the surface of any object reflects different wavelengths of light, we see color. This interpretation of wavelengths is consistent among all humans, with the exception of people who experience color blindness. We process this information about light through our eyes, as the light stimulates the retina, the optic nerve and other glands. This penetration into our body results in the stimulation of body functions by different colors. Each color carries its own wavelength and energy. For example, red is the longest wavelength with the slowest frequency of vibration, with warm and stimulating energy. At the other end of the spectrum, violet has the shortest wavelength and fastest vibration, making it a calming and cleansing color. With their own energies, it's no wonder that colors affect our mood and their respective properties are applied in various therapies and in working magic.

Favorite colors define our personality. When you buy a gift or flowers for a loved one or a close friend, you show you care by selecting an item in her favorite color. A bride uses her favorite color in the décor and theme of her wedding. When you wear colors that suit you, you receive compliments about your appearance. Different practitioners master their knowledge of color to heal, decorate, dress, paint, or perform magic. The Witch harnesses the energies and properties of color to enhance her magical work. The artist manipulates color to create a visual type of magic. Spiritual counsellors and healers interpret personal energy fields, known as auras, as colors. Interior designers blend and contrast color to create mood and space. In meditation and healing, color results in emotional changes and mood shifts. Over tens of thousands of years, and across numerous cultures, color has played a role in healing, ritual, tradition, mood enhancement, symbolism, and magic. It appears not only in nature, but also in man-made dyes, fabrics, powders, paint, and in visualization and meditation, creating a plethora of resources to help us harness the visual, magical, and healing properties of color.

Since the advent of color movies, the contrast of black-and-white cinematography with color has been used effectively to communicate change, awakening, and adventure. Who can forget that moment in *The Wizard of Oz* when Dorothy's transition to her dream and life-changing journey appears in color?

Mood and Behavior

Psychologists recognize that color affects behavior and learning. Without realizing it, we associate color with emotions in our everyday speech. How many times have you heard a person use the term "feeling off-color" to describe a feeling of imbalance or illness? We talk about feeling "green with envy," "seeing red" when angry, or feeling "blue" when sad. In a state of happiness we are "tickled pink." Because color affects how we feel, it affects our performance, emotional health, spiritual well-being, and even our physiology.

Not all colors appeal to everyone. Our favorite colors are sometimes described as our "soul colors," which suggests that we are attracted to colors that define our strengths and preferences. Likewise, colors we dislike can reveal hidden weaknesses and areas for potential improvement. If you are not fond of yellow, for example, this may indicate a loss of personal power. On the other hand, an attraction to yellow is often an indicator that you can manage challenges with confidence.

Color Therapy

Color therapy is based on the understanding that colors generate different vibrations that stimulate the mind and body in various ways. In meditation, focus on the color you wish to invoke for healing. Close your eyes and imagine your chosen color flowing into your body and through your aura, creating a healing and soothing effect with each breath. Use this table to identify some simple ways to enhance your mood or improve your health with color therapy.

Red	Heals fatigue, energizes
Orange	Soothes nerves and promotes positive energy and happiness

Yellow	Assists with nerves and digestive system and helps you express your true self
Green	A balancing, relaxing color that promotes harmony
Blue	A calm color that helps with mental clarity and lowers blood pressure
Purple	Enhances inner peace while addressing stress

In their shades, colors belong to one of three categories: active, passive, and neutral. Active colors such as red, orange, and yellow energize and stimulate. Passive colors of blue, green, and purple balance and restore, making them a popular choice in the bedroom or bathroom. Neutral colors such as grey, white, and beige do not stimulate or calm, but effectively dilute the effects of the passive and active colors. Many food outlets decorate and brand in red and orange to stimulate appetite. Bright reds and yellows are believed to increase blood pressure, so it's unlikely you will ever see these colors in a hospital or medical center.

In ancient Egypt, colored water was drunk to absorb the benefits of color therapy. This water, called "solarized water," was made by infusing clear water with a crystal of a chosen color or wrapping colored fabric around a jug or glass of water and leaving it in the sun for thirty minutes before drinking. Another treatment known as chromatherapy or color acupuncture uses an instrument to capture and direct light rays through color filters to stimulate energy points on the body.

Magical Application

Color is an important magical correspondence used in a significant proportion of spellcraft. The variety of applications is vast. You can use color with ribbon, candles, crystals, fabric, paper, herb pouches, clothing, and visualization. Some Witches even transcribe their spells into their Books of Shadows with colored ink to further imbue their spell with the desired energies. If you have not yet used color for magic, refer to this list of basic correspondences.

Red	Passion, vitality, creativity, health
Pink	Love, romance, friendship
Orange	Encouragement, endurance
Yellow	Confidence, communication, happiness, self-esteem, travel
Green	Prosperity, success, finance, luck, fertility, growth
Blue	Healing, protection, peace, understanding, truth, harmony
Purple	Spirituality, meditation, inner power, psychic ability
Brown	Security, home, comfort, grounding
Grey	Invisibility, neutralizing
Silver	Intuition, dreams, stability
Gold	Luck, justice, money, power
White	Purity, truth, protection, cleansing, healing, peace
Black	Absorbing negativity, banishing

For example, for job interview success, plait green and yellow ribbons as part of your spell and keep the ribbon in your pocket or purse on the day

of the interview. Or if you feel affected by negative
energies or attitudes, engrave a black candle with a
symbol of what you wish to banish or diminish from
your life. Surround yourself with a circle of four
white candles. Burn the candle as you imagine the
negativity being absorbed into the flame whilst the
white candles protect you.

Chakra Points

The numerous energy points in our body are called
chakra points. The main points that run from the
base of the spine to the top of the head correspond
to the seven colors of the rainbow spectrum. Each
major chakra point is an energy centre that aligns
with a particular color and part of the body. Chakra
healing aims to balance each energy centre to maintain a healthy mind, body, and spirit. In this process,
a chakra point may be identified as being out of
balance through under-activity or over-activity. Sta-
bilizing a chakra draws on several techniques that
include music, exercise, crystals, scent, and color.
The therapist uses either the corresponding color
or the complementary opposite color to correct the
imbalance: an overactive chakra point is treated with
a complementary opposite color, while a less active
chakra point benefits from treatment that uses the
corresponding color.

The base chakra, at the bottom of the spine,
corresponds to the color red. If you lack confidence,
stimulate this chakra point with red clothing or visualizing red healing light. But if you are irritable and
find it difficult to relax, you can balance the base
chakra with the complementary opposite color of

green. The sacral chakra in the lower stomach corresponds to orange. The stomach chakra that relates
to digestion and stomach conditions is stimulated
with yellow. Green is the color that nurtures the
heart chakra, which governs the heart and lungs.
The throat chakra, corresponding to blue, is the
source of communication and creativity. A blue-pur-
ple color relates to the brow chakra, and the crown
chakra, associated with purple or white, is the area
that balances the material and spiritual being.

The Aura

Another area where color plays an interesting role is
in the human aura. We each emit an aura that is an
egg-shaped energy field of color that surrounds our
body. Different colors seen in the aura represent
various emotional, physical, and mental indicators
of strengths and weaknesses.

A healthy aura is luminous and in perfect harmony, featuring the colors of the rainbow. Clear and
vivid colors are an indicator of positive energy and
thoughts. The colors become dark, murky, or grey
when a person is unwell, diseased, or emitting negative energy. An aura healer or therapist can often
identify weaknesses in an aura well before an illness
manifests and provide information that can help
you address a health issue before it arises.

Color Across Cultures and Traditions

Across cultures, color represents symbols and beliefs.
Throughout history, color has been used to define
spiritual authority, social hierarchy, conflict, peace,
birth, death, fertility, and prosperity. One culture

may interpret a color to be lucky while in contrast another tradition may find it offensive. In eastern cultures, it is believed that color protects people from ghosts and evil spirits. In many cultures, purple is associated with royalty because until recently the dye color was expensive to produce. It was custom in many countries to wrap a newborn baby in a purple cloth to attract wealth and success. While white is a color for funerals and mourning in China, it remains the traditional bridal color, representing purity, for marriage in Western countries.

The colors in almost every nation's flag hold cultural significance to unite and inspire its people with a common cause. The flag of the indigenous people of Australia, the Aboriginals, is black and red with a yellow circle. The black represents their race, the red the Earth, and the yellow is the Sun. In its simplicity, it symbolizes the identity of the Australian Aboriginal people and their sacred connection to the land.

In religion, color represents an interpretation of belief. Colors in Asian religions represent good and evil. In the Japanese religion of Shinto, priests use color to symbolize their different ranks. A Hindu teacher wears a yellow robe. Many religious ministers of patriarchal religions wear black, which is also the color of mourning in Western countries. In tribal societies, color was used to differentiate groups and hierarchy through accessories and body paint. In tribal life, it was particularly popular to use body paint as disguise to communicate with the spirit world. We continue to associate certain colors with festivities. Green and red remind us of Yule or Christmas, while orange and black are the ubiquitous colors of Halloween or Samhain. In Wicca, the triple goddess is linked to three colors: white for the maiden, red for the fertile mother, and black for the crone. Rituals associated with these life-cycle milestones feature the respective colors to symbolize a transition from one phase to the next.

Although we often take our colorful surroundings for granted, color plays a vital role in our day-to-day existence. Each color carries its own energy and enters our bodies through our eyes. In turn, this provides a stimulus that affects our mood and sense of harmony. It's not surprising that color plays a part as a critical magical correspondence in ritual and spell craft. The effects on our mood are often unconscious, and you are not likely to notice that it is the color that has soothed or energized you. In its numerous applications, particularly in healing and balancing, color carries an ability to stabilize imbalances and improve our overall well-being.

Cord & Knot Magic

by Sorita D'Este

Cord magic is a very simple and effective technique for casting spells. You can use cords or ribbons to perform cord magic, and both are easy to obtain inexpensively in a whole range of colors. You can perform cord spells in any circumstance, though it is beneficial to cast a circle and call the elements and the Goddess and God to add energy to your spell.

There are three very important things to consider before performing a cord spell. The first of these is deciding what exactly you want to perform the spell for, and deciding on an appropriate visualization to perform while you cast the spell. This enables your mind to concentrate its power and focus on the intent of your spell. The second consideration is which color your cord will be, and the third is how many knots you will use. Both these considerations focus your mind on the nature of your spell, as you need to determine the correct correspondences to focus the energy appropriately.

Color Correspondences

White: purity, healing, blessing, wisdom, innocence

Red: energy, passion, vitality, willpower, success

Orange: creativity, courage, emotional strength

Yellow: communication, wealth, travel

Green: growth, fertility, harmony in relationships

Blue: healing, protection, serenity, spiritual harmony

Indigo: success in long term plans, improving perception

Purple: luck, spiritual development, psychic abilities

Pink: love, romance, friendship, tranquility

Brown: grounding, stability, endurance

Black: binding, depression, grief, protection

Once you have decided on the color to use, you will need to decide how many knots you need to tie into the cord. The number of knots is again determined by the nature of the magical working you have decided to perform. So think carefully and consider carefully what will work best for you.

1 is the number of unity, for focus, acceptance

2 is the number of duality, for partnerships, balance

3 is the number of Saturn, for solidity, timing, stability

4 is the number of Jupiter, for expansion, general health

5 is the number of Mars, for energy, passion, courage

6 is the number of the Sun, for success, wealth, charisma

7 is the number of Venus, for love, fertility, growth

8 is the number of Mercury, for communication, healing

9 is the number of the Moon, for the emotions, tides

10 is the number of the Earth, for endurance, grounding

11 is the number of Uranus, for magic, change

When performing your cord spell, knots are tied in the cord or ribbon to fix the spell and focus your intent. You can repeat the words of the spell as you tie each knot to strengthen the effect, or you can use a traditional spell such as the following:

By knot of one, the spell is begun
By knot of two, it cometh true
By knot of three, so mote it be
By knot of four, the open door
By knot of five, it comes alive
By knot of six, the spell is fixed
By knot of seven, it has the power of heaven
By knot of eight, the open gate
By knot of nine, the _____ is mine

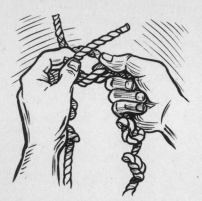

How To Do Cord Spells

Before you perform the spell you will have worked out the intent of the spell and the visualization you are going to use, decided on what color cord you are going to use, and how many knots you will tie in it. As with other spells, you should time your cord magic for when the Moon and planets are best aspected.

If the spell is personal, you may decide to wear the ribbon or cord beforehand for a few days to charge it with your own energy. If you have allowed a time frame for the spell to work in, be sure not to untie any knots in the cord or ribbon before this time.

Cord Spell for Success

When doing spells, it also helps the effect if you give the spell avenues to become manifest. So buy the odd instant lottery ticket or take the offer of that bit of extra work. Remember not to expect something for nothing, and be open to opportunities, and the spell will work much more effectively for you.

A gold cord is needed for this spell, or yellow if you cannot get gold. Gold and yellow are the colors of the Sun, which symbolizes wealth and success. Likewise six is the number of the Sun, so six knots are tied in the cord to strengthen the attractive influence to the solar energies.

You are seeking to attract success, so during the waxing Moon is the best time to cast the spell. A day between the New and Full Moon is the ideal time, as the Moon waxes to fullness, so the influence of the spell will increase. As the spell is solar, it is best cast during the day.

1. Take the gold cord in your hands and concentrate on your desire for more success in your life. Say, "It is my intent to attract more success into my life. So mote it be."

2. Focus your desire for your circumstances to improve. Visualize a simple, appropriate image, like a gold coin, in your head and keep it there for the duration of the spell casting.

3. As you tie the first knot near one end of the cord repeat your intent: "It is my intent to attract more success into my life."

4. Repeat this for the remaining five knots, keeping the mental image in your head the whole time.

5. Now bind the spell, so its effects are contained and will draw the positive attractive energies to you. Say, "I call on earth to bind this spell, air to speed its passage well, fire bring spirit from above, water fill this spell with love. By all the power of land and sea, this spell bound around shall be, no harm nor return to cause on me, as I do will so mote it be." As you do this, tie an imaginary golden cord into a knot in the air in front of you, so the physical action mirrors the intent of the words.

6. Place the cord somewhere you spend a lot of time and where it will not be touched by others.

Spell for Health

This spell is for general health, so it uses a blue cord with four knots. Wear the cord or ribbon around a wrist or ankle for a few days before performing the spell to get it attuned to your energies. The waxing Moon is the best time to do this, as the energies are increasing to their maximum.

The cord will act as a focus for energies that contribute to your health. Taking more care to eat and live healthily will give the energies a strong base to act from, boosting the effect of the spell.

1. Hold the blue cord in your hands, visualize yourself healthy and say, "It is my will to be healthy."

2. As you tie the first knot, say, "By knot of one, the spell is begun," keeping the mental image of a healthy you in mind.

3. Tie the second knot, saying, "By knot of two, it cometh true," still maintaining the mental image.

4. Tie the third knot, saying, "By knot of three, I will be healthy."

5. Tie the fourth knot, saying, "By knot of four, ill health no more."

6. Bind the spell as before, but visualize a blue knot when performing the spell binding.

7. You may choose to wear this cord or to put it somewhere safe where you spend a lot of time.

Spell for Protection

This spell is for protection, and uses a black ribbon with three knots. Black is the color of protection, and is also the best color for absorbing negativity. This is why it is the funeral color, as it helps people in dealing with grief and depression. Three is the number of Saturn, which gives form and stability. This combination gives a strong and stable form of protection, both from external influences and from negative personal states.

Much of the negativity around you is undirected. Whether you are in a hectic office or on public transport, it is easy to pick up on this negativity and draw it like a magnet. This spell provides a barrier to keep such energies at bay, and can also help you in personal situations where you feel threatened by making you aware that you can stop other people's negativity from affecting you.

1. Take the black ribbon in your hands and concentrate on your desire to be protected from negativity. Visualize a mirror around your aura facing outwards, so that negativity is reflected away from you back to its source. Say, "I will not allow others to negatively influence me."

2. Tie the first knot near one end of the ribbon and repeat your intent: "I will not allow others to negatively influence me."

3. Repeat this for the second and third knots, keeping the mental image of your aura in your head the whole time.

4. Now bind the spell, as before, and wear the ribbon under your clothes on your ankle or wrist when you are out.

5. After a month, put one end of the ribbon in a bowl of salt and untie the knots, saying, "I release all negativity held in this ribbon." This will transfer the negativity into the salt, which will neutralize it, and which you should then dispose of. You can then repeat the spell anew if you feel it is still needed.

An Instant Croning Ritual

by Tammy Sullivan

For the female Witch, reaching the Crone stage in life is equal to reaching one's peak of wisdom. Historically, Croning rituals were performed at a specific age instead of at the onset of menopause. However, unless you are affiliated with a tradition that requires a specific age, it is not a rule you must follow. Sometimes, due to health concerns, we may not be able to wait nature out and allow the body to reach this stage at a certain age. So once the body is no longer in the Mother stage, and you feel you can uphold the title of Crone, it is fine to adapt yourself to the Crone persona. Many Witches choose a new magical name for themselves at this time. It's not necessary to do so, but perfectly acceptable. Customarily, a Croning ritual also includes a rebirthing procedure. Rebirth has not been incorporated into the ritual presented here due to the fact that it is geared for the solitary Witch, but taking a new magical name can serve the rebirthing function.

The following ritual allows for the celebration of reaching the Crone stage in life, the acceptance of the title *Crone* (which is a huge honor), and also includes magical work to help focus on the spirit of the Crone. However, it is meant as an example of a way to pattern your own ideas into a ritual format. While it can be performed as is, a Croning ritual is meant to be tailored to suit the individual. Therefore, any little tweaks you need to incorporate into the ritual to personalize it will be just fine. Don't be afraid to make it your own. If you prefer a more structured ritual, add that in. If you want it more relaxed, take out parts. Some Witches have Croned themselves over a cup of coffee, and that is perfectly acceptable and valid.

You must also define the word *Crone* for yourself. What is the primary virtue of a Crone to you? Is it patience? Or perhaps it's confidence? Search your heart and mind to identify all of the characteristics that you associate with the word. Once you are a Crone you will have joined the ranks of some of the strongest and most admired women in the world. Which women best fit into that role for you? What qualities do you most admire and hope to emulate?

It's wise to have a short speech prepared or be ready to speak from the heart. You may wish to give testimony as to your character. Spend some time discussing past successes, fond memories, and anything that reminds you of the joy of your Mother time in your speech. Remember that a Crone has the confidence to state both her positive and negative attributes without losing security. A Crone accepts that she is who she is—and she is a fireball of power. Comprehension, self-expression, eating habits, concern for the health and safety of the self and others—all of these things improve with age.

If you choose to incorporate the full ceremony of Pagan ritual, you may wish to prepare your Moon cakes and circle area earlier in the day so that you can go straight from a cleansing bath to a purified space. Again, the key word is comfort. Your comfort level will directly affect your healing process, so it's best to keep it at its highest possible level.

I personally like the colors of black and silver to glorify the Crone aspect of the ceremony. Navy, emerald, or rich wine colors work well too—just keep the shades on the deep side.

If you like, you may sip wine, ale, herbal tea, or mead. I prefer wine because it is another thing that improves with age.

You will need seven candles (four black, two silver, and one gold), patchouli incense, sandalwood oil, a bowl of salt and a bowl of water, a libation dish, a chalice, and a treasured piece of jewelry or personal trinket.

Place the black candles on the cardinal direction points. Place the silver candle on the left side of the altar area and the gold on the right; these candles will serve as the God and Goddess representation. The second silver candle is placed in the center of the God and Goddess candles. Place the Moon cakes and wine onto the altar. Light the incense.

Walk to the northern point and light the candle while saying, "I call to the element of earth, the body of the Great Spirit and my foundation. I invite you to my circle." Walk to the east and light the candle. Say, "I call to the element of air, the mind of the Great Spirit and my intellect. I invite you to my circle." Walk to the south and light the candle. Say, " I call to the element of fire, the energy of the Great Spirit and that which animates me. I invite you to my circle." Walk to the west and light the candle. Say, "I call to the element of water, the blood of the Great Spirit and my emotions. I invite you to my circle." Take the incense and walk the circle. Mix salt and water in a chalice (you may use your finger). Walk the boundary of the circle once more while asperging the salt water. As you do so say, "Sealed with love and good vibrations, this circle is blessed."

Walk to the altar. It is time to invite the God and Goddess. Say, "I call to the eternal energy of the God and the Goddess. You, who are all things, are also present within me. Today is a special day for your child. I wish to share it now with you." Pour a sip of the wine into the libation dish and invite the Lord and Lady to share it with you. Do the same with the Moon cakes. Allow yourself plenty of time to simply relax and enjoy the presence of the Lord and Lady. When you are ready announce, "No longer Maiden, Mother no more. Today I embrace the title of Crone. I will uphold the name with honor." Now is the time to speak or recite what the word *Crone* actually means to you and how you are prepared to handle yourself accordingly. You may read poetry or sing—anything that your heart says to do. Also, acknowledge the blessings that come with age. Dab the sandalwood oil onto your third eye, your heart, and your lower stomach. Announce your new name in an introductory manner. For example, you could say, "I will be known as ____." Take the trinket you have selected and hold it in your right hand. Announce that from that day forward, the item will serve as a reminder that as you walk with the Crone, she walks within you. Perform the following meditation.

Mirror Light

All is dark. You sit comfortably in the darkness and know that you are safe. Breathe deeply and evenly. Slowly, a warm light begins to glow through your stomach. It lights the room and you find yourself in a dim tunnel. There is a bright white light at the end. You walk toward it. You notice the walls of the tunnel. They are solid rock and cool to the touch. As you reach the mouth of the tunnel you spy a tall, older woman. Her hair is a glorious shade of silvery-white and her eyes are sharp with intelligence. Her energy fairly crackles around you and you know that you are safe. She glows with a loving light. She greets you by name and introduces herself. As you look into her eyes you see all of the clouds that have blocked your objectivity clear away. You see many of the answers you seek. The lady asks you to place your trinket in her hand. You gently do as she asks. She closes her fist and channels energy into it until it glows with her light. She hands it back to you. She places her hand on the area of your stomach that is glowing and very slowly fades into it. You turn and walk back to where you began. Open your eyes and breathe deeply for a few minutes.

Anything that was shown to you should be written into your personal Book of Shadows at this time. Anoint the trinket with the sandalwood oil and put it on.

Say farewell to the God and Goddess and put out the altar candles. Walk to the west and say, "Farewell element of water. Blessed be." Put out the candle. Walk to the south and say, "Farewell element of fire. Blessed be." Put out the candle. Walk to the east and say, "Farewell element of air. Blessed be." Put out the candle. Walk to the north and say, "Farewell element of Earth. Blessed be." Visualize the circle energy dissipating.

I highly recommend using some sort of mirrored trinket. The charm seems to carry more power when you know the Crone is reflected back to you and through you.

Now go out and celebrate! Bask in the glory of the beautiful, wise, and perfect Crone: you.

Household Omens

by Muse

Were you worried about bad luck the last time you broke a mirror or opened an umbrella in the house? Are you guilty of uttering the words, "someone is walking over my grave" when you get goosebumps? Did you honestly think someone was talking about you the last time your ears rang? If any of these apply to you, you are guilty of practicing augury—a.k.a. divination. You paid attention to seemingly inconsequential events or details and deduced the past, present, or future from it.

We all grew up with old wives' tales and urban legends that forbade us from stepping on cracks lest we break our mothers' backs, or told us to throw table salt over our shoulders to ward off the devil when the salt spilled. Omens and superstitions have been around since the dawn of time. The human belief in external powers and supernatural forces extends into every culture known to man. There is an undying belief that looking out for signs can provide protection against the seemingly random events that happen in life. From these signs, we can attempt to control our frighteningly uncontrollable futures.

Omens and Superstitions

Some omens are so common that we no longer think to question them. For example, everyone knows that breaking a mirror causes seven years of bad luck. Stepping on a crack is also a sign of bad luck, as is walking under a ladder. In America, a black cat crossing your path is bad luck. If your ear itches, someone is talking about you. Goosebumps means someone is walking over your grave. Spilling salt will bring the devil's attention unless you throw some over your left shoulder. Finding a penny, especially heads up, is very good luck. A groom seeing his bride in her dress on their wedding day is bad luck. The number seven is lucky, and the number thirteen is unlucky. The Full Moon brings out the crazy in people. When an eyelash falls out, you can make a wish and it will come true. Blowing on dice makes them lucky.

Just looking around your house you can find omens every day. The omens listed below are from all over the world. Every culture has its own omens and its own meanings to coincide with them. In America especially, the melting pot of many cultures, these omens and superstitions abound in our everyday lives. But even in the older countries, ancient beliefs and superstitions stayed alive through the ages because they had meaning and gave the people hope of a glimpse into the future.

The following omens and superstitions are common enough that you may have experienced quite a few without noticing them at the time.

Money

If bubbles appear in a cup of coffee, you accidentally knock over a sugar bowl, or tea leaves float to the top of the cup, money will soon come your way.

Visitors

You will receive visitors if a broom falls over, someone drops silverware, a bee enters your home, or your eyebrow itches.

If a dog is lying down facing away from the door, expect a visitor. But if it is facing the door, expect someone in the house to leave.

Death

Death is coming if a clock stops or falls to the floor, a picture frame falls to the floor, or an owl screeches near a home.

A sure sign of death is for a bird to fly into the house or tap on the window.

Seeing a lone fox near your home is an omen of disaster and death.

Good Luck

You will have good luck if you find a button, dream of a dove, or find a spider in the evening.

Sneezing three times brings good luck.

Seeing a rainbow is very good luck.

White spots on the fingernails are good luck.

Bad Luck

You will have bad luck if you put your shirt on backward, get out of bed on the left side, meet a cat first thing when you leave the house in the morning, or find a spider first thing in the morning.

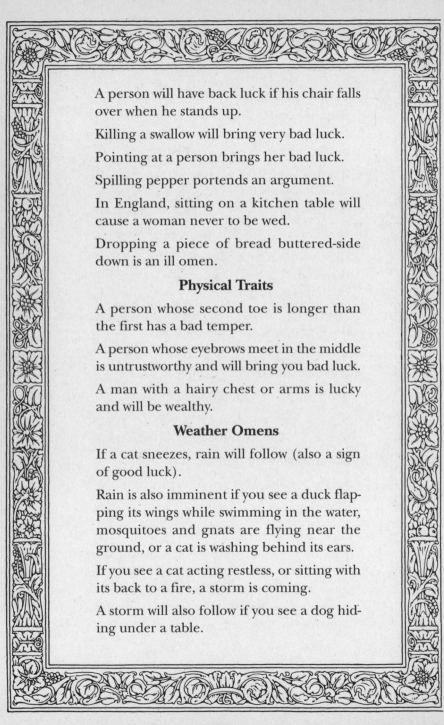

A person will have back luck if his chair falls over when he stands up.

Killing a swallow will bring very bad luck.

Pointing at a person brings her bad luck.

Spilling pepper portends an argument.

In England, sitting on a kitchen table will cause a woman never to be wed.

Dropping a piece of bread buttered-side down is an ill omen.

Physical Traits

A person whose second toe is longer than the first has a bad temper.

A person whose eyebrows meet in the middle is untrustworthy and will bring you bad luck.

A man with a hairy chest or arms is lucky and will be wealthy.

Weather Omens

If a cat sneezes, rain will follow (also a sign of good luck).

Rain is also imminent if you see a duck flapping its wings while swimming in the water, mosquitoes and gnats are flying near the ground, or a cat is washing behind its ears.

If you see a cat acting restless, or sitting with its back to a fire, a storm is coming.

A storm will also follow if you see a dog hiding under a table.

Animals

Seeing three white dogs together or seeing a spotted dog (such as a Dalmatian) will bring good luck.

While in America a black cat crossing your path is bad luck, in Britain it is good luck.

Keeping a chameleon as a pet wards off evil.

If you are bitten by a fox, you will not live more than seven more years.

Seeing a rabbit running down the street foretells a fire.

Rats leaving a house for no reason forewarns the collapse of the house.

Bird Omens

Bird omens are some of the easiest to identify because birds are common no matter where you live. Ravens and crows especially foretell the future. Alexander the Great was supposedly guided across the desert by two ravens sent from the heavens. Ravens have been housed in the Tower of London for over nine hundred years, and it is said that if the ravens ever leave the Tower, England will fall. In Wales, if a Raven perches on a house, it is good luck. Seeing two ravens is also a sign of good luck. Seeing a single crow perched on a house, however, is very bad luck. Finding a dead crow is good luck. A rhyme for crows goes:

One for sorrow,
Two for joy,

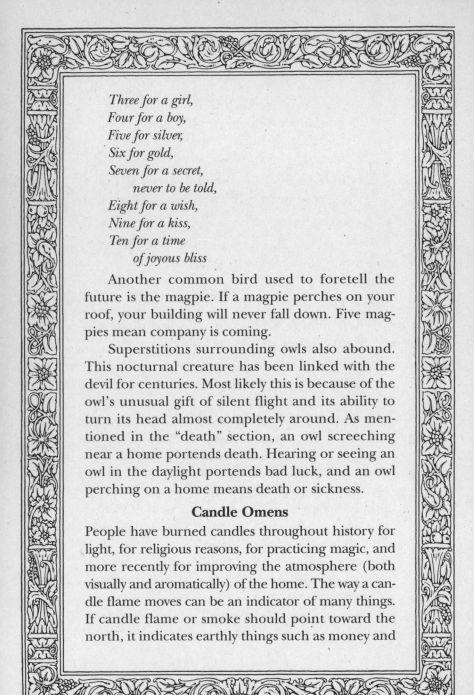

Three for a girl,
Four for a boy,
Five for silver,
Six for gold,
Seven for a secret,
*   never to be told,*
Eight for a wish,
Nine for a kiss,
Ten for a time
*   of joyous bliss*

Another common bird used to foretell the future is the magpie. If a magpie perches on your roof, your building will never fall down. Five magpies mean company is coming.

Superstitions surrounding owls also abound. This nocturnal creature has been linked with the devil for centuries. Most likely this is because of the owl's unusual gift of silent flight and its ability to turn its head almost completely around. As mentioned in the "death" section, an owl screeching near a home portends death. Hearing or seeing an owl in the daylight portends bad luck, and an owl perching on a home means death or sickness.

Candle Omens

People have burned candles throughout history for light, for religious reasons, for practicing magic, and more recently for improving the atmosphere (both visually and aromatically) of the home. The way a candle flame moves can be an indicator of many things. If candle flame or smoke should point toward the north, it indicates earthly things such as money and the home. Toward the east, it indicates the realm of intelligence. The south means movement, strength, and passion. The west is the realm of emotion and relationships. Pay attention to other signs appearing around the same time you look to the candle for answers. For example, if you have trouble lighting the candle, and then when it is lit it leans toward the north, look for trouble with money. Or, if you find a spider in the evening (a sign of good luck) and then notice your candle flame leaning toward the west, it is auspicious for love.

Counteractive Charms

As common as many omens are, charms to counteract them also thrive. One famous anti-curse and anti-bad-luck charm is writing the "Abracadabra" charm on a piece of paper. As the words faded, so would the curse or bad luck:

ABRACADABRA
ABRACADABR
ABRACADAB
ABRACADA
ABRACAD
ABRACA
ABRAC
ABRA
ABR
AB
A

More Charms

An amulet in the shape of a hand repels the evil eye.

A cross repels evil as well.

A charm in the shape of a pair of dice is good luck, and so is a four-leafed clover or a rabbit's foot.

It is an old custom to put two pins crossed under the doormat in order to ward off evil spirits. A broom placed behind a door or across a threshold also bars evil spirits from entering. Keeping a nail in your pocket or somewhere in the home guards against the evil eye.

In Conclusion

Omens and superstitions flourish, even in today's rational age. All it takes is a little observation to see signs of the future, signs of success or failure, even signs of the past. Pay attention to odd events during the day and night. There is energy all around us, and if we listen closely, it will tell us secrets and give us a glimpse into the future.

Innovative Invocations:
Designing Unique Quarter Calls
by Elizabeth Barrette

I invoke the east and the elemental powers of air. Hail and well met!

. . . ho hum.

When you first start practicing magic, everything is exciting. Every circle seems to hum with power, every incantation sends a thrill up your spine. They hold your interest because they're new to you, even if they're not particularly original. It's good to start with the basics, of course, and popular methods tend to become popular because they work. After you've been practicing for a year or two, though, you begin to wonder if there's something more. And after you've been at it for a decade, you may feel like tearing out your hair if you hear the same old thing one more time.

Most rituals open with the casting of the circle, usually by invoking the elements. This creates a boundary for magical and sacred space. A generic set of quarter calls will generate a perfectly good circle, but there is so much more that can be done. Here are a few ideas on customizing these invocations for intermediate and advanced practitioners.

Identifying Ritual Themes

Each ritual focuses on one or more themes—it has to be "about" something or "for" some purpose. By identifying the themes, you can make the ceremony more cohesive. Every motif you employ should relate to this underlying idea. Ask yourself why you're doing this ritual, and what you hope to accomplish with it.

Some themes recur so often in magic that whole fields of spellcraft have sprung up around them. Magic for prosperity, love, health and healing, protection, and purification rank among the primary themes. Check the table of contents in any good Book of Shadows and you'll usually find spells listed by themes like this. Do any of these relate to the magic you're planning to do?

Themes relate to the elements in different ways. Sometimes one element really dominates a theme and the others may seem like a

distraction. Other times several elements work but one clashes. You can't easily leave out an element or two—it tends to upset the balance—although it is possible to do a ritual focused on a single element. This is where "aspecting" comes in handy.

Aspecting is the process of focusing on specific facets or aspects of an element so you can tailor a ritual to your specific needs. With aspecting, you can invoke the parts of an element that best match what you're doing, and avoid the ones that conflict. Identifying the ritual theme lets you see how to choose the right aspects.

For example, there are themes that suggest a strong connection to certain correspondences—not the elements themselves, but other things associated with them that share the same energy. Suppose you want to do a ritual honoring totems. The elements might not seem to have much to do with that. But wait! Elemental correspondences include the animals ruled by each element. You could invoke cranes (who fly, and are sacred in Japan) in the east; lions (who are fierce, and live in Africa) in the south, salmon (who swim,, and are sacred in Celtic cultures) in the west; and polar bears (who are sturdy, and live near the pole) in the north. Now you've covered the directions, and the particular quality of each element, while sticking close to your theme.

Most traditions in the contemporary Pagan community recognize the four elements of western magic: air, fire, water, and earth. Each element has its own characteristic qualities, and properties that it can grant or attract. They are often collated into a table of correspondences, which you can use for inspiration in designing rituals.

Air

Self: mind
Personality: intellectual, logical, social

Life phase: birth, childhood

Season: spring

Time of day: dawn

Altar tools: athame, feather, bell, incense

Direction: east

Astrological signs: Gemini, Libra, Aquarius

Tarot: suit of swords

Magical techniques: fanning, chanting, sweeping the aura with feathers

Colors: white, crystal, pale blue, lavender, gray, yellow

Animals: birds, butterflies and other flying insects, bats, flying squirrels

Spirits: angels, sylphs, fairies

Plants: dandelion, maple, sweet pea, ash, violet, lavender, lemon, rosemary

Stones: quartz, blue topaz

Themes: school, divination, decision-making, inspiration, computer time, psychic gifts

Fire

Self: heart

Personality: passionate, assertive, energetic, courageous, active, creative

Life phase: adolescence, young adulthood

Season: summer

Time of day: noon

Altar tools: wand, candles and candleholders, incense

Direction: south

Astrological signs: Aries, Leo, Sagittarius

Tarot: suit of wands

Magical techniques: censing, burning things, leaping over bonfires

Colors: red, orange, yellow, gold

Animals: lions, tigers, wolves

Spirits: salamanders, dragons, djinni

Plants: cinnamon, ginger, chili peppers, lime, orange

Stones: garnet, ruby

Themes: passionate love, creativity, power, courage, transformation, blood, healing, destruction, temper

Water

Self: soul

Personality: intuitive, responsive, emotional, sensitive, romantic

Life phase: parenthood, maturity

Season: autumn

Time of day: twilight

Altar tools: chalice, bowls, cauldron

Direction: west

Astrological signs: Cancer, Scorpio, Pisces

Tarot: suit of cups

Magical techniques: passing the chalice, sprinkling with water, dropping things into water

Colors: deep blue, ultramarine, violet

Animals: fish, dolphins, otters, frogs, penguins

Spirits: undines, mermaids

Plants: watercress, iris, water lilies, seaweed, willow

Stones: aquamarine, turquoise, coral, pearl

Themes: romantic love, intuition, fertility, menstruation, purification, feelings, the subconscious

Earth

Self: body

Personality: practical, loyal, physical, prosperous

Life phase: elderhood, death

Season: winter

Time of day: night

Altar tools: pentacle, stone, platter, table

Direction: north

Astrological signs: Taurus, Virgo, Capricorn

Tarot: suit of coins

Magical techniques: dancing, burying things

Colors: brown, black, gray, green

Animals: horses, moles, badgers

Spirits: gnomes, kobolds

Plants: potato, wheat, oak, pine, cedar, sage, cypress

Stones: agate, geode, holey stones

Themes: prosperity, security, endurance, family, nature, death, plants, animals, rocks, deep time

When you find a single correspondence that fits well with your theme, try using that to invoke the quarters. Say that you want to compose a Croning ritual for an elder in your coven. She has a particular passion for flowers, and has requested that you work them into the ritual somehow. If you're working outside, you might cast the circle by laying flowers on the ground; indoors, you could put a different bouquet in each of the quarters, in vases of elemental colors. Use these to add detail and interest to the invocations. Your east invocation might go something like this:

Soft breeze of the east,
Bring us the scent of your blossoms:
Sweet pea for freshness of thought,
Daisy for new perspectives.
Let thoughts remain limber as the ash
That shades the wild flowers.
So mote it be!

Invoking Para-Elemental Powers

The elements are magical, spiritual expressions of things readily found in the natural world. However, nature is rarely as pure as these ideals. The physical manifestations of the elements often mingle. Other times they appear in different versions of the original element. On a metaphysical level, then, these overlaps and variations appear as "para-elemental" forces. You can aspect the four elements by using para-elemental forms that relate to your theme.

Air & Fire

Heat waves: the shimmer of light through atmosphere bent by crossing different temperatures and densities; ideal for casting illusions.

Smoke: the footprints of fire as it moves through air; good for blessings, covering other scents, creating a cozy hearthside mood.

Starlight: distant sparks in the night sky evoke the most mystical and ethereal qualities of both elements; perfect for rituals that need a sense of wonder or detachment.

Steam: water heated to gaseous form, this is the most energetic combination; when you need a lot of power, consider invoking steam.

Volcanic gas vents: the poisonous breath of our planet's fiery core; a good metaphor for malicious gossip.

Air & Water

Cloud: the highest and most ephemeral blend of air and water; a good match for spells of the mind or intuition, especially if you like cloudgazing, and also perfect for summoning rain.

Fog: thick, obscuring blankets of hovering droplets; ideal for protection, concealment, muffling, binding, wards, and shields.

Hurricane: a terrible swirl of cloud and wind; mainly useful in spells to ward hurricanes away from populated areas, but its power can be drained into more productive purposes.

Mist: delicate, translucent veils of water droplets close to the ground; good for creating a mystical or romantic mood.

Air & Earth

Breath: the air from a living body; this most intimate combination of air and earth is ideal for blessings and expressions of personal power.

Dust devil: a whimsical twist of wind and particles (which can also be hay, leaves, etc., as well as soil) dancing along the ground; brings a sense of whimsy and mischief; ideal for honoring trickster deities.

Hail: destructive barrage of ice pellets; use to ward against damaging hail; a metaphor for a cluster of disasters.

Sandstorm: a scouring assault of wind-driven sand; can make effective shields or concealment, but risky, and better invoked only for warding off sandstorms.

Tornado: a violent twist of wind and debris, easier to deflect than disperse; useful as a metaphor for chaotically destructive people, or in invocations to ward off tornados.

Treetops: canopy habitat where the upper reaches of earthy trees extend into the sky, especially in rainforests; uniquely balanced between the energies, both grounded and inspired.

Fire & Water

Acid rain: poisonous rain that chemically "burns" whatever it touches; useful in rituals for environmental awareness, but also as a metaphor for pervasive problems that slowly eat away resources.

Hot spring: hot water rising from deep sources; a source of power from within, less intense than Fire alone.

Fire & Earth

Lava: molten rock flowing on the surface; a source of fast, strong energy, with more staying power than fire alone.

Magma: molten rock deep within the planet; slow, steady, intense energy ideal for sustained spells.

Volcano: violent, explosive eruptions of molten rock or slower simmering hot spots; the most extreme source of fire and earth energy, sacred to many deities including Vulcan and Pele.

Water & Earth

Beach: anywhere a body of water touches land; the gentlest and most lifegiving combination of water and earth, perfect for abundance and family magic, spells that ebb and flow over time like the tides or the course of a river, or letting go of the past.

Ice: water become solid as rock; the most stable aspect of water; terrific for dispassionate bindings or slippery shields.

Mud: water mixed with dust or soil; the most direct blend of earth and water, often inconvenient but rarely harmful, good for seasonal autumn or spring spells.

Quicksand: deceptive mix of water and sand; sometimes useful in illusions, or as a metaphor for situations that suck you in and make it hard to escape.

Slush: a pesky mix of snow, ice, water, and dirt with a sticky consistency; most common in urban areas, thus useful in spells with a modern flavor.

Snow: frozen water in drifts; among the lightest and most mobile forms of earth, as it intersects with water; good when you need flexible stability.

Swamp: habitat characterized by soil saturated with water; a broad union between the elements, good for tolerance or assimilation—and due to its filtration effect, splendid for purification.

Wellspring: water arising from hidden sources below; an unexpected gift, thus ideal for rituals of gratitude or inner resources.

You can invoke para-elemental forces in a ritual in much the same way you would the primary elements. They work in the four cardinal directions, depending on which association you prefer to emphasize, but also for cross-quarter directions, so you could invoke Beach in the west, north, or northwest. As an example, here is a Beach invocation suitable for a family-oriented ritual:

In the northwest,
Ocean embraces the sand,
Slow dance of water and land.
Cover stress, wash away strife,
And bring new life.
Hail and well met!

Note that some of these para-elemental aspects are beneficial or neutral, while others can be quite destructive. In magic, it's useful to understand harmful effects for the purpose of damage control. If you need to dismantle a hurricane, that will be much more possible (though not necessarily easier) to accomplish if you know that hurricanes are an elemental combination of water and air. Find a way to separate the two—such as running the hurricane to ground over an unpopulated area—and it will lose most of its power. As you can see from the lists above, weatherwitching typically involves two or more elements; it is among the most quintessentially para-elemental of magical disciplines.

When you find that one element matches your ritual theme especially well, you can aspect it through the other primary elements by using para-elemental forces. (You can also base a ritual on one of the para-elemental forms, much as you would a primary element.) This also provides a convenient way to avoid direct conflicts if some element clashes with your theme. For instance, I once led a well-blessing ritual—which of course had a strong match to water—but fire was a serious mismatch, and air and earth weren't particularly close. So we aspected water through the four quarters by using para-elemental combinations of Water with the other elements. We invoked Fog and Cloud in the east, Steam and Hot Springs in the south, Rain and Wells in the west, Ice and Mud in the north. By honoring water in so many of its forms, and acknowledging the other elements in more harmonious guises, we added power and cohesion to the ritual. It worked beautifully.

Other Options

The set of four elements (air, fire, water, earth) used in western magic is the most popular system in Paganism today, appearing in a variety of traditions. However, other options exist. Most often, people simply expand on the first four elements. The fifth element is more ephemeral than the others, and goes by such names as spirit or crystal. Its direction is the center, or within.

This element governs such themes as spirituality, personal evolution, and mystical knowledge. Another candidate for the fifth element is "surprise." This is a good one to invoke when you need to prepare for the unexpected.

A few systems expand considerably further. One of my favorites appears in the song "1-1-1" by the band Elvendrums: earth, air, fire, water, life, light, magic. This works especially well in rituals where you have several attendees and you want to get them all involved, because it takes seven callers to cast a circle this way. Conversely, for a smaller group, there are concise sets that take fewer callers. Celtic culture mentions the "three realms" of land, sea, and sky. The three realms are perfect for a ritual relying on the mystical symbolism of the number three.

In East Asia, the magical system of Feng Shui is based on a set of five elements: fire, earth, metal, water, wood. Feng Shui seeks to create an auspicious balance of these energies. It is most often applied in the home or office, and so this set of elements is ideal for spells involving business or family matters.

Not all circle castings need necessarily invoke directional or elemental powers. You can venture further afield by casting your circle with any cohesive set of magical motifs. For example, I once wrote a Hawaiian ritual honoring the volcano goddess Pele, in which we invoked the seven principles of Huna. These magical concepts form the basis of Hawaiian shamanism, and, along with other touches of the Hawaiian language, added a strong cultural flavor to that ritual. If you're designing a ritual based on a specific culture, look around for a set of associations that might inspire your invocations.

Whatever structure you choose, the opening invocations will set the tone for your ritual. Make sure they match your theme and goal—but leave room to get creative. Try different things and see how they work for you or your coven, especially if you have a series of similar rituals such as esbat observances. Watch for inspiration in mythology, music, other people's rituals—whatever you encounter in your magical explorations. Everything is research!

Magical Journaling
for the Reluctant

by Elizabeth Genco

I'm guessing that you know the drill by now: "Keep a journal!" all the teachers implore. And I do mean *all* the teachers. If you've ever been in a class that requires some kind of inner work, from junior-high English to undergraduate psychology to any flavor of Western esotericism, you've probably been told to keep a journal.

And maybe you've tried. Dear Gods, how you've tried. But you can't seem to get over a . . . stumbling block, shall we say.

Truth is, you hate keeping a journal. You don't know what to write. You feel silly writing. You just don't *wanna*.

Or maybe that's a little extreme. You don't "hate" keeping a journal, per se, but you just can't seem to get around to it. You've tried, and now beautiful books with only three or four pages of writing in them skulk around in dusty corners of your living space. Your intentions are good, but the habit just doesn't want to stick, so you figure—why bother?

Or maybe your disdain doesn't have anything to do with the act of writing itself. No, you're not keeping a journal because the last time you let yourself spill all over the page, some jerk—maybe even some jerk close to you—found your journal and read it. Maybe the subsequent arguments made your life a living nightmare, or maybe you just haven't been able to get over the violation. Subject yourself to that again? Thanks, but no thanks.

I have kept journals for years. My first conscious memories of journal keeping are from age eight or nine, though I probably started earlier (I don't even know where all of them are, which is kind of terrifying, but I try not to let it bother me). I have often said that journaling is what taught me how to write (keeping me out of therapy is just an added bonus), and I love writing, so applying my existing tools to a new spiritual practice wasn't all that difficult. But I've watched many of my spiritual friends try to keep a journal and struggle all the way. When they ultimately give up, the words of all those old teachers ring in their ears. They feel like failures.

Nothing could be further from the truth. *Any* journal keeping is successful journal keeping. There are no quotas or monthly minimums. As I said, I've kept a journal for years, but within those years, I have gone long stretches—again, years—without touching a notebook. Oddly, sometimes the more I had going on in my life, the less I wrote in a journal. During those periods, there was nothing I could do to convince myself to pick up a pen. To take a particularly loaded example, I remember thinking, "Gee, I should write this down," after losing my virginity (kind of a milestone, don't you think?), and then not doing it. Oh, well. My notebook was there, the next time I wanted it. Despite my nonchalance, I've got minor regrets that I didn't make a few notes after that fateful night. The truth is, I can barely remember it.

The ability to "remember stuff" is a big, big benefit of keeping a journal; this is especially true in the magical realm. If you engage in magical or spiritual practices, your perceptions have undoubtedly been thrown wide open. Magical work contains a lot of information; unless you're one of the lucky (read: rare) ones with a

razor-sharp memory, you're not going to be able to remember it all. Writing it down creates a tangible record that you can refer to later. And when you do return to your journals, I promise that you're going to find all kinds of neat stuff that you don't even remember writing down. Now, *that's* the stuff, right there.

A journal tracks your overall development as well as your experiences. Your inner landscape can shift dramatically over time as you work magic. Using a journal, you can see how far you've come (or not come, as the case may be, and make adjustments accordingly). You'll be able to see what worked and what didn't, and perhaps understand why. Using your journal to keep track of goals can help you steer yourself in your desired direction.

If you've had the ugly experience of having your journal found and read, I can certainly understand why you might never want to keep one again. Take comfort in the fact that the problem is entirely under your control. To keep your journal secure, you can store it in a strong box with a lock, or hide it in a safe place. Even better, try keeping your journal a secret if you can. If you have nosy family members, write in your book during the times you have reserved for privacy, such as when you're working magic. If you can keep your kids out of your purse, that's a good place for it. If the spectre of "if anyone ever found it" really upsets you, take some extra care to make sure than nobody does. You might have to brainstorm to find what's right for you, but chances are very good that just a few well-chosen practices will keep your journal out of the wrong hands.

Finally, you don't *have* to keep a journal. A journal is an incredibly useful tool, but obviously the world is not going to end if you don't keep one. I hereby give you permission to bid the old "keep a journal!" naggers *adieu*. Some folks just aren't interested, and that's fine. But if you're not quite ready to abandon the idea, or if my words have convinced you to give it another try, here are some tips, all geared toward easing you into the process.

Don't set any expectations for yourself. Ultimately, your only schedule for journal-keeping is whenever the heck you feel like it. You can write in your book once a day, once a week, once a month, once a quarter, once a year, or once every five years. Or never. No demands or expectations means that you don't get to kick yourself when your practice turns out to be something other than what you envisioned. In this case, if you *don't* envision, you have the freedom to develop the practice that will work best for you.

Along with low expectations, establish the following ground rule at the outset: that there will be no ground rules. You can keep your journal however you'd like. The only "rule" that I follow is one of simple administrivia: I always note the date on my entries. For sanity's sake (finding old entries without being able to trace them can drive one nuts), I highly suggest that you do the same. But that's about it. I try to note the phase of the Moon at every entry, too, but, I'll be honest—after a decade, that just hasn't stuck. Oh, well.

When I first began practicing Wicca, I kept my magical journal in a notebook separate from my "mundane" journal. This is a fine practice, and makes total sense. However, over time, my "magical" inner landscape became more and more entwined with the "mundane" one. Result? I wrote in my "magical" journal less and less. Finally, I just scrapped the magical journal and wrote everything in one. While some folks suggest that you keep your magical notebook separate from a mundane journal, I posit that anyone just trying to get in the hang of journal keeping will probably find a single notebook much more palatable than multiple notebooks. You don't have to make that distinction.

Speaking of notebooks, a few words on selecting the right one: it all boils down to picking something that you're going to use. Buying a new notebook can be a real treat (me, I like to prolong the magic; as such, I have a "notebook stash" filled with books that I can't possibly use within the next, oh, twenty years), but take a few minutes to consider what would work best for you. Some folks like to write in the prettiest notebooks they can find. Others choke at the prospect of "messing up" such pristine objects and feel more comfortable (read: less inhibited) scribbling away in a little spiral-bound number from the dollar store. Use what works, and don't think about it too hard. It's only a notebook.

The same thing goes for pens. Use what's comfortable, and don't think about it too hard. (May I suggest the Pilot G2 gel pen in a basic black?)

There are a million ways to keep a magical journal and you are limited only by your imagination. But if you're short on ideas as to how to start, try this: simply jot down a brief paragraph after your private rituals. You can include the phase of the Moon, a short description of what you performed, what actually transpired, and a sentence or two on how you're feeling that day. Once you're in the habit, you can expand the practice to include short entries on all the other experiences relating to your spiritual life: notes on dreams, spells, coincidences, divinations, etc. Soon you might find that you're writing a lot! But first, start small.

Keeping track of magical workings is a common use of magical journals. In your journal, note the purpose of the spell, astrological information (the date and time cast, the moon phase), your location, ingredients used, deities called, and how you performed the spell. Leave some space for recording your results later.

List-making is another simple, non-threatening journal activity. The lists can be of anything. Some suggestions: spells to try, deities to research, books to read (or at least flip through in the bookstore), classes or groves to check out, to-do lists, supply inventories ("was I out of mugwort or lavender?"), shops to visit (in person or online), shopping lists, favorite chants, magical techniques.

Start a list of personal correspondences. What is *your* personal symbolism for things like colors, herbs, or gemstones? Your correspondences can be based on research, personal experience, gut instinct, or all three.

Another powerful list-making technique is goal-setting. Writing goals down is the first step to bringing them into being. Consider what you would like to accomplish during the next turn of the wheel, or five years down the road, and record those goals in your journal. Samhain is a great time for goal-setting—you could even design a short ritual to create the list, or dedicate yourself to achieving the items on it. Again, think small and set realistic expectations. You can set goals for smaller periods of time too, of course.

If you're going through a rough patch, or find yourself frequently in a funk, you can use your journal to chart your moods. Every day (or every day you feel like it), take a quick check of your moods that day and write them down, also noting the day's key events in a sentence or two. If you want to take it even further, you can record the weather and the Moon phase as well. After a couple of weeks or a month, take a look at your notes and see if any patterns emerge.

Good luck, and have fun keeping your magical journal!

Living Together Pagan:
Solitary In a Group

by Brenna Lyons

At a recent social event, a group of friends regaled me with the tale of the break-up of a ritual and study group. The split was due primarily to several philosophical differences, including whether or not the God should be "called" in addition to the Goddess at rituals, and in what order the elements should be invoked. Overall, the split was neither pretty nor kind.

It is amazing to me that, in a community that praises pursuit of one's personal path and self-discovery of individual connection to deity and others, such intolerance of similar yet dissimilar beliefs can still become so vicious.

It has long been said that herding Pagans is akin to herding cats. It is also typically noted that Pagans are known to be tolerant of each other's paths, even when those paths do not coincide.

Why, then, is there such animosity when Pagans interact? As a solitary, I find myself on the outside of this issue looking in. To me, all Pagans are essentially solitaries acting inside or outside a group.

Working Within a Group

When one is a member of a group, she often expects, perhaps rightly and perhaps wrongly, that everyone within that group will share her beliefs and practice as she practices. It is unlikely that you will form a group of any notable size with people whose paths converge so closely, but the unrealistic expectation often exists. That leaves the individual with several choices: compromise or accept change in ritual, refuse to compromise and/or leave the group.

Compromise is not as difficult as it sounds. As a solitary, I find that I accept compromise whenever I engage in a public ritual.

Perhaps one ritual can model the practice of persons A and C, and another ritual can model the practice of persons B and D. Or elements of the practitioners may be melded into a single ritual to make a truly unique and beautiful whole.

The problems with compromise come when there is one member of the group whose views oppose the rest but wants equal compromise as if she represented half of the total group size, or when the paths are so divergent that the practitioners of one would have a difficult time celebrating in the manner the other path does. In such a case, leaving the group in favor of another or forming a new group might be best.

In my personal experience, situations where there can be no compromise can rarely be saved.

Who Is Right and Who Is Wrong?

Can you ever really be wrong in worship? Well, I imagine gross errors, when you claim a particular and well-known path but fail to uphold the basic tenets of the path, would be wrong in that respect, since your professed path is obviously not your actual path. But beyond that, can you be wrong in how you choose to practice?

I would argue that you cannot.

Every Pagan steps foot on a path that is part design and part inspiration. Even within a specific base such as Wicca, practitioners do not always agree.

Search for ritual candle colors, and you will find that green may be used for money, fertility, health issues, nature, and several other things. Some suggest blue for tranquility and others purple.

Why does this happen? The practice of a Pagan path is as individual as the person and the path she finds herself on. Is the color you choose important for the magical properties of the color as reported by a noted authority you trust, much of which finds a basis in psychology or cultural perception? Or is it important for the focus it affords you?

Is one right and the other wrong? I find it hard not to pity the individual who answers "yes" to this question.

The correct path to take is the one that draws your heart and puts you at peace with the ritual you intend to perform. Therefore the "correct" practice for any individual would be the one that gives the individual what she needs to practice at ease.

If an acclaimed book names your birth colors as red and black and your stone a Moonstone, but green and white call to you, rose quartz warms to your skin in a soothing manner, and opal energizes you, you must question whether "going by the book" will cause such discord that you will find no comfort in your workings. If it will, perhaps the "generally accepted correlations" are not for you.

If the color green for money works for you, because you know it's right "by the book," you use it. If yellow and white work for you, because they are colors that allow you mental clarity and focus in your rituals, no matter your task, who is to argue that it is wrong for you, the solitary who must forge your own path?

For this reason, if for no other, telling someone her practice is wrong because it doesn't adhere to your personal dogma or even to respected sources is nonsensical. The energies around us do not touch us all in the same way. We are not all attuned to them in the same way. Our paths are not the same path, so our perceptions and modes of communing with the deities or energies will not necessarily coincide.

Public Rituals

When attending a ritual, you are not guaranteed to agree with the gross form of the ritual. Like the argument of candle colors, you must choose which elements of a ritual are essential to your personal peace and which are not. Perhaps calling both the God and Goddess, though it is not to your personal tastes, doesn't concern you, but the calling of the elements in a particular order puts you at ease.

Simply put, it does you little good to continuously attend rituals that clash with your personal comfort. If you are not at ease, your energies will be a negating or disruptive force within the whole. In that way, neither you nor the others around you will be getting as much from the ritual as might be, because the individual is ill at ease.

If you know a ritual feels incomplete to you if both God and Goddess are not called, you will want to seek out groups that hold rituals that call both. If you know the rituals of a certain group feel discordant to you, you are likewise better served seeking out another group for rituals. That doesn't mean you cannot form friendships with the original group or that you cannot celebrate with them, but perhaps staying far outside their ritual circles would be best for you.

If a ritual is not to your tastes, you should still be gracious to your hosts. Thank them for their effort on your behalf, but continue searching for the group that is the proper fit for you. The fact that this group is not that fit is neither your fault nor theirs. It is simply the nature of Paganism that paths do not always coincide or even run parallel to each other.

Us vs. Them

Many Pagans forget that we are a community. We are diverse, rich, and steeped in lore. We are strong in numbers and in determination. Our strength should be in celebrating our unity, respecting each other regardless of path or even whether someone chooses to be "openly Pagan" or not.

Look again at the analogy of herding cats. Cats are independent creatures—headstrong, proud and intelligent. They are not sheep to be fleeced easily, not cattle to be led blindly to fate. But there is more to cats than even that.

Cats are fiercely loyal to a community of mothers, sisters, and children. In the face of an enemy, be it another cat or another breed of animal, they band together to protect their own. They raise children together in a tight-knit community, yet they go their own ways when needed. They fight amongst themselves at times, but when there is threat from without or within they are one, a single unit to be reckoned with.

Do you wonder now why Pagans are often said to have an affinity for cats?

It's not so much that one must herd Pagans as it is that one must impress a common goal or problem upon what amounts to a myriad of strong, independent, intelligent solitary people on paths that may weave around those of the others. If the resolution offered for said difficulty is reasonable, rational, and palatable, a large number of the cats may take up the community mantle. If it's not, they won't.

The key to living together as Pagans is to know our strengths and to respect them. We are strong, we are many, we are proud—and we are Pagan.

Almanac Section

Calendar

Time Changes

Lunar Phases

Moon Signs

Full Moons

Sabbats

World Holidays

Incense of the Day

Color of the Day

Almanac Listings

In these listings you will find the date, day, lunar phase, Moon sign, color and incense for the day, and festivals from around the world.

The Date

The date is used in numerological calculations that govern magical rites.

The Day

Each day is ruled by a planet that possesses specific magical influences:

MONDAY (MOON): Peace, sleep, healing, compassion, friends, psychic awareness, purification, and fertility.

TUESDAY (MARS): Passion, sex, courage, aggression, and protection.

WEDNESDAY (MERCURY): The conscious mind, study, travel, divination, and wisdom.

THURSDAY (JUPITER): Expansion, money, prosperity, and generosity.

FRIDAY (VENUS): Love, friendship, reconciliation, and beauty.

SATURDAY (SATURN): Longevity, exorcism, endings, homes, and houses.

SUNDAY (SUN): Healing, spirituality, success, strength, and protection.

The Lunar Phase

The lunar phase is important in determining the best times for magic.

THE WAXING MOON (from the New Moon to the Full) is the ideal time for magic to draw things toward you.

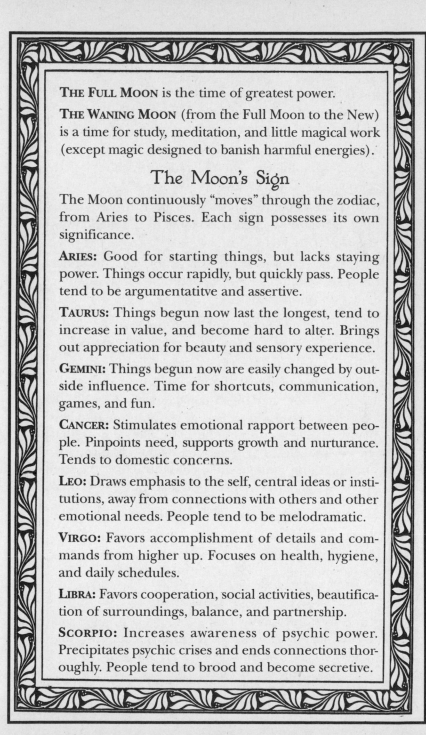

THE FULL MOON is the time of greatest power.

THE WANING MOON (from the Full Moon to the New) is a time for study, meditation, and little magical work (except magic designed to banish harmful energies).

The Moon's Sign

The Moon continuously "moves" through the zodiac, from Aries to Pisces. Each sign possesses its own significance.

ARIES: Good for starting things, but lacks staying power. Things occur rapidly, but quickly pass. People tend to be argumentatitve and assertive.

TAURUS: Things begun now last the longest, tend to increase in value, and become hard to alter. Brings out appreciation for beauty and sensory experience.

GEMINI: Things begun now are easily changed by outside influence. Time for shortcuts, communication, games, and fun.

CANCER: Stimulates emotional rapport between people. Pinpoints need, supports growth and nurturance. Tends to domestic concerns.

LEO: Draws emphasis to the self, central ideas or institutions, away from connections with others and other emotional needs. People tend to be melodramatic.

VIRGO: Favors accomplishment of details and commands from higher up. Focuses on health, hygiene, and daily schedules.

LIBRA: Favors cooperation, social activities, beautification of surroundings, balance, and partnership.

SCORPIO: Increases awareness of psychic power. Precipitates psychic crises and ends connections thoroughly. People tend to brood and become secretive.

SAGITTARIUS: Encourages flights of imagination and confidence. This is an adventurous, philosophical, and athletic Moon sign. Favors expansion and growth.

CAPRICORN: Develops strong structure. Focus on traditions, responsibilities, and obligations. A good time to set boundaries and rules.

AQUARIUS: Rebellious energy. Time to break habits and make abrupt change. Personal freedom and individuality is the focus.

PISCES: The focus is on dreaming, nostalgia, intuition, and psychic impressions. A good time for spiritual or philanthropic activities.

Color and Incense

The color and incense for the day are based on information from *Personal Alchemy* by Amber Wolfe, and relate to the planet that rules each day. This information can be taken into consideration along with other factors when planning works of magic or when blending magic into mundane life. Please note that the incense selections are not hard-and-fast. If you can not find or do not like the incense listed for the day, choose a similar scent that appeals to you.

Festivals and Holidays

Festivals are listed throughout the year. The exact dates of many of these ancient festivals are difficult to determine; prevailing data has been used.

Time Changes

The times and dates of all astrological phenomena in this almanac are based on **Eastern Standard Time (EST).** If you live outside of EST, you will need to make the following changes:

Pacific Standard Time: Subtract three hours.

Mountain Standard Time: Subtract two hours.

Central Standard Time: Subtract one hour.

Alaska/Hawaii: Subtract five hours.

Daylight Saving Time: Add an hour. In 2005, Congress extended the length of Daylight Saving Time by one month, effective this year. Daylight Saving Time now runs from March 11, 2007 to November 4, 2007.

2007 Sabbats and Full Moons

January 3	Full Moon 8:57 am
February 2	Imbolc
February 2	Full Moon 12:45 am
March 3	Full Moon 6:17 pm
March 20	Ostara (Spring Equinox)
April 2	Full Moon 1:15 pm
May 1	Beltane
May 2	Full Moon 6:09 am
May 31	Full Moon 9:04 pm
June 21	Litha (Summer Solstice)
June 30	Full Moon 9:49 am
July 29	Full Moon 8:48 pm
August 1	Lammas
August 28	Full Moon 6:35 am
September 23	Mabon (Fall Equinox)
September 26	Full Moon 3:45 pm
October 26	Full Moon 12:51 am
October 31	Samhain
November 24	Full Moon 9:30 am
December 22	Yule (Winter Solstice)
December 23	Full Moon 8:15 pm

January

1 Monday
New Year's Day • Kwanzaa ends
Waxing Moon
Moon Phase: Second Quarter
Color: Gray

Moon Sign: Gemini
Incense: Clary sage

2 Tuesday
First Writing (Japanese)
Waxing Moon
Moon Phase: Second Quarter
Color: Red

Moon Sign: Gemini
Moon enters Cancer 10:14 am
Incense: Bayberry

3 Wednesday
St. Genevieve's Day
Waxing Moon
Moon Phase: Full Moon 8:57 am
Color: Yellow

Moon Sign: Cancer
Incense: Honeysuckle

4 Thursday
Frost Fairs on the Thames
Waning Moon
Moon Phase: Third Quarter
Color: Green

Moon Sign: Cancer
Moon enters Leo 4:14 pm
Incense: Jasmine

5 Friday
Epiphany Eve
Waning Moon
Moon Phase: Third Quarter
Color: White

Moon Sign: Leo
Incense: Rose

6 Saturday
Epiphany
Waning Moon
Moon Phase: Third Quarter
Color: Brown

Moon Sign: Leo
Incense: Sage

7 Sunday
Rizdvo (Ukrainian)
Waning Moon
Moon Phase: Third Quarter
Color: Yellow

Moon Sign: Leo
Moon enters Virgo 1:18 am
Incense: Hyacinth

8   Monday
Midwives' Day
Waning Moon
Moon Phase: Third Quarter
Color: Lavender

Moon Sign: Virgo
Incense: Hyssop

---

9   Tuesday
Feast of the Black Nazarene (Filipino)
Waning Moon
Moon Phase: Third Quarter
Color: White

Moon Sign: Virgo
Moon enters Libra 1:15 pm
Incense: Ylang ylang

---

10   Wednesday
Business God's Day (Japanese)
Waning Moon
Moon Phase: Third Quarter
Color: Brown

Moon Sign: Libra
Incense: Marjoram

☾   Thursday
Carmentalia (Roman)
Waning Moon
Moon Phase: Fourth Quarter 7:44 am
Color: Turquoise

Moon Sign: Libra
Incense: Myrrh

---

12   Friday
Revolution Day (Tanzanian)
Waning Moon
Moon Phase: Fourth Quarter
Color: Pink

Moon Sign: Libra
Moon enters Scorpio 11:08 pm
Incense: Mint

---

13   Saturday
Twentieth Day (Norwegian)
Waning Moon
Moon Phase: Fourth Quarter
Color: Gray

Moon Sign: Scorpio
Incense: Pine

---

14   Sunday
Feast of the Ass (French)
Waning Moon
Moon Phase: Fourth Quarter
Color: Orange

Moon Sign: Scorpio
Moon enters Sagittarius 1:11 pm
Incense: Eucalyptus

15 Monday
Birthday of Martin Luther King, Jr. (observed)   Moon Sign: Sagittarius
Waning Moon   Incense: Lily
Moon Phase: Fourth Quarter
Color: White

16 Tuesday
Apprentices Day   Moon Sign: Sagittarius
Waning Moon   Moon enters Capricorn 8:49 pm
Moon Phase: Fourth Quarter   Incense: Geranium
Color: Black

17 Wednesday
St. Anthony's Day (Mexican)   Moon Sign: Capricorn
Waning Moon   Incense: Lavender
Moon Phase: Fourth Quarter
Color: Topaz

Thursday
Assumption Day   Moon Sign: Capricorn
Waning Moon   Incense: Clove
Moon Phase: New Moon 11:01 pm
Color: Purple

19 Friday
Kitchen God Feast (Chinese)   Moon Sign: Capricorn
Waxing Moon   Moon enters Aquarius 1:15 am
Moon Phase: First Quarter   Incense: Thyme
Color: Rose

20 Saturday
Islamic New Year   Moon Sign: Aquarius
Waxing Moon   Sun enters Aquarius 6:01 am
Moon Phase: First Quarter   Incense: Sandalwood
Color: Blue

21 Sunday
St. Agnes Day   Moon Sign: Aquarius
Waxing Moon   Moon enters Pisces 3:48 am
Moon Phase: First Quarter   Incense: Juniper
Color: Gold

January

22 Monday
Saint Vincent's Day (French)
Waxing Moon
Moon Phase: First Quarter
Color: Silver

Moon Sign: Pisces
Incense: Rosemary

23 Tuesday
St. Ildefonso's Day
Waxing Moon
Moon Phase: First Quarter
Color: Gray

Moon Sign: Pisces
Moon enters Aries 5:52 am
Incense: Ginger

24 Wednesday
Alasitas Fair (Bolivian)
Waxing Moon
Moon Phase: First Quarter
Color: White

Moon Sign: Aries
Incense: Lilac

☽ Thursday
Burns' Night (Scottish)
Waxing Moon
Moon Phase: Second Quarter 6:01 pm
Color: Crimson

Moon Sign: Aries
Moon enters Taurus 8:28 am
Incense: Nutmeg

26 Friday
Republic Day (Indian)
Waxing Moon
Moon Phase: Second Quarter
Color: Coral

Moon Sign: Taurus
Incense: Violet

27 Saturday
Vogelgruff (Swiss)
Waxing Moon
Moon Phase: Second Quarter
Color: Indigo

Moon Sign: Taurus
Moon enters Gemini 12:10 pm
Incense: Patchouli

28 Sunday
St. Charlemagne's Day
Waxing Moon
Moon Phase: Second Quarter
Color: Amber

Moon Sign: Gemini
Moon enters Aquarius 6:09 pm
Incense: Frankincense

January

29 Monday
Australia Day
Waxing Moon
Moon Phase: Second Quarter
Color: Ivory

Moon Sign: Gemini
Moon enters Cancer 5:16 pm
Incense: Neroli

30 Tuesday
Three Hierarchs' Day (Eastern Orthodox)
Waxing Moon
Moon Phase: Second Quarter
Color: Maroon

Moon Sign: Cancer
Incense: Cedar

31 Wednesday
Independence Day (Nauru)
Waxing Moon
Moon Phase: Second Quarter
Color: Yellow

Moon Sign: Cancer
Incense: Bay laurel

Homemade Butter

Put heavy cream in a jar with a lid, and seal the lid tightly. Shake the cream for fifteen to twenty minutes—perhaps you can pass it around the circle at a ritual gathering. It will turn into the most delicious homemade butter, which can be enjoyed at your Imbolc feast.

—Sharynne NicMhacha

February

1   **Thursday**
St. Brigid's Day (Irish)   Moon Sign: Cancer
Waxing Moon   Moon enters Leo 12:14 pm
Moon Phase: Second Quarter   Incense: Carnation
Color: White

  Friday
Imbolc • Groundhog Day   Moon Sign: Leo
Waxing Moon   Incense: Vanilla
Moon Phase: Full Moon 12:45 am
Color: Purple

3   **Saturday**
St. Blaise's Day   Moon Sign: Leo
Waning Moon   Moon enters Virgo 9:34 am
Moon Phase: Third Quarter   Incense: Magnolia
Color: Brown

4   **Sunday**
Independence Day (Sri Lankan)   Moon Sign: Virgo
Waning Moon   Incense: Almond
Moon Phase: Third Quarter
Color: Orange

5   **Monday**
Festival de la Alcaldesa (Italian)   Moon Sign: Virgo
Waning Moon   Moon enters Libra 9:15 pm
Moon Phase: Third Quarter   Incense: Narcissus
Color: Gray

6   **Tuesday**
Bob Marley's Birthday (Jamaican)   Moon Sign: Libra
Waning Moon   Incense: Cinnamon
Moon Phase: Third Quarter
Color: Red

7   **Wednesday**
Full Moon Poya (Sri Lankan)   Moon Sign: Libra
Waning Moon   Incense: Lavender
Moon Phase: Third Quarter
Color: White

February

8 Thursday
Mass for Broken Needles (Japanese)
Waning Moon
Moon Phase: Third Quarter
Color: Crimson

Moon Sign: Libra
Moon enters Scorpio 10:09 am
Incense: Apricot

9 Friday
St. Marion's Day (Lebanese)
Waning Moon
Moon Phase: Third Quarter
Color: Rose

Moon Sign: Scorpio
Incense: Cypress

◐ Saturday
Gasparilla Day (Florida)
Waning Moon
Moon Phase: Fourth Quarter 4:51 pm
Color: Blue

Moon Sign: Scorpio
Moon enters Sagittarius 10:01 pm
Incense: Ivy

11 Sunday
Foundation Day (Japanese)
Waning Moon
Moon Phase: Fourth Quarter
Color: Amber

Moon Sign: Sagittarius
Incense: Heliotrope

12 Monday
Lincoln's Birthday (actual)
Waning Moon
Moon Phase: Fourth Quarter
Color: Lavender

Moon Sign: Sagittarius
Incense: Hyssop

13 Tuesday
Parentalia (Roman)
Waning Moon
Moon Phase: Fourth Quarter
Color: White

Moon Sign: Sagittarius
Moon enters Capricorn 6:42 am
Incense: Basil

14 Wednesday
Valentine's Day
Waning Moon
Moon Phase: Fourth Quarter
Color: Brown

Moon Sign: Capricorn
Incense: Marjoram

15 Thursday
Lupercalia (Roman)
Waning Moon
Moon Phase: Fourth Quarter
Color: Turquoise

Moon Sign: Capricorn
Moon enters Aquarius 11:34 am
Incense: Balsam

---

16 Friday
Fumi-e (Japanese)
Waning Moon
Moon Phase: Fourth Quarter
Color: Coral

Moon Sign: Aquarius
Incense: Alder

Saturday
Quirinalia (Roman)
Waning Moon
Moon Phase: New Moon 11:14 am
Color: Indigo

Moon Sign: Aquarius
Moon enters Pisces 1:30 pm
Incense: Rue

---

18 Sunday
Chinese New Year (boar)
Waxing Moon
Moon Phase: First Quarter
Color: Gold

Moon Sign: Pisces
Sun enters Pisces 8:09 pm
Incense: Marigold

---

19 Monday
Presidents' Day (observed)
Waxing Moon
Moon Phase: First Quarter
Color: White

Moon Sign: Pisces
Moon enters Aries 2:06 pm
Incense: Lily

---

20 Tuesday
Mardi Gras
Waxing Moon
Moon Phase: First Quarter
Color: Maroon

Moon Sign: Aries
Incense: Ginger

---

21 Wednesday
Ash Wednesday
Waning Moon
Moon Phase: First Quarter
Color: Yellow

Moon Sign: Aries
Moon enters Taurus 3:03 pm
Incense: Honeysuckle

February

22 Thursday
Caristia (Roman)
Waxing Moon
Moon Phase: First Quarter
Color: Green

Moon Sign: Taurus
Incense: Mulberry

23 Friday
Terminalia (Roman)
Waxing Moon
Moon Phase: First Quarter
Color: Pink

Moon Sign: Taurus
Moon enters Gemini 5:42 pm
Incense: Orchid

24 Saturday
Regifugium (Roman)
Waxing Moon
Moon Phase: Second Quarter 2:56 am
Color: Gray

Moon Sign: Gemini
Incense: Pine

25 Sunday
Saint Walburga's Day (German)
Waxing Moon
Moon Phase: Second Quarter
Color: Yellow

Moon Sign: Gemini
Moon enters Cancer 10:47 pm
Incense: Eucalyptus

26 Monday
Zamboanga Festival (Filipino)
Waxing Moon
Moon Phase: Second Quarter
Color: Ivory

Moon Sign: Cancer
Incense: Clary sage

27 Tuesday
Threepenny Day
Waxing Moon
Moon Phase: Second Quarter
Color: Black

Moon Sign: Cancer
Incense: Bayberry

28 Wednesday
Kalevala Day (Finnish)
Waxing Moon
Moon Phase: Second Quarter
Color: Topaz

Moon Sign: Cancer
Moon enters Leo 6:29 am
Incense: Lilac

March

1 **Thursday**
Matronalia (Roman)
Waxing Moon
Moon Phase: Second Quarter
Color: Purple

Moon Sign: Leo
Incense: Myrrh

---

2 **Friday**
St. Chad's Day (English)
Waxing Moon
Moon Phase: Second Quarter
Color: White

Moon Sign: Leo
Moon enters Virgo 4:32 pm
Incense: Yarrow

Saturday
Doll Festival (Japanese)
Waxing Moon
Moon Phase: Full Moon 6:17 pm
Color: Blue

Moon Sign: Virgo
Incense: Sage

---

4 **Sunday**
Purim
Waning Moon
Moon Phase: Third Quarter
Color: Gold

Moon Sign: Virgo
Incense: Juniper

---

5 **Monday**
Isis Festival (Roman)
Waning Moon
Moon Phase: Third Quarter
Color: Lavender

Moon Sign: Virgo
Moon enters Libra 4:25 am
Incense: Rosemary

---

6 **Tuesday**
Alamo Day
Waning Moon
Moon Phase: Third Quarter
Color: White

Moon Sign: Libra
Incense: Geranium

---

7 **Wednesday**
Bird and Arbor Day
Waning Moon
Moon Phase: Third Quarter
Color: Yellow

Moon Sign: Libra
Moon enters Scorpio 5:16 pm
Incense: Lavender

March

8 Thursday
International Women's Day
Waning Moon
Moon Phase: Third Quarter
Color: Crimson

Moon Sign: Scorpio
Incense: Jasmine

---

9 Friday
Forty Saints' Day (Romanian)
Waning Moon
Moon Phase: Third Quarter
Color: Purple

Moon Sign: Scorpio
Incense: Mint

---

10 Saturday
Tibet Day
Waning Moon
Moon Phase: Third Quarter
Color: Black

Moon Sign: Scorpio
Moon enters Sagittarius 5:37 am
Incense: Sandalwood

◑ Sunday
Daylight Saving Time begins
Waning Moon
Moon Phase: Fourth Quarter 11:54 pm
Color: Orange

Moon Sign: Sagittarius
Incense: Hyacinth

---

12 Monday
Receiving the Water (Buddhist)
Waning Moon
Moon Phase: Fourth Quarter
Color: Silver

Moon Sign: Sagittarius
Moon enters Capricorn 4:34 pm
Incense: Neroli

---

13 Tuesday
Purification Feast (Balinese)
Waning Moon
Moon Phase: Fourth Quarter
Color: Scarlet

Moon Sign: Capricorn
Incense: Ylang ylang

---

14 Wednesday
Mamuralia (Roman) • Purim
Waning Moon
Moon Phase: Fourth Quarter
Color: Brown

Moon Sign: Capricorn
Moon enters Aquarius 10:53 pm
Incense: Bay laurel

March ♈

15 Thursday
Phallus Festival (Japanese)
Waning Moon
Moon Phase: Fourth Quarter
Color: White

Moon Sign: Aquarius
Incense: Nutmeg

16 Friday
St. Urho's Day (Finnish)
Waning Moon
Moon Phase: Fourth Quarter
Color: Coral

Moon Sign: Aquarius
Incense: Violet

17 Saturday
St. Patrick's Day
Waning Moon
Moon Phase: Fourth Quarter
Color: Brown

Moon Sign: Aquarius
Moon enters Pisces 1:30 am
Incense: Magnolia

☽ Sunday
Sheelah's Day (Irish)
Waning Moon
Moon Phase: New Moon 10:42 pm
Color: Yellow

Moon Sign: Pisces
Incense: Frankincense

19 Monday
St. Joseph's Day (Sicilian)
Waxing Moon
Moon Phase: First Quarter
Color: Ivory

Moon Sign: Pisces
Moon enters Aries 1:41 am
Incense: Hyssop

20 Tuesday
Ostara • Spring Equinox
Waxing Moon
Moon Phase: First Quarter
Color: Red

Moon Sign: Aries
Sun enters Aries 8:07 pm
Incense: Cedar

21 Wednesday
Juarez Day (Mexican)
Waxing Moon
Moon Phase: First Quarter
Color: White

Moon Sign: Aries
Moon enters Taurus 1:15 am
Incense: Honeysuckle

March ♈

22 Thursday
Hilaria (Roman)
Waxing Moon
Moon Phase: First Quarter
Color: Green

Moon Sign: Taurus
Incense: Clove

23 Friday
Pakistan Day
Waxing Moon
Moon Phase: First Quarter
Color: Rose

Moon Sign: Taurus
Moon enters Gemini 2:06 am
Incense: Rose

24 Saturday
Day of Blood (Roman)
Waxing Moon
Moon Phase: First Quarter
Color: Gray

Moon Sign: Gemini
Incense: Patchouli

◖ Sunday
Tichborne Dole (English)
Waxing Moon
Moon Phase: Second Quarter 2:16 pm
Color: Amber

Moon Sign: Gemini
Moon enters Cancer 5:49 am
Incense: Heliotrope

26 Monday
Prince Kuhio Day (Hawaiian)
Waxing Moon
Moon Phase: Second Quarter
Color: White

Moon Sign: Cancer
Incense: Narcissus

27 Tuesday
Smell the Breezes Day (Egyptian)
Waxing Moon
Moon Phase: Second Quarter
Color: Maroon

Moon Sign: Cancer
Moon enters Leo 1:04 pm
Incense: Cinnamon

28 Wednesday
Oranges and Lemons Service (English)
Waxing Moon
Moon Phase: Second Quarter
Color: Topaz

Moon Sign: Leo
Incense: Lilac

29 Thursday
St. Eustace's Day
Waxing Moon
Moon Phase: Second Quarter
Color: Turquoise

Moon Sign: Leo
Moon enters Virgo 11:27 pm
Incense: Apricot

30 Friday
Seward's Day (Alaskan)
Waxing Moon
Moon Phase: Second Quarter
Color: Pink

Moon Sign: Virgo
Incense: Thyme

31 Saturday
The Borrowed Days (Ethiopian)
Waxing Moon
Moon Phase: Second Quarter
Color: Blue

Moon Sign: Virgo
Incense: Rue

Birch Wine

1 gallon birch sap
3 lbs. (6¾ cups) sugar
1 lb. (4 cups packed) raisins
1½ tbsp. crude tartar

You can make as many gallons at a time as you wish, following the proportions listed above. Boil the sap, sugar, and raisins for twenty minutes and then put them in a tub along with the tartar. When the mixture has fermented for a few days, strain it and put it into a cask or containers. When the liquid has stopped fermenting, take out the raisins and seal up the container. Let stand five months, and then bottle. Store in a cool place with the bottle kept upright.

—Sharynne NicMhacha

April ♈

1 Sunday
April Fools' Day • Palm Sunday
Waxing Moon
Moon Phase: Second Quarter
Color: Yellow

Moon Sign: Virgo
Moon enters Libra 11:43 am
Incense: Almond

---

2 Monday
The Battle of Flowers (French)
Waxing Moon
Moon Phase: Full Moon 1:15 pm
Color: White

Moon Sign: Libra
Incense: Lily

---

3 Tuesday
Passover begins
Waning Moon
Moon Phase: Third Quarter
Color: Red

Moon Sign: Libra
Incense: Basil

---

4 Wednesday
Megalesia (Roman)
Waning Moon
Moon Phase: Third Quarter
Color: Brown

Moon Sign: Libra
Moon enters Scorpio 12:35 am
Incense: Marjoram

---

5 Thursday
Tomb-Sweeping Day (Chinese)
Waning Moon
Moon Phase: Third Quarter
Color: Green

Moon Sign: Scorpio
Incense: Balsam

---

6 Friday
Good Friday • Orthodox Good Friday
Waning Moon
Moon Phase: Third Quarter
Color: Rose

Moon Sign: Scorpio
Moon enters Sagittarius 12:56 pm
Incense: Alder

---

7 Saturday
Festival of Pure Brightness (Chinese)
Waning Moon
Moon Phase: Third Quarter
Color: Gray

Moon Sign: Sagittarius
Incense: Pine

April

8 Sunday
Easter • Orthodox Easter
Waning Moon
Moon Phase: Third Quarter
Color: Gold

Moon Sign: Sagittarius
Moon enters Capricorn 11:36 pm
Incense: Marigold

9 Monday
Valour Day (Filipino)
Waning Moon
Moon Phase: Third Quarter
Color: Lavender

Moon Sign: Capricorn
Incense: Rosemary

10 Tuesday
Passover ends
Waning Moon
Moon Phase: Fourth Quarter 2:04 pm
Color: White

Moon Sign: Capricorn
Incense: Ginger

11 Wednesday
Heroes Day (Costa Rican)
Waning Moon
Moon Phase: Fourth Quarter
Color: Topaz

Moon Sign: Capricorn
Moon enters Aquarius 7:23 am
Incense: Lavender

12 Thursday
Cerealia (Roman)
Waning Moon
Moon Phase: Fourth Quarter
Color: Turquoise

Moon Sign: Aquarius
Incense: Mulberry

13 Friday
Thai New Year
Waning Moon
Moon Phase: Fourth Quarter
Color: Pink

Moon Sign: Aquarius
Moon enters Pisces 11:38 am
Incense: Orchid

14 Saturday
Sanno Festival (Japanese)
Waning Moon
Moon Phase: Fourth Quarter
Color: Blue

Moon Sign: Pisces
Incense: Ivy

April

15 Sunday
Plowing Festival (Chinese)
Waning Moon
Moon Phase: Fourth Quarter
Color: Amber

Moon Sign: Pisces
Moon enters Aries 12:46 pm
Incense: Juniper

16 Monday
Zurich Spring Festival (Swiss)
Waning Moon
Moon Phase: Fourth Quarter
Color: Ivory

Moon Sign: Aries
Incense: Narcissus

Tuesday
Yayoi Matsuri (Japanese)
Waning Moon
Moon Phase: New Moon 7:36 am
Color: Scarlet

Moon Sign: Aries
Moon enters Taurus 12:11 pm
Incense: Cedar

18 Wednesday
Flower Festival (Japanese)
Waxing Moon
Moon Phase: First Quarter
Color: White

Moon Sign: Taurus
Incense: Bay laurel

19 Thursday
Cerealia last day (Roman) • Passover ends
Waxing Moon
Moon Phase: First Quarter
Color: Purple

Moon Sign: Taurus
Moon enters Gemini 11:51 am
Incense: Carnation

20 Friday
Drum Festival (Japanese)
Waxing Moon
Moon Phase: First Quarter
Color: Coral

Moon Sign: Gemini
Sun enters Taurus 7:07 am
Incense: Cypress

21 Saturday
Tiradentes Day (Brazilian)
Waxing Moon
Moon Phase: First Quarter
Color: Indigo

Moon Sign: Gemini
Moon enters Cancer 1:50 pm
Incense: Magnolia

April

22 Sunday
Earth Day
Waxing Moon
Moon Phase: First Quarter
Color: Orange

Moon Sign: Cancer
Incense: Heliotrope

23 Monday
St. George's Day (English)
Waxing Moon
Moon Phase: First Quarter
Color: Silver

Moon Sign: Cancer
Moon enters Leo 7:38 pm
Incense: Clary sage

◐ Tuesday
St. Mark's Eve
Waxing Moon
Moon Phase: Second Quarter 2:35 am
Color: Black

Moon Sign: Leo
Incense: Ylang ylang

25 Wednesday
Robigalia (Roman)
Waxing Moon
Moon Phase: Second Quarter
Color: Yellow

Moon Sign: Leo
Incense: Honeysuckle

26 Thursday
Arbor Day
Waxing Moon
Moon Phase: Second Quarter
Color: Crimson

Moon Sign: Leo
Moon enters Virgo 5:24 am
Incense: Jasmine

27 Friday
Humabon's Conversion (Filipino)
Waxing Moon
Moon Phase: Second Quarter
Color: Purple

Moon Sign: Virgo
Incense: Vanilla

28 Saturday
Floralia (Roman)
Waxing Moon
Moon Phase: Second Quarter
Color: Black

Moon Sign: Virgo
Moon enters Libra 5:44 pm
Incense: Sage

29 Sunday
Green Day (Japanese)
Waxing Moon
Moon Phase: Second Quarter
Color: Yellow

Moon Sign: Libra
Incense: Hyacinth

30 Monday
Walpurgis Night • May Eve
Waxing Moon
Moon Phase: Second Quarter
Color: White

Moon Sign: Libra
Incense: Hyssop

Honey Cakes

2⅓ cups sifted sugar
1 cup honey
5½ cups sifted flour
1⅔ cups citron
2 tbsp. diced orange peel
3 tbsp. powdered ginger
3 tbsp. cinnamon

Melt the sugar and honey together over low heat. Mix in flour, citron, orange peel, and powdered ginger and cinnamon. Roll the pastry on a floured board and cut into flower shapes or symbols. Cook at 350°–375° until done.

—Sharynne NicMhacha

May

1 Tuesday
Beltane • May Day
Waxing Moon
Moon Phase: Second Quarter
Color: Scarlet

Moon Sign: Libra
Moon enters Scorpio 6:41 am
Incense: Basil

Wednesday
Big Kite Flying (Japanese)
Waxing Moon
Moon Phase: Full Moon 6:09 am
Color: Brown

Moon Sign: Scorpio
Incense: Lavender

3 Thursday
Holy Cross Day
Waning Moon
Moon Phase: Third Quarter
Color: Green

Moon Sign: Scorpio
Moon enters Sagittarius 6:47 pm
Incense: Myrrh

4 Friday
Bona Dea (Roman)
Waning Moon
Moon Phase: Third Quarter
Color: White

Moon Sign: Sagittarius
Incense: Yarrow

5 Saturday
Cinco de Mayo (Mexican)
Waning Moon
Moon Phase: Third Quarter
Color: Gray

Moon Sign: Sagittarius
Incense: Patchouli

6 Sunday
Martyrs' Day (Lebanese)
Waning Moon
Moon Phase: Third Quarter
Color: Orange

Moon Sign: Sagittarius
Moon enters Capricorn 5:21 am
Incense: Eucalyptus

7 Monday
Pilgrimage of St. Nicholas (Italian)
Waning Moon
Moon Phase: Third Quarter
Color: Lavender

Moon Sign: Capricorn
Incense: Neroli

May

8 Tuesday
Liberation Day (French)
Waning Moon
Moon Phase: Third Quarter
Color: Red

Moon Sign: Capricorn
Moon enters Aquarius 1:48 pm
Incense: Cedar

9 Wednesday
Lemuria (Roman)
Waning Moon
Moon Phase: Third Quarter
Color: Yellow

Moon Sign: Aquarius
Incense: Lilac

◑ Thursday
First Day of Bird Week (Japanese)
Waning Moon
Moon Phase: Fourth Quarter 12:27 am
Color: Purple

Moon Sign: Aquarius
Moon enters Pisces 7:31 pm
Incense: Carnation

11 Friday
Ukai Season Opens (Japanese)
Waning Moon
Moon Phase: Fourth Quarter
Color: Pink

Moon Sign: Pisces
Incense: Violet

12 Saturday
Florence Nightingale's Birthday
Waning Moon
Moon Phase: Fourth Quarter
Color: Brown

Moon Sign: Pisces
Moon enters Aries 10:19 pm
Incense: Sandalwood

13 Sunday
Mother's Day
Waning Moon
Moon Phase: Fourth Quarter
Color: Yellow

Moon Sign: Aries
Incense: Frankincense

14 Monday
Carabao Festival (Spanish)
Waning Moon
Moon Phase: Fourth Quarter
Color: Silver

Moon Sign: Aries
Moon enters Taurus 10:48 pm
Incense: Narcissus

May

15 Tuesday
Festival of St. Dympna (Belgian)
Waning Moon
Moon Phase: Fourth Quarter
Color: White

Moon Sign: Taurus
Incense: Geranium

16 Wednesday
St. Honoratus' Day
Waning Moon
Moon Phase: New Moon 3:27 pm
Color: Topaz

Moon Sign: Taurus
Moon enters Gemini 10:34 pm
Incense: Marjoram

17 Thursday
Norwegian Independence Day
Waxing Moon
Moon Phase: First Quarter
Color: Turquoise

Moon Sign: Gemini
Incense: Clove

18 Friday
Las Piedras Day (Uruguayan)
Waxing Moon
Moon Phase: First Quarter
Color: Coral

Moon Sign: Gemini
Moon enters Cancer 11:38 pm
Incense: Thyme

19 Saturday
Pilgrimage to Treguier (French)
Waxing Moon
Moon Phase: First Quarter
Color: Blue

Moon Sign: Cancer
Incense: Ivy

20 Sunday
Pardon of the Singers (British)
Waxing Moon
Moon Phase: First Quarter
Color: Gold

Moon Sign: Cancer
Incense: Almond

21 Monday
Victoria Day (Canadian)
Waxing Moon
Moon Phase: First Quarter
Color: Ivory

Moon Sign: Cancer
Moon enters Leo 3:56 am
Sun enters Gemini 6:12 am
Incense: Clary sage

May ♊

22 Tuesday
Heroes' Day (Sri Lankan)
Waxing Moon
Moon Phase: First Quarter
Color: Black

Moon Sign: Leo
Incense: Basil

○ Wednesday
Shavuot
Waxing Moon
Moon Phase: Second Quarter 5:02 pm
Color: White

Moon Sign: Leo
Moon enters Virgo 12:26 pm
Incense: Bay laurel

24 Thursday
Culture Day (Bulgarian)
Waxing Moon
Moon Phase: Second Quarter
Color: Crimson

Moon Sign: Virgo
Incense: Apricot

25 Friday
Lady Godiva's Day
Waxing Moon
Moon Phase: Second Quarter
Color: Rose

Moon Sign: Virgo
Incense: Vanilla

26 Saturday
Pepys' Commemoration (English)
Waxing Moon
Moon Phase: Second Quarter
Color: Indigo

Moon Sign: Virgo
Moon enters Libra 12:16 am
Incense: Pine

27 Sunday
St. Augustine of Canterbury's Day
Waxing Moon
Moon Phase: Second Quarter
Color: Amber

Moon Sign: Libra
Incense: Marigold

28 Monday
Memorial Day (observed)
Waxing Moon
Moon Phase: Second Quarter
Color: Lavender

Moon Sign: Libra
Moon enters Scorpio 1:11 pm
Incense: Hyssop

May

29 Tuesday
Royal Oak Day (English)
Waxing Moon
Moon Phase: Second Quarter
Color: Gray

Moon Sign: Scorpio
Incense: Ylang ylang

30 Wednesday
Memorial Day (actual)
Waxing Moon
Moon Phase: Second Quarter
Color: Yellow

Moon Sign: Scorpio
Incense: Honeysuckle

Thursday
Flowers of May
Waxing Moon
Moon Phase: Full Moon 9:04 pm
Color: White

Moon Sign: Scorpio
Moon enters Sagittarius 1:06 am
Incense: Mulberry

Cranachan

Scotch-cut oats
Heavy cream
Sugar
Rum
Vanilla
Fresh berries

Partially grind the scotch-cut oats in a coffee grinder. Toast these in an iron pan over a low heat until golden. Beat a bowlful of heavy cream until it is a stiff froth, and stir in a handful of the toasted oats. Make sure the cream predominates (not too many oats). Sweeten to taste, and flavor with rum and/or vanilla. Layer in a tall glass between fresh berries or a frozen berry mixture sweetened with a little honey.

—Sharynne NicMhacha

June
♊

1 Friday
National Day (Tunisian)
Waning Moon
Moon Phase: Third Quarter
Color: Coral

Moon Sign: Sagittarius
Incense: Cypress

---

2 Saturday
Rice Harvest Festival (Malaysian)
Waning Moon
Moon Phase: Third Quarter
Color: Blue

Moon Sign: Sagittarius
Moon enters Capricorn 11:09 am
Incense: Rue

---

3 Sunday
Memorial to Broken Dolls (Japanese)
Waning Moon
Moon Phase: Third Quarter
Color: Yellow

Moon Sign: Capricorn
Incense: Juniper

---

4 Monday
Full Moon Day (Burmese)
Waning Moon
Moon Phase: Third Quarter
Color: White

Moon Sign: Capricorn
Moon enters Aquarius 7:15 pm
Incense: Rosemary

---

5 Tuesday
Constitution Day (Danish)
Waning Moon
Moon Phase: Third Quarter
Color: Scarlet

Moon Sign: Aquarius
Incense: Bayberry

---

6 Wednesday
Swedish Flag Day
Waning Moon
Moon Phase: Third Quarter
Color: Brown

Moon Sign: Aquarius
Incense: Lilac

---

7 Thursday
St. Robert of Newminster's Day
Waning Moon
Moon Phase: Third Quarter
Color: Turquoise

Moon Sign: Aquarius
Moon enters Pisces 1:24 am
Incense: Balsam

June

○ **Friday**
St. Medard's Day (Belgian)
Waning Moon
Moon Phase: Fourth Quarter 7:43 am
Color: Purple

Moon Sign: Pisces
Incense: Mint

9 Saturday
Vestalia (Roman)
Waning Moon
Moon Phase: Fourth Quarter
Color: Gray

Moon Sign: Pisces
Moon enters Aries 5:26 am
Incense: Sandalwood

10 Sunday
Time-Observance Day (Chinese)
Waning Moon
Moon Phase: Fourth Quarter
Color: Gold

Moon Sign: Aries
Incense: Heliotrope

11 Monday
Kamehameha Day (Hawaiian)
Waning Moon
Moon Phase: Fourth Quarter
Color: Silver

Moon Sign: Aries
Moon enters Taurus 7:29 am
Incense: Lily

12 Tuesday
Independence Day (Filipino)
Waning Moon
Moon Phase: Fourth Quarter
Color: White

Moon Sign: Taurus
Incense: Ginger

13 Wednesday
St. Anthony of Padua's Day
Waning Moon
Moon Phase: Fourth Quarter
Color: Yellow

Moon Sign: Taurus
Moon enters Gemini 8:24 am
Incense: Honeysuckle

☽ **Thursday**
Flag Day
Waning Moon
Moon Phase: New Moon 11:13 pm
Color: Green

Moon Sign: Gemini
Incense: Carnation

June

15 Friday
St. Vitus's Day Fires
Waxing Moon
Moon Phase: First Quarter
Color: Rose

Moon Sign: Gemini
Moon enters Cancer 9:45 am
Incense: Rose

16 Saturday
Bloomsday (Irish)
Waxing Moon
Moon Phase: First Quarter
Color: Black

Moon Sign: Cancer
Incense: Magnolia

17 Sunday
Father's Day
Waxing Moon
Moon Phase: First Quarter
Color: Amber

Moon Sign: Cancer
Moon enters Leo 1:25 pm
Incense: Eucalyptus

18 Monday
Independence Day (Egyptian)
Waxing Moon
Moon Phase: First Quarter
Color: Lavender

Moon Sign: Leo
Incense: Clary sage

19 Tuesday
Juneteenth
Waxing Moon
Moon Phase: First Quarter
Color: Red

Moon Sign: Leo
Moon enters Virgo 8:45 pm
Incense: Cinnamon

20 Wednesday
Flag Day (Argentinian)
Waxing Moon
Moon Phase: First Quarter
Color: Topaz

Moon Sign: Virgo
Incense: Bay laurel

21 Thursday
Litha • Summer Solstice
Waxing Moon
Moon Phase: First Quarter
Color: Purple

Moon Sign: Virgo
Sun enters Cancer 2:06 pm
Incense: Myrrh

June

○ Friday
Rose Festival (English)
Waxing Moon
Moon Phase: Second Quarter 9:15 am
Color: White

Moon Sign: Virgo
Moon enters Libra 7:43 am
Incense: Alder

23 Saturday
St. John's Eve
Waxing Moon
Moon Phase: Second Quarter
Color: Indigo

Moon Sign: Libra
Incense: Pine

24 Sunday
St. John's Day
Waxing Moon
Moon Phase: Second Quarter
Color: Gold

Moon Sign:Libra
Moon enters Scorpio 8:26 pm
Incense: Hyacinth

25 Monday
Fiesta of Santa Orosia (Spanish)
Waxing Moon
Moon Phase: Second Quarter
Color: Gray

Moon Sign: Scorpio
Incense: Narcissus

26 Tuesday
Pied Piper Day (German)
Waxing Moon
Moon Phase: Second Quarter
Color: Black

Moon Sign: Scorpio
Incense: Basil

27 Wednesday
Day of the Seven Sleepers (Islamic)
Waxing Moon
Moon Phase: Second Quarter
Color: White

Moon Sign: Scorpio
Moon enters Sagittarius 8:23 am
Incense: Lavender

28 Thursday
Paul Bunyan Day
Waxing Moon
Moon Phase: Second Quarter
Color: Green

Moon Sign: Sagittarius
Incense: Clove

June

29 Friday
Saint Peter and Paul's Day
Waxing Moon
Moon Phase: Second Quarter
Color: Pink

Moon Sign: Sagittarius
Moon enters Capricorn 6:05 pm
Incense: Orchid

Saturday
The Burning of the Three Firs (French)
Waxing Moon
Moon Phase: Full Moon 9:49 am
Color: Brown

Moon Sign: Capricorn
Incense: Sage

Strawberry Pudding

½ cup (1 stick) butter
⅓ cup sugar
1 cup sifted flour
2 beaten eggs
2 tbsp. strawberry jam
½ tsp. baking soda
1 tsp. milk

Cream together butter and sugar, then beat in the eggs and
flour alternately. Add strawberry jam. Dissolve the baking
soda in milk and add. Mix thoroughly and put in a greased
bowl. (The bowl should be a little more than half full).
Cover with greased wax paper and steam for 1½ hours.

—Sharynne NicMhacha

July

1 Sunday
Canada Day
Waning Moon
Moon Phase: Third Quarter
Color: Yellow

Moon Sign: Capricorn
Incense: Almond

2 Monday
Heroes' Day (Zambian)
Waning Moon
Moon Phase: Third Quarter
Color: Lavender

Moon Sign: Capricorn
Moon enters Aquarius 1:24 am
Incense: Neroli

3 Tuesday
Indian Sun Dance (Native American)
Waning Moon
Moon Phase: Third Quarter
Color: Red

Moon Sign: Aquarius
Incense: Ylang ylang

4 Wednesday
Independence Day
Waning Moon
Moon Phase: Third Quarter
Color: Brown

Moon Sign: Aquarius
Moon enters Pisces 6:52 am
Incense: Marjoram

5 Thursday
Tynwald (Nordic)
Waning Moon
Moon Phase: Third Quarter
Color: Turquoise

Moon Sign: Aquarius
Incense: Jasmine

6 Friday
Khao Phansa Day (Thai)
Waning Moon
Moon Phase: Third Quarter
Color: White

Moon Sign: Aquarius
Moon enters Aries 10:56 am
Incense: Yarrow

◐ Saturday
Weaver's Festival (Japanese)
Waning Moon
Moon Phase: Fourth Quarter 12:53 pm
Color: Blue

Moon Sign: Aries
Incense: Ivy

July

8 Sunday
St. Elizabeth's Day (Portuguese)
Waning Moon
Moon Phase: Fourth Quarter
Color: Orange

Moon Sign: Aries
Moon enters Taurus 1:54 pm
Incense: Marigold

9 Monday
Battle of Sempach Day (Swiss)
Waning Moon
Moon Phase: Fourth Quarter
Color: White

Moon Sign: Taurus
Incense: Lily

10 Tuesday
Lady Godiva Day (English)
Waning Moon
Moon Phase: Fourth Quarter
Color: Black

Moon Sign: Taurus
Moon enters Gemini 4:10 pm
Incense: Cedar

11 Wednesday
Revolution Day (Mongolian)
Waning Moon
Moon Phase: Fourth Quarter
Color: Topaz

Moon Sign: Gemini
Incense: Bay laurel

12 Thursday
Lobster Carnival (Nova Scotian)
Waning Moon
Moon Phase: Fourth Quarter
Color: Purple

Moon Sign: Gemini
Moon enters Cancer 6:39 pm
Incense: Apricot

13 Friday
Festival of the Three Cows (Spanish)
Waning Moon
Moon Phase: Fourth Quarter
Color: Rose

Moon Sign: Cancer
Incense: Rose

Saturday
Bastille Day (French)
Waning Moon
Moon Phase: New Moon 8:04 am
Color: Brown

Moon Sign: Cancer
Moon enters Leo 10:43 pm
Incense: Patchouli

July

15 Sunday
St. Swithin's Day
Waxing Moon
Moon Phase: First Quarter
Color: Gold

Moon Sign: Leo
Incense: Juniper

16 Monday
Our Lady of Carmel
Waxing Moon
Moon Phase: First Quarter
Color: Gray

Moon Sign: Leo
Incense: Rosemary

17 Tuesday
Rivera Day (Puerto Rican)
Waxing Moon
Moon Phase: First Quarter
Color: Scarlet

Moon Sign: Leo
Moon enters Virgo 5:39 am
Incense: Basil

18 Wednesday
Gion Matsuri Festival (Japanese)
Waxing Moon
Moon Phase: First Quarter
Color: White

Moon Sign: Virgo
Incense: Lilac

19 Thursday
Flitch Day (English)
Waxing Moon
Moon Phase: First Quarter
Color: Crimson

Moon Sign: Virgo
Moon enters Libra 3:53 pm
Incense: Mulberry

20 Friday
Binding of Wreaths (Lithuanian)
Waxing Moon
Moon Phase: First Quarter
Color: Pink

Moon Sign: Libra
Incense: Vanilla

21 Saturday
National Day (Belgian)
Waxing Moon
Moon Phase: First Quarter
Color: Indigo

Moon Sign: Libra
Incense: Pine

July

○ **Sunday**
St. Mary Magdalene's Day
Waxing Moon
Moon Phase: Second Quarter 2:29 am
Color: Amber

Moon Sign: Libra
Moon enters Scorpio 4:18 am
Incense: Frankincense

23 Monday
Mysteries of Santa Cristina (Italian)
Waxing Moon
Moon Phase: Second Quarter
Color: Silver

Moon Sign: Scorpio
Sun enters Leo 1:00 am
Incense: Hyssop

24 Tuesday
Pioneer Day (Mormon)
Waxing Moon
Moon Phase: Second Quarter
Color: White

Moon Sign: Scorpio
Moon enters Sagittarius 4:29 pm
Incense: Bayberry

25 Wednesday
St. James' Day
Waxing Moon
Moon Phase: Second Quarter
Color: Yellow

Moon Sign: Sagittarius
Incense: Lavender

26 Thursday
St. Anne's Day
Waxing Moon
Moon Phase: Second Quarter
Color: Green

Moon Sign: Sagittarius
Incense: Balsam

27 Friday
Sleepyhead Day (Finnish)
Waxing Moon
Moon Phase: Second Quarter
Color: Coral

Moon Sign: Sagittarius
Moon enters Capricorn 2:21 am
Incense: Thyme

28 Saturday
Independence Day (Peruvian)
Waxing Moon
Moon Phase: Second Quarter
Color: Black

Moon Sign: Capricorn
Incense: Sandalwood

July

☺ **Sunday**
Pardon of the Birds (French)
Waxing Moon
Moon Phase: Full Moon 8:48 pm
Color: Yellow

Moon Sign: Capricorn
Moon enters Aquarius 9:13 am
Incense: Eucalyptus

---

30 Monday
Micmac Festival of St. Ann
Waning Moon
Moon Phase: Third Quarter
Color: Ivory

Moon Sign: Aquarius
Incense: Clary sage

---

31 Tuesday
Weighing of the Aga Khan
Waning Moon
Moon Phase: Third Quarter
Color: Red

Moon Sign: Aquarius
Moon enters Pisces 1:40 pm
Incense: Ginger

Lammas Toffee

2 cups packed brown sugar
½ cup (1 stick) butter
1⅓ cup corn syrup
2 tsp. vinegar
1 tsp. baking soda

This traditional sweet, often called "Yellow Man" was sold at Lammas fairs. Dissolve together brown sugar, butter, corn syrup, and vinegar, then boil without stirring until a drop removed from the mixture hardens in cold water. Remove from heat and quickly stir in baking soda, which will foam up. Pour into a greased tin to cool. Break into chunks and enjoy!

—Sharynne NicMhacha

August

1   **Wednesday**
Lammas
Waning Moon
Moon Phase: Third Quarter
Color: Brown

Moon Sign: Pisces
Incense: Honeysuckle

---

2   **Thursday**
Porcingula (Native American)
Waning Moon
Moon Phase: Third Quarter
Color: Turquoise

Moon Sign: Pisces
Moon enters Aries 4:43 pm
Incense: Nutmeg

---

3   **Friday**
Drimes (Greek)
Waning Moon
Moon Phase: Third Quarter
Color: White

Moon Sign: Aries
Incense: Violet

---

4   **Saturday**
Cook Islands Constitution Celebration
Waning Moon
Moon Phase: Third Quarter
Color: Gray

Moon Sign: Aries
Moon enters Taurus 7:16 pm
Incense: Pine

◗   **Sunday**
Benediction of the Sea (French)
Waning Moon
Moon Phase: Fourth Quarter 5:19 pm
Color: Orange

Moon Sign: Taurus
Incense: Hyacinth

---

6   **Monday**
Hiroshima Peace Ceremony
Waning Moon
Moon Phase: Fourth Quarter
Color: Lavender

Moon Sign: Taurus
Moon enters Gemini 10:01 pm
Incense: Narcissus

---

7   **Tuesday**
Republic Day (Ivory Coast)
Waning Moon
Moon Phase: Fourth Quarter
Color: Scarlet

Moon Sign: Gemini
Incense: Geranium

8   **Wednesday**
Dog Days (Japanese)
Waning Moon
Moon Phase: Fourth Quarter
Color: White

Moon Sign: Gemini
Incense: Bay laurel

---

9   **Thursday**
Nagasaki Peace Ceremony
Waning Moon
Moon Phase: Fourth Quarter
Color: Green

Moon Sign: Gemini
Moon enters Cancer 1:36 am
Incense: Mulberry

---

10   **Friday**
St. Lawrence's Day
Waning Moon
Moon Phase: Fourth Quarter
Color: Pink

Moon Sign: Cancer
Incense: Orchid

---

11   **Saturday**
Puck Fair (Irish)
Waning Moon
Moon Phase: Fourth Quarter
Color: Blue

Moon Sign: Cancer
Moon enters Leo 6:42 am
Incense: Rue

☽   **Sunday**
Fiesta of Santa Clara
Waning Moon
Moon Phase: New Moon 7:02 pm
Color: Yellow

Moon Sign: Leo
Incense: Juniper

---

13   **Monday**
Women's Day (Tunisian)
Waxing Moon
Moon Phase: First Quarter
Color: Silver

Moon Sign: Leo
Moon enters Virgo 2:03 pm
Incense: Neroli

---

14   **Tuesday**
Festival at Sassari
Waxing Moon
Moon Phase: First Quarter
Color: Gray

Moon Sign: Virgo
Incense: Basil

August

15 Wednesday
Assumption Day
Waxing Moon
Moon Phase: First Quarter
Color: Topaz

Moon Sign: Virgo
Incense: Marjoram

16 Thursday
Festival of Minstrels (European)
Waxing Moon
Moon Phase: First Quarter
Color: White

Moon Sign: Virgo
Moon enters Libra 12:04 am
Incense: Balsam

17 Friday
Feast of the Hungry Ghosts (Chinese)
Waxing Moon
Moon Phase: First Quarter
Color: Rose

Moon Sign: Libra
Incense: Cypress

18 Saturday
St. Helen's Day
Waxing Moon
Moon Phase: First Quarter
Color: Indigo

Moon Sign: Libra
Moon enters Scorpio 12:13 pm
Incense: Ivy

19 Sunday
Rustic Vinalia (Roman)
Waxing Moon
Moon Phase: First Quarter
Color: Gold

Moon Sign: Scorpio
Incense: Almond

☾ Monday
Constitution Day (Hungarian)
Waxing Moon
Moon Phase: Second Quarter 7:54 pm
Color: Ivory

Moon Sign: Scorpio
Incense: Rosemary

21 Tuesday
Consualia (Roman)
Waxing Moon
Moon Phase: Second Quarter
Color: Red

Moon Sign: Scorpio
Moon enters Sagittarius 12:44 am
Incense: Ylang ylang

August

22 Wednesday
Feast of the Queenship of Mary (English)
Waxing Moon
Moon Phase: Second Quarter
Color: Yellow

Moon Sign: Sagittarius
Incense: Lavender

23 Thursday
National Day (Romanian)
Waxing Moon
Moon Phase: Second Quarter
Color: Purple

Moon Sign: Sagittarius
Moon enters Capricorn 11:20 am
Sun enters Virgo 8:08 am
Incense: Apricot

24 Friday
St. Bartholomew's Day
Waxing Moon
Moon Phase: Second Quarter
Color: Coral

Moon Sign: Capricorn
Incense: Thyme

25 Saturday
Feast of the Green Corn (Native American)
Waxing Moon
Moon Phase: Second Quarter
Color: Black

Moon Sign: Capricorn
Moon enters Aquarius 6:35 pm
Incense: Magnolia

26 Sunday
Pardon of the Sea (French)
Waxing Moon
Moon Phase: Second Quarter
Color: Amber

Moon Sign: Aquarius
Incense: Eucalyptus

27 Monday
Summer Break (English)
Waxing Moon
Moon Phase: Second Quarter
Color: Gray

Moon Sign: Aquarius
Moon enters Pisces 10:34 pm
Incense: Lily

☺ Tuesday
St. Augustine's Day
Waxing Moon
Moon Phase: Full Moon 6:35 am
Color: Scarlet

Moon Sign: Pisces
Incense: Bayberry

29 **Wednesday**
St. John's Beheading
Waning Moon
Moon Phase: Third Quarter
Color: White

Moon Sign: Pisces
Incense: Lilac

30 **Thursday**
St. Rose of Lima Day (Peruvian)
Waning Moon
Moon Phase: Third Quarter
Color: Crimson

Moon Sign: Pisces
Moon enters Aries 12:24 am
Incense: Carnation

31 **Friday**
Unto These Hills Pageant (Cherokee)
Waning Moon
Moon Phase: Third Quarter
Color: Purple

Moon Sign: Aries
Incense: Alder

~❦~

Fresh Blueberry Jam

7 lbs. (8 pints) fresh blueberries
1 lb. (6 cups) rhubarb, cut into 1-inch
   lengths
5 lbs. (11½ cups) sugar

Wash and pick the blueberries clean. Put the rhubarb and sugar in a pot. Heat slowly, and boil for ten minutes. Add the blueberries and simmer, skimming often, until the fruit is tender. Test the jam by dropping it from a spoon into cold water, and when it sets properly, pour into warm, dry jars. When the jam is cooled, put on the jar lids and store in a cool place.

—Sharynne NicMhacha

September

1 Saturday
Greek New Year
Waning Moon
Moon Phase: Third Quarter
Color: Brown

Moon Sign: Aries
Moon enters Taurus 1:35 am
Incense: Patchouli

2 Sunday
St. Mamas's Day
Waning Moon
Moon Phase: Third Quarter
Color: Yellow

Moon Sign: Taurus
Incense: Frankincense

☾ Monday
Labor Day (observed)
Waning Moon
Moon Phase: Fourth Quarter 10:32 pm
Color: Lavender

Moon Sign: Taurus
Moon enters Gemini 3:30 am
Incense: Hyssop

4 Tuesday
Los Angeles' Birthday
Waning Moon
Moon Phase: Fourth Quarter
Color: Red

Moon Sign: Gemini
Incense: Basil

5 Wednesday
Roman Circus
Waning Moon
Moon Phase: Fourth Quarter
Color: Topaz

Moon Sign: Gemini
Moon enters Cancer 7:08 am
Incense: Lavender

6 Thursday
The Virgin of Remedies (Spanish)
Waning Moon
Moon Phase: Fourth Quarter
Color: Green

Moon Sign: Cancer
Incense: Nutmeg

7 Friday
Festival of the Durga (Hindu)
Waning Moon
Moon Phase: Fourth Quarter
Color: White

Moon Sign: Cancer
Moon enters Leo 12:59 pm
Incense: Vanilla

September ♍

8 Saturday
Birthday of the Virgin Mary
Waning Moon
Moon Phase: Fourth Quarter
Color: Gray

Moon Sign: Leo
Incense: Sage

9 Sunday
Chrysanthemum Festival (Japanese)
Waning Moon
Moon Phase: Fourth Quarter
Color: Orange

Moon Sign: Leo
Moon enters Virgo 9:10 pm
Incense: Heliotrope

10 Monday
Festival of the Poets (Japanese)
Waning Moon
Moon Phase: Fourth Quarter
Color: White

Moon Sign: Virgo
Incense: Clary sage

☽ Tuesday
Coptic New Year
Waning Moon
Moon Phase: New Moon 8:44 am
Color: Maroon

Moon Sign: Virgo
Incense: Cinnamon

12 Wednesday
National Day (Ethiopian)
Waxing Moon
Moon Phase: First Quarter
Color: Yellow

Moon Sign: Virgo
Moon enters Libra 7:31 am
Incense: Honeysuckle

13 Thursday
Rosh Hashanah • Ramadan begins
Waxing Moon
Moon Phase: First Quarter
Color: Turquoise

Moon Sign: Libra
Incense: Clove

14 Friday
Holy Cross Day
Waxing Moon
Moon Phase: First Quarter
Color: Rose

Moon Sign: Libra
Moon enters Scorpio 7:37 pm
Incense: Cypress

15 **Saturday**
Birthday of the Moon (Chinese)
Waxing Moon
Moon Phase: First Quarter
Color: Blue

Moon Sign: Scorpio
Incense: Sandalwood

16 **Sunday**
Mexican Independence Day
Waxing Moon
Moon Phase: First Quarter
Color: Gold

Moon Sign: Scorpio
Incense: Marigold

17 **Monday**
Von Steuben's Day
Waxing Moon
Moon Phase: First Quarter
Color: Silver

Moon Sign: Scorpio
Moon enters Sagittarius 8:21 am
Incense: Rosemary

18 **Tuesday**
Dr. Johnson's Birthday
Waxing Moon
Moon Phase: First Quarter
Color: White

Moon Sign: Sagittarius
Incense: Cedar

◖ **Wednesday**
St. Januarius' Day (Italian)
Waxing Moon
Moon Phase: Second Quarter 12:48 pm
Color: Topaz

Moon Sign: Sagittarius
Moon enters Capricorn 7:51 pm
Incense: Lilac

20 **Thursday**
St. Eustace's Day
Waxing Moon
Moon Phase: Second Quarter
Color: Purple

Moon Sign: Capricorn
Incense: Myrrh

21 **Friday**
Christ's Hospital Founder's Day (British)
Waxing Moon
Moon Phase: Second Quarter
Color: Pink

Moon Sign: Capricorn
Incense: Mint

September ♎

22 **Saturday**
Yom Kippur
Waxing Moon
Moon Phase: Second Quarter
Color: Indigo

Moon Sign: Capricorn
Moon enters Aquarius 4:18 am
Incense: Pine

23 **Sunday**
Mabon • Fall Equinox
Waxing Moon
Moon Phase: Second Quarter
Color: Amber

Moon Sign: Aquarius
Sun enters Libra 5:51 am
Incense: Almond

24 **Monday**
Schwenkenfelder Thanksgiving (Germ.-Amer.)
Waxing Moon
Moon Phase: Second Quarter
Color: Ivory

Moon Sign: Aquarius
Moon enters Pisces 8:55 am
Incense: Neroli

25 **Tuesday**
Doll's Memorial Service (Japanese)
Waxing Moon
Moon Phase: Second Quarter
Color: Gray

Moon Sign: Pisces
Incense: Ginger

☺ **Wednesday**
Feast of Santa Justina (Mexican)
Waxing Moon
Moon Phase: Full Moon 3:45 pm
Color: Yellow

Moon Sign: Pisces
Moon enters Aries 10:22 am
Incense: Marjoram

27 **Thursday**
Sukkot begins
Waning Moon
Moon Phase: Third Quarter
Color: White

Moon Sign: Aries
Incense: Jasmine

28 **Friday**
Confucius' Birthday
Waning Moon
Moon Phase: Third Quarter
Color: Coral

Moon Sign: Aries
Moon enters Taurus 10:17 am
Incense: Rose

29 Saturday

Michaelmas   Moon Sign: Taurus
Waning Moon   Incense: Rue
Moon Phase: Third Quarterr
Color: Black

30 Sunday

St. Jerome's Day   Moon Sign: Taurus
Waning Moon   Moon enters Gemini 10:34 am
Moon Phase: Third Quarter   Incense: Juniper
Color: Yellow

Elderberry Sweet

fresh elderberries
sugar
cloves
cornstarch

Gather fresh elderberries (making sure you can identify them properly) and remove all stems and leaves. Place in a large pan of boiling water to extract the juice. Crush with a wooden spoon and strain through muslin to extract the berry juice. To each pint of juice add 1⅛ cup sugar and half a dozen cloves. Bring to a boil, then simmer gently for five minutes. Thicken with cornstarch (just under ¾ cup for each pint of juice). Strain into a glass dish and cover with stewed apples and whipped cream when it has set.

—Sharynne NicMhacha

October

1 Monday
Armed Forces Day (South Korean)
Waning Moon
Moon Phase: Third Quarter
Color: Gray

Moon Sign: Gemini
Incense: Narcissus

---

2 Tuesday
Old Man's Day (Virgin Islands)
Waning Moon
Moon Phase: Third Quarter
Color: Red

Moon Sign: Gemini
Moon enters Cancer 12:57 pm
Incense: Geranium

---

3 Wednesday
Sukkot ends
Waning Moon
Moon Phase: Fourth Quarter 6:06 am
Color: Brown

Moon Sign: Cancer
Incense: Bay laurel

---

4 Thursday
St. Francis' Day
Waning Moon
Moon Phase: Fourth Quarter
Color: Turquoise

Moon Sign: Cancer
Moon enters Leo 6:27 pm
Incense: Nutmeg

---

5 Friday
Republic Day (Portuguese)
Waning Moon
Moon Phase: Fourth Quarter
Color: White

Moon Sign: Leo
Incense: Thyme

---

6 Saturday
Dedication of the Virgin's Crowns (English)
Waning Moon
Moon Phase: Fourth Quarter
Color: Black

Moon Sign: Leo
Incense: Ivy

---

7 Sunday
Kermesse (German)
Waning Moon
Moon Phase: Fourth Quarter
Color: Orange

Moon Sign: Leo
Moon enters Virgo 3:03 am
Incense: Hyacinth

October ♎

8 Monday
Columbus Day (observed)
Waning Moon
Moon Phase: Fourth Quarter
Color: Lavender

Moon Sign: Virgo
Incense: Hyssop

9 Tuesday
Alphabet Day (South Korean)
Waning Moon
Moon Phase: Fourth Quarter
Color: White

Moon Sign: Virgo
Moon enters Libra 1:57 pm
Incense: Ylang ylang

10 Wednesday
Health Day (Japanese)
Waning Moon
Moon Phase: Fourth Quarter
Color: Topaz

Moon Sign: Libra
Incense: Lilac

☽ Thursday
Medetrinalia (Roman)
Waning Moon
Moon Phase: New Moon 1:01 am
Color: Green

Moon Sign: Libra
Incense: Balsam

12 Friday
National Day (Spanish)
Waxing Moon
Moon Phase: First Quarter
Color: Rose

Moon Sign: Libra
Moon enters Scorpio 2:13 am
Incense: Vanilla

13 Saturday
Ramadan ends
Waxing Moon
Moon Phase: First Quarter
Color: Gray

Moon Sign: Scorpio
Incense: Pine

14 Sunday
Battle Festival (Japanese)
Waxing Moon
Moon Phase: First Quarter
Color: Yellow

Moon Sign: Scorpio
Moon enters Sagittarius 2:58 pm
Incense: Eucalyptus

15 Monday
The October Horse (Roman)
Waxing Moon
Moon Phase: First Quarter
Color: White

Moon Sign: Sagittarius
Incense: Clary sage

16 Tuesday
The Lion Sermon (British)
Waxing Moon
Moon Phase: First Quarter
Color: Black

Moon Sign: Sagittarius
Incense: Bayberry

17 Wednesday
Pilgrimage to Paray-le-Monial
Waxing Moon
Moon Phase: First Quarter
Color: Brown

Moon Sign: Sagittarius
Moon enters Capricorn 3:03 am
Incense: Honeysuckle

18 Thursday
Brooklyn Barbeque
Waxing Moon
Moon Phase: First Quarter
Color: Crimson

Moon Sign: Capricorn
Incense: Apricot

◖ Friday
Our Lord of Miracles Procession (Peruvian)
Waxing Moon
Moon Phase: Second Quarter 4:33 am
Color: Pink

Moon Sign: Capricorn
Moon enters Aquarius 12:52 pm
Incense: Violet

20 Saturday
Colchester Oyster Feast
Waxing Moon
Moon Phase: Second Quarter
Color: Blue

Moon Sign: Aquarius
Incense: Sage

21 Sunday
Feast of the Black Christ
Waxing Moon
Moon Phase: Second Quarter
Color: Amber

Moon Sign: Aquarius
Moon enters Pisces 7:02 pm
Incense: Heliotrope

October ♏

22 Monday
Goddess of Mercy Day (Chinese)
Waxing Moon
Moon Phase: Second Quarter
Color: Silver

Moon Sign: Pisces
Incense: Narcissus

23 Tuesday
Revolution Day (Hungarian)
Waxing Moon
Moon Phase: Second Quarter
Color: Maroon

Moon Sign: Pisces
Moon enters Aries 9:24 pm
Sun enters Scorpio 3:15 pm
Incense: Basil

24 Wednesday
United Nations Day
Waxing Moon
Moon Phase: Second Quarter
Color: Yellow

Moon Sign: Aries
Incense: Lavender

25 Thursday
St. Crispin's Day
Waxing Moon
Moon Phase: Second Quarter
Color: Purple

Moon Sign: Aries
Moon enters Taurus 9:07 pm
Incense: Jasmine

☻ Friday
Quit Rent Ceremony (England)
Waxing Moon
Moon Phase: Full Moon 12:51 am
Color: Coral

Moon Sign: Taurus
Incense: Orchid

27 Saturday
Feast of the Holy Souls
Waning Moon
Moon Phase: Third Quarter
Color: Indigo

Moon Sign: Taurus
Moon enters Gemini 8:11 pm
Incense: Magnolia

28 Sunday
Ochi Day (Greek)
Waning Moon
Moon Phase: Third Quarter
Color: Gold

Moon Sign: Gemini
Incense: Marigold

29 Monday
Iroquois Feast of the Dead
Waning Moon
Moon Phase: Third Quarter
Color: Ivory

Moon Sign: Gemini
Moon enters Cancer 8:49 pm
Incense: Rosemary

30 Tuesday
Meiji Festival (Japanese)
Waning Moon
Moon Phase: Third Quarter
Color: Red

Moon Sign: Cancer
Incense: Cinnamon

31 Wednesday
Halloween • Samhain
Waning Moon
Moon Phase: Third Quarter
Color: White

Moon Sign: Cancer
Incense: Marjoram

Colcannon for Samhain Divination

3 lbs. potatoes
2½ cups chopped cabbage
1 small onion
butter
salt and pepper

Boil potatoes, drain, and mash well. Cook chopped cabbage and mix in with the potatoes. Chop one small onion and cook gently in butter until soft, and mix into the potatoes and cabbage. Season with salt and pepper, and serve on hot plates with a well of butter in the middle of each mound. Mix small tokens into the colcannon for Samhain-tide divination; whoever receives the symbolic item can divine from it something of the year to come. A coin denotes wealth, a wishbone represents heart's desire, a horseshoe means good luck, and so on.

—Sharynne NicMhacha

November

○ **Thursday**
All Saints' Day
Waning Moon
Moon Phase: Fourth Quarter 5:18 pm
Color: Green

Moon Sign: Cancer
Moon enters Leo 12:48 am
Incense: Mulberry

2 Friday
All Souls' Day
Waning Moon
Moon Phase: Fourth Quarter
Color: Pink

Moon Sign: Leo
Incense: Rose

3 Saturday
Saint Hubert's Day (Belgian)
Waning Moon
Moon Phase: Fourth Quarter
Color: Brown

Moon Sign: Leo
Moon enters Virgo 8:44 am
Incense: Sandalwood

4 Sunday
Daylight Saving Time ends
Waning Moon
Moon Phase: Fourth Quarter
Color: Yellow

Moon Sign: Virgo
Incense: Juniper

5 Monday
Guy Fawkes Night (British)
Waning Moon
Moon Phase: Fourth Quarter
Color: Gray

Moon Sign: Virgo
Moon enters Libra 6:47 pm
Incense: Neroli

6 Tuesday
Election Day
Waning Moon
Moon Phase: Fourth Quarter
Color: Black

Moon Sign: Libra
Incense: Geranium

7 Wednesday
Mayan Day of the Dead
Waning Moon
Moon Phase: Fourth Quarter
Color: Topaz

Moon Sign: Libra
Incense: Lilac

8 Thursday
The Lord Mayor's Show (English)   Moon Sign: Libra
Waning Moon   Moon enters Scorpio 7:18 am
Moon Phase: Fourth Quarter   Incense: Myrrh
Color: White

☽ Friday
Lord Mayor's Day (British)   Moon Sign: Scorpio
Waning Moon   Incense: Yarrow
Moon Phase: New Moon 6:03 pm
Color: Purple

10 Saturday
Martin Luther's Birthday   Moon Sign: Scorpio
Waxing Moon   Moon enters Sagittarius 7:59 pm
Moon Phase: First Quarter   Incense: Rue
Color: Blue

11 Sunday
Veterans Day   Moon Sign: Sagittarius
Waxing Moon   Incense: Hyacinth
Moon Phase: First Quarter
Color: Orange

12 Monday
Tesuque Feast Day (Native American)   Moon Sign: Sagittarius
Waxing Moon   Incense: Lily
Moon Phase: First Quarter
Color: Lavender

13 Tuesday
Festival of Jupiter (Roman)   Moon Sign: Sagittarius
Waxing Moon   Moon enters Capricorn 8:00 am
Moon Phase: First Quarter   Incense: Bayberry
Color: Maroon

14 Wednesday
The Little Carnival (Greek)   Moon Sign: Capricorn
Waxing Moon   Incense: Marjoram
Moon Phase: First Quarter
Color: Yellow

November

15 Thursday
St. Leopold's Day
Waxing Moon
Moon Phase: First Quarter
Color: Turquoise

Moon Sign: Capricorn
Moon enters Aquarius 6:30 pm
Incense: Clove

16 Friday
St. Margaret of Scotland's Day
Waxing Moon
Moon Phase: First Quarter
Color: Coral

Moon Sign: Aquarius
Incense: Alder

☽ Saturday
Queen Elizabeth's Day
Waxing Moon
Moon Phase: Second Quarter 5:32 pm
Color: Indigo

Moon Sign: Aquarius
Incense: Magnolia

18 Sunday
St. Plato's Day
Waxing Moon
Moon Phase: Second Quarter
Color: Gold

Moon Sign: Aquarius
Moon enters Pisces 2:14 am
Incense: Frankincense

19 Monday
Garifuna Day (Belizian)
Waxing Moon
Moon Phase: Second Quarter
Color: Ivory

Moon Sign: Pisces
Incense: Rosemary

20 Tuesday
Commerce God Ceremony (Japanese)
Waxing Moon
Moon Phase: Second Quarter
Color: Red

Moon Sign: Pisces
Moon enters Aries 6:24 am
Incense: Cedar

21 Wednesday
Repentance Day (German)
Waxing Moon
Moon Phase: Second Quarter
Color: Brown

Moon Sign: Aries
Incense: Bay laurel

November

22 Thursday
Thanksgiving Day
Waxing Moon
Moon Phase: Second Quarter
Color: Purple

Moon Sign: Aries
Moon enters Taurus 7:18 am
Sun enters Sagittarius 11:50 am
Incense: Jasmine

23 Friday
St. Clement's Day
Waxing Moon
Moon Phase: Second Quarter
Color: Rose

Moon Sign: Taurus
Incense: Mint

Saturday
Feast of the Burning Lamps (Egyptian)
Waxing Moon
Moon Phase: Full Moon 9:30 am
Color: Blue

Moon Sign: Taurus
Moon enters Gemini 6:29 am
Incense: Patchouli

25 Sunday
Saint Catherine of Alexandria's Day
Waning Moon
Moon Phase: Third Quarter
Color: Orange

Moon Sign: Gemini
Incense: Almond

26 Monday
Festival of Lights (Tibetan)
Waning Moon
Moon Phase: Third Quarter
Color: Silver

Moon Sign: Gemini
Moon enters Cancer 6:07 am
Incense: Clary sage

27 Tuesday
Saint Maximus' Day
Waning Moon
Moon Phase: Third Quarter
Color: Gray

Moon Sign: Cancer
Incense: Ylang ylang

28 Wednesday
Day of the New Dance (Tibetan)
Waning Moon
Moon Phase: Third Quarter
Color: Topaz

Moon Sign: Cancer
Moon enters Leo 8:23 am
Incense: Honeysuckle

November

29 Thursday
Tubman's Birthday (Liberian)
Waning Moon
Moon Phase: Third Quarter
Color: Crimson

Moon Sign: Leo
Incense: Apricot

30 Friday
St. Andrew's Day
Waning Moon
Moon Phase: Third Quarter
Color: White

Moon Sign: Leo
Moon enters Virgo 2:44 pm
Incense: Vanilla

Apple Pudding

¾ lb. apples
¾ cup (1½ stick) butter
4 beaten eggs
grated peel of 1 lemon
sugar
1 tsp. brandy
1 tsp. orange-flower water
ginger cookies
puff pastries
candied lemon or orange peel, sliced

Pare and grate apples. Beat butter until creamed, and mix with apples, eggs, lemon peel, sugar to taste, brandy and orange-flower water, and several moistened and crumbled ginger cookies. Bake in puff pastry shells (store-bought shells are fine) at 350°, and when almost done strew finely sliced candied lemon or orange peel on the top.

—Sharynne NicMhacha

December

○ **Saturday**
Big Tea Party (Japanese)
Waning Moon
Moon Phase: Fourth Quarter 7:44 am
Color: Brown

Moon Sign: Virgo
Incense: Pine

---

2 **Sunday**
Republic Day (Laotian)
Waning Moon
Moon Phase: Fourth Quarter
Color: Yellow

Moon Sign: Virgo
Incense: Almond

---

3 **Monday**
St. Francis Xavier's Day
Waning Moon
Moon Phase: Fourth Quarter
Color: Gray

Moon Sign: Virgo
Moon enters Libra 1:01 am
Incense: Narcissus

---

4 **Tuesday**
St. Barbara's Day
Waning Moon
Moon Phase: Fourth Quarter
Color: Red

Moon Sign: Libra
Incense: Basil

---

5 **Wednesday**
Hanukkah begins
Waning Moon
Moon Phase: Fourth Quarter
Color: Topaz

Moon Sign: Libra
Moon enters Scorpio 1:31 pm
Incense: Honeysuckle

---

6 **Thursday**
St. Nicholas' Day
Waning Moon
Moon Phase: Fourth Quarter
Color: Turquoise

Moon Sign: Scorpio
Incense: Clove

---

7 **Friday**
Burning the Devil (Guatemalan)
Waning Moon
Moon Phase: Fourth Quarter
Color: White

Moon Sign: Scorpio
Incense: Rose

8 Saturday
Feast of the Immaculate Conception
Waning Moon
Moon Phase: Fourth Quarter
Color: Blue

Moon Sign: Scorpio
Moon enters Sagittarius 2:11 am
Incense: Rue

---

9 Sunday
St. Leocadia's Day
Waning Moon
Moon Phase: New Moon 12:40 pm
Color: Orange

Moon Sign: Sagittarius
Incense: Hyacinth

---

10 Monday
Nobel Day
Waxing Moon
Moon Phase: First Quarter
Color: Lavender

Moon Sign: Sagittarius
Moon enters Capricorn 1:50 pm
Incense: Lily

---

11 Tuesday
Pilgrimage at Tortugas
Waxing Moon
Moon Phase: First Quarter
Color: White

Moon Sign: Capricorn
Incense: Ginger

---

12 Wednesday
Hanukkah ends
Waxing Moon
Moon Phase: First Quarter
Color: Yellow

Moon Sign: Capricorn
Incense: Lavender

---

13 Thursday
St. Lucy's Day (Swedish)
Waxing Moon
Moon Phase: First Quarter
Color: Purple

Moon Sign: Capricorn
Moon enters Aquarius 12:01 am
Incense: Carnation

---

14 Friday
Warriors' Memorial (Japanese)
Waxing Moon
Moon Phase: First Quarter
Color: Pink

Moon Sign: Aquarius
Incense: Vanilla

December

15 Saturday
Consualia (Roman)
Waxing Moon
Moon Phase: First Quarter
Color: Indigo

Moon Sign: Aquarius
Moon enters Pisces 8:15 am
Incense: Ivy

---

16 Sunday
Posadas (Mexican)
Waxing Moon
Moon Phase: First Quarter
Color: Yellow

Moon Sign: Pisces
Incense: Juniper

☽ Monday
Saturnalia (Roman)
Waxing Moon
Moon Phase: Second Quarter 5:17 am
Color: Ivory

Moon Sign: Pisces
Moon enters Aries 1:52 pm
Incense: Rosemary

---

18 Tuesday
Feast of the Virgin of Solitude
Waxing Moon
Moon Phase: Second Quarter
Color: Black

Moon Sign: Aries
Incense: Cedar

---

19 Wednesday
Opalia (Roman)
Waxing Moon
Moon Phase: Second Quarter
Color: Brown

Moon Sign: Aries
Moon enters Taurus 4:38 pm
Incense: Lilac

---

20 Thursday
Commerce God Festival (Japanese)
Waxing Moon
Moon Phase: Second Quarter
Color: Crimson

Moon Sign: Taurus
Incense: Jasmine

---

21 Friday
Independence Day (Kazakhstani)
Waxing Moon
Moon Phase: Second Quarter
Color: Purple

Moon Sign: Taurus
Moon enters Gemini 5:14 pm
Incense: Cypress

December

22 Saturday
Yule • Winter Solstice
Waxing Moon
Moon Phase: Second Quarter
Color: Blue

Moon Sign: Gemini
Sun enters Capricorn 1:08 am
Incense: Sage

Sunday
Larentalia (Roman) • Hanukkah ends
Waxing Moon
Moon Phase: Full Moon 8:15 pm
Color: Amber

Moon Sign: Gemini
Moon enters Cancer 5:18 pm
Incense: Frankincense

---

24 Monday
Christmas Eve
Waning Moon
Moon Phase: Third Quarter
Color: Silver

Moon Sign: Cancer
Incense: Neroli

---

25 Tuesday
Christmas Day
Waning Moon
Moon Phase: Third Quarter
Color: White

Moon Sign: Cancer
Moon enters Leo 6:52 pm
Incense: Cinnamon

---

26 Wednesday
Kwanzaa begins
Waning Moon
Moon Phase: Third Quarter
Color: Topaz

Moon Sign: Leo
Incense: Bay laurel

---

27 Thursday
Boar's Head Supper (English)
Waning Moon
Moon Phase: Third Quarter
Color: Green

Moon Sign: Leo
Moon enters Virgo 11:44 pm
Incense: Balsam

---

28 Friday
Holy Innocents' Day
Waning Moon
Moon Phase: Third Quarter
Color: Rose

Moon Sign: Virgo
Incense: Vanilla

29 Saturday
St. Thomas à Becket
Waning Moon
Moon Phase: Third Quarter
Color: Gray

Moon Sign: Virgo
Incense: Sandalwood

30 Sunday
Republic Day (Madagascar)
Waning Moon
Moon Phase: Third Quarter
Color: Gold

Moon Sign: Virgo
Moon enters Libra 8:37 am
Incense: Heliotrope

◑ Monday
New Year's Eve
Waning Moon
Moon Phase: Fourth Quarter 2:51 am
Color: White

Moon Sign: Libra
Incense: Clary sage

Scottish Athol Brose

scotch-cut oats
water
2 tbs. heather honey
½ cup whiskey
½ cup cream

This is a beverage traditionally made at New Year's.
Grind several cups of scotch-cut oats in a coffee grinder.
Add cold water to form a thick paste. After half an hour,
strain through a fine sieve to obtain the liquid from the
oats. Using a silver spoon, mix ½ cup of the oat liquid with
heather honey, whiskey, and cream. Serve in wine glasses.

—Sharynne NicMhacha

Fire Magic

Fire Magic

by James Kambos

Fire magic is one of the most ancient and widely used forms of magic in existence. The origins of fire magic can be traced back to prehistoric times. To understand why fire has played such an important part in religious and spiritual beliefs, you must first realize the role fire has played in the development of the human race.

Before fire, there was ice—and our early ancestors, like the other creatures of our Earth, were at the mercy of nature. Then, at least 50,000 years ago, one of the most significant events in human history took place: man and woman learned how to tame the sacred flame.

In Western occult tradition the four elements are fire, water, air, and earth. Together they are the building blocks of life as we know it. However, it is fire that has captured the imagination of humankind since our ancestors first appeared on Earth. Perhaps it is because fire represents pure energy and the primal life-force.

The moment man and woman mastered fire is when fire magic began. Armed with the knowledge of how to control this most vital element, the human race elevated itself above all other forms of animal life. With fire, prehistoric cave dwellers were able to protect themselves from the fang of the wild beast and the bite of the frigid wind. With the sacred flame, our ancestors drove back the darkness, and the cave floor became the first hearth. And around the fire on bitter cold nights, long ago forgotten, early people gathered. Around the flames primitive man and woman felt secure. Friendships were kindled; clans developed. Fire enabled these early nomads to settle and live in one place. From this, civilization began.

Today, when we ignite a ritual fire, light a candle in church, or burn incense on an altar, we are practicing a form of fire magic. But on a deeper level we are responding to an ancient instinct. Like our primitive forebears, we also have an enduring need to tend the legendary flame.

Prometheus and the Legend of Fire

Many cultures have various myths and legends concerning fire and how it was first discovered by mortals. One of the most enduring myths about fire comes from ancient Greece.

Prometheus and his brother Epimetheus were members of a giant race of Greek gods called Titans. The council of gods assigned them the task of giving all the animals of Earth the skills and powers they needed to survive. By the time they got to the human race, there were no powers left to give.

Brave Prometheus however, felt sorry for humankind, and decided to give early man and woman the gift of fire. Zeus was outraged that Prometheus stole precious fire from the gods and gave it to mere mortals. To punish Prometheus, Zeus had him chained to a mountain, where he was attacked by vultures every day for centuries. There he remained until he was rescued by Hercules.

This legend made Prometheus the hero of mortal man and illustrates how important fire was to the ancients. The American sculptor Paul Manship was so inspired by the myth of Prometheus that it led him to create his masterpiece, also called *Prometheus*. This spectacular statue of the Titan fire-giver is in Rockefeller Center in New York City.

Spirits of Fire

The two beings most closely associated with fire are the Jinn (genies), and the salamanders. Both have been linked to fire magic for centuries.

According to ancient occult tradition, the Jinn were created from pure smokeless fire. The Jinn were shapeshifters and able to take many forms. Those who took human form functioned as humans; however, they had no blood in their veins. Instead, fire, the element from which they were created, was believed to run through their bodies—and if wounded they were said to burst into flames.

The Jinn were considered to be intelligent beings and were believed to inhabit the Earth long before the human race. Given their association with fire, they were known for having extraordinary magical abilities. Middle Eastern occultists credit them with teaching humans the magical art of scrying.

Many believe the human-looking Jinn coexist with humans even today, and have the ability to act as guardian spirits. For as long as there is fire magic, there will always be the Jinn.

The salamander has also had an ancient relationship with fire. The Greeks and Romans believed the salamander's body to be so cold that it could withstand even the hottest blaze. For this reason, the salamander became known as an elemental of fire, and symbolizes its energy.

Salamanders are actually shy, timid creatures, but as an elemental of fire they have much to teach us. They represent vitality, strength, courage, imagination, and mental and physical swiftness. Passion also falls under the domain of the salamander. To connect with the salamanders, or to strengthen any of the qualities I've mentioned, anoint a red candle with olive oil. Light the candle, and as the flame grows, concentrate on your desired qualities growing. Times to commune with these elementals are noon or midnight. Simply enjoying the Sun on a warm day at high noon is also a good idea. After your session, leave a sprinkling of basil or cinnamon as a symbol of thanks.

Some of the old world magicians believed that each of the sacred elements were individual kingdoms, ruled by kings. The king of the salamanders was called Djin, which also happens to be an old spelling for Jinn. This demonstrates how these ancient spirits of fire have been interconnected down through the ages.

Fire Magic and the Sabbats

Fire magic in some form can be found in many sabbat rituals and observances. It could be as simple as lighting a candle or incense, or smoldering herbs in a cauldron. And, if space and safety are not a concern, a traditional ritual bonfire is an exciting way to celebrate a sabbat. Many years ago sabbat bonfires were very common. Not only did they provide a focal point for a ritual, they also provided light and warmth, and were used to prepare food.

Here are some suggestions on ways to incorporate fire magic into sabbat rituals throughout the year.

Imbolc: Since Imbolc is a celebration of the strengthening Sun, fire magic has a major role in this sabbat. For this holiday try lighting as many white or cream-colored candles as you can. Place some in east- and west-facing windows, and, to create more sparkle, include a few small mirrors here and there. If you want fragrance, vanilla-scented candles or incense would be a nice idea.

Ostara: Rebirth is the theme for this holiday, which celebrates the spring equinox. To include fire in your Ostara ritual, begin by lighting one yellow pillar candle. Observe the flame as it grows. From the main candle, light as many pastel-colored candles as you wish, including the colors violet, light green, and pink. As you light each candle, think of the Sun growing in warmth.

Beltane: Fire has always been a central theme at Beltane, and purification is one of its key ideas. Traditionally great bonfires were lit; between the fires, livestock were led to cleanse them as insurance against disease. Humans as well would walk between the fires in an act of purification. The woods used to kindle Beltane fires are birch, oak, fir, willow, ash, apple, grape vine, and hawthorn. As a fertility rite, ashes from the Beltane fires were then spread over the fields. Since most of us don't have the space to perform such rituals today, try burning some small wood chips in a cauldron. Then, as an offering, sprinkle the cooled ashes outdoors.

Midsummer (Summer Solstice): During this solar festival the Sun is at its zenith. Bonfires blazed during the night long ago to encourage the Sun to take its place in the heavens. Large wooden hoops were set ablaze to welcome the Sun's return. (My mother, who lived in Greece as a child, remembers this ritual taking place in her village as recently as 1930.) Folk dances were frequently done around the Midsummer fires. It is said that larkspur sprinkled in a Midsummer fire will protect against spirits, and give the magician a chance to increase his psychic awareness. Try this as part of your Midsummer fire ritual: Light a tall gold candle; from its flame light four smaller candles, one for each season (select a color for each of the smaller candles appropriate for that season). Place the small candles around the

gold candle. Visualize the Sun at the height of its power, giving its energy to each of the seasons.

Lammas: This harvest celebrates grains such as oats, wheat, and corn. Some European villages lit bonfires at night, fueled by some of the dried grain stalks. Breads were frequently taken to church, where they would be blessed. To capture the essence of this holiday, upon your altar light two gold candles. Between them place a loaf of bread or cornbread. Slice the bread. Leave one slice between the candles as an offering to Father Sun, whose energy made the harvest possible. Serve the rest of the bread; eat it before the burning candles. Think of how the heat from the fire made the baking of the bread possible.

Mabon: Now we arrive at the autumn equinox, the first of the dark sabbats. Fire magic takes on special meaning now, as the dark season looms before us. At Mabon you may include fire magic in your celebration in several ways. Now is a good time to smudge and cleanse ritual tools. To do this, smolder a bit of willow and cedar in a cauldron. Let the smoke waft over any items you wish to cleanse. To cleanse your own spirit, or to remove a bad habit from your life, write the problem on a piece of white paper. Then crumple the paper in your hand as if you're angry. Toss the paper in the Mabon fire, or your cauldron. As the smoke rises, see your problems drifting away.

At Mabon we turn inward toward hearth and home. If it is cool enough and you have a fireplace, starting a fire would be a natural way to include the fire element in your sabbat ritual. Or, simply light rust-colored candles. End a Mabon ritual by serving nut bread and your favorite beverage. Sit before the fire or flickering candles, and think of the ways you wish to improve your life during the dark months ahead.

Samhain: This was the ancient Celtic New Year, and the beginning of the dark half of the year. At Samhain, fire magic was extremely important. On the eve of Samhain in old Europe, all household fires were extinguished and great needfires were begun throughout the countryside. From these needfires the household fires were rekindled. This was done to symbolize that the fires would continue to burn throughout the dark days of winter.

The fires at Samhain also served to light the way for the spirits which were active on this night. A bit of this fire magic is still with us in the form of the jack-o'-lantern. With its silly or scary face, and warm glowing light, the jack-o'-lantern serves to scare away evil spirits. But at the same time it lights the way for the spirits of our ancestors as they visit on this All Hallows' Eve. To observe the traditional Samhain needfires today on a smaller scale, burn patchouli incense and light a fire in your cauldron. From the cauldron fire, light one orange and one black candle. Meditate on your ancestors and let the candles burn down.

Yule: This is the winter solstice, the longest night of the year. At Yule we celebrate the rebirth of the Sun God. To light the way for his return, fire magic was performed by burning the Yule log. The ritual burning of the Yule log was done to encourage the returning strength of the Sun, and to light Mother Earth's way back to the lushness of summer. Since most of us don't have a hearth big enough to accommodate the large Yule logs of long ago, there are other ways to observe Yule. Decorate your altar with pine, holly, and mistletoe. Light red and green candles to represent the eternal life cycle. In simple ritual, let the candles burn, and hang the mistletoe to purify your home. When the holiday is over, burn the pine and holly if possible and then sprinkle the ashes upon the sleeping earth.

Candle Magic

An article about fire magic would not be complete without mentioning candle magic. Candles offer a convenient way to practice fire magic. Just by lighting a candle, you can transform an ordinary room into a place of mystery, and the soft glow of candlelight creates the perfect atmosphere for magic. And not only that, but many of us don't have fireplaces, so candles can take the place of the hearth.

Candle magic in some form is still used today by many cultures and religions. Birthday-cake candles, for instance, were originally burned to thank the deities for prosperity and another year of life. Votive candles, Christmas candles, and the candles lit on each night during the Jewish celebration of Hanukkah are all forms of candle rituals.

Many forms of candle magic exist. It may be as simple as lighting a candle, concentrating on your goal, and then extinguishing the flame. Or it may involve using many candles, anointing

them with oils, and praying over them for several nights. Due to space limitations, my intent here is not to be exhaustive, but to get you started in the right direction.

The reason candle magic works is due to the energy released by the flame. Early occultists believed that the three parts of a burning candle corresponded to the human form. The wax symbolized the human body, the wick represented the mind, and the flame signified the spirit.

To use a candle for spell-casting, first select a virgin candle in a color appropriate to your magical goal. When in doubt about color, white is always a good choice. Charge the candle by rubbing it from the middle to the wick, then from the middle to the bottom. As you do this, think of your desire. Some magicians anoint the candle as they rub it with oils of their choice; olive oil is a good all-purpose oil for this. Next, light the candle. Speak words of power, chant, and visualize your need manifesting itself into your life.

At this point the flame will "speak" to you in the following manner: if the flame burns steadily, your wish will come to you; if the flame sputters, then returns to a steady flame, you will have some delays in achieving your goal, but it will come to you; if the flame sputters out completely, or sparks, forces are working against you at this time. In this case, try working your spell at a later date.

To end any candle-burning ritual, thank the divine for hearing you and the element of fire for aiding you. Never blow out a candle flame, as this will offend the fire elementals. Instead, extinguish the flame with a snuffer. And as a safety precaution, never leave a burning candle unattended.

Fireside Magic

From cave to cabin, from ancient temple to modern condo, the dancing flames upon a hearth have ignited the imagination of humanity since before recorded history.

The very act of starting a fire is in itself magical. Consider the wood. The wood was once a tree. It was nourished from the roots by the rain and Mother Earth. It reached for the heavens and received the life-giving light of Father Sun. When you kindle a fire you are connecting with all the elements. And from the fire, wood returns to us the warmth and energy of the Sun.

To increase the magical power of any fire, consider the magical meanings of these popular varieties of wood.

Apple: Burn applewood when working love, fertility, or past-life spells.

Ash: Ash burns very hot. Use when you need to add a burst of energy to a spell.

Birch: Burn to connect with the Goddess.

Hawthorn: Burn to fulfill a wish, or work with the Fairy realm.

Hickory: An excellent wood to burn when you want to break a curse.

Maple: Burn to achieve peace or prosperity.

Oak: Use for health and fertility spells, or to connect with the God.

Pine: This wood symbolizes eternity and the Wheel of the Year.

Each wood will burn differently and with its own scent.

Firegazing

One of the favorite pastimes enjoyed centuries ago while sitting before the fire was firegazing. It is the act of seeing the future while looking at the flames. Technically it is known as *pyromancy*. To do this, the seer would sit before the fire as it burned steadily. The ever-changing flames would then induce an altered state of awareness. Omens were sought in the movement, color, and smoke coming from both ember and flame. If you are new to firegazing, limit your sessions to about ten minutes. After a few times, you'll notice your fire scrying abilities improving. The fire meditation that follows is another form of firegazing. On a quiet night, intone these words while following their directions:

When you feel the need to inquire,
Sit before the ancient fire.
Upon the flames, sprinkle yarrow, mint, and marigold.
With these, your answer will be told.
Hold your eyes steady as you gaze

Deeply into the dancing blaze.
In the yellow flames, in the orange flames,
Do you see an image, a face, or name?
If the flames fail to speak,
Try again, but wait a week.

A Fire Spell for Creativity

Fire can literally spark creativity. Try this fireside spell to get your creative juices flowing:

After you build your fire, light a red taper candle from its flame. Allow a few drops of the red candle wax to drip on the fire. This will "feed" the fire spirits and act as an offering. Set the candle aside and let it burn. Next, as you sit in front of the fire, wrap red string or yarn around a small grapevine wreath. With each turn of yarn feel your creativity increasing. When you've made one complete turn around the wreath, place the wreath into the fire. It is done.

A Spell for a Winter's Eve

This last spell is similar to fire magic performed in Colonial America, when the winter nights were long and neighbors lived far apart.

To bring you a wish which lies deep in your heart
Sit before the winter fire, as it begins to spark.
Upon the flames place these:
One walnut crushed, a branch of hawthorn
And bark from the mighty oak.
Then speak your wish as they begin to smoke
What you want shall come to pass—
Let the fire die, until it is ember and ash.

Connecting with Deity

by Kristin Madden

Power and spiritual guidance do not come directly from us. Rather, they flow through us from the divine. In order to craft effective magic and create the lives we desire, we must connect with divinity in some way. Establishing a conscious and direct connection with Deity is one of the greatest benefits of a Pagan path, and the experience of this completes us in ways that no other relationship really can.

Once you connect with Deity, you gain first-hand experience of the reality of the gods or spirit allies you believe in. No longer is this simply a matter of faith; you know it in your body, mind, and soul. You don't just need to trust that they exist: you've experienced them and you know it. This dramatically changes your perception of spirituality, yourself, and life in general. It is such a wonderful and powerful feeling that it can get rather addictive!

How this connection develops is unique to the individual, as it should be. However, there are common methods that can get you started and make the way easier. Once that relationship is established, the spirits will guide you directly into a deeper, more personal connection with them.

Getting To Know You

Any time you associate with another being, there is an initial period of getting to know each other. Ideally, this takes the two of you beyond your first impressions into a deeper understanding and appreciation of who you each are, as individuals and in relationship to each other. A similar thing happens when you begin to work with a spirit guide or deity.

In the beginning, you may know something about this being through stories or myths. You possess a largely cultural perspective and that is a great place to start. Explore the history of this being. Uncover who they were at the beginning, how they changed, and how the peoples that have honored them perceived them. Learn the stories that relate to them and consider not only how scholars interpret them, but also how these stories affect you and what you think they may mean.

As I said, this is a great place to start, but it has a tendency to lead to a very academic perspective. You may be able to tell someone the exact number of statues and inscription to Epona that have been found, and in how many countries, but this type of study is only one side of the story. You need to balance this with direct experience. This transforms what you know into a holistic understanding of these beloved spirits.

So how do you go abut getting to know your patron goddess or the spirit animal that has wandered into your life?

Altars

One wonderful way to begin is to build an altar or shrine to this being. An altar can be as elaborate or as simple—and perhaps not so obvious—as you need it to be. A very subtle symbol or picture propped up on a shelf can be a powerful altar. It all depends on your intent and focus.

A more portable altar can be equally subtle or obvious. A power object, picture, or other symbol of your deity may be kept in a small pouch, a plastic box, or an elaborately decorated wooden altar-in-a-box. You might want to add plants or stones that are said to be sacred to this deity.

If you can, set aside a special table or a shelf that can be devoted to this deity. Cover it with an appropriate and beautiful cloth. Place associated power objects, along with statues, drawings, and other depictions of this spirit, on the altar. You might like to add a special candle or incense burner to help you induce a sacred state of mind when meditating here. Create a regular practice of prayer or meditation that you will perform at this altar, and be sure to keep your altar clean.

This practice sets up a give-and-take relationship between you and your deity. It establishes a cycle of balanced energy that only strengthens as you use it. You have created a semi-permanent sacred space devoted to this deity. As you meditate there, you not only give but also receive energy, guidance, blessings, and more. And all this energy anchors itself in the objects of your altar, which hold and possibly magnify that energy.

Use of this space conditions you to the objects on your altar and to the methods you use for meditation and attunement there. In time, you will find that all you need to do is light your candle or gaze at your picture and your consciousness automatically begins to enter that meditative state in which you are most receptive to this deity.

Divination

The various methods of divination are designed to allow us greater access to spirit guidance. The cards, pendulum, or runes act as a psychic canvas, externalizing this guidance so that we might more easily understand it. Not just for divining the future, these wonderful methods can provide a glimpse into your inner self, insight into situations and people around you, and a means of communicating with your deities.

The most obvious way to use divination methods to connect with spirit guidance is to use them in the most common way: you sit with them, holding a question or situation in mind, and then read them in the appropriate way. Divination cards are laid out in a particular spread. Runes are thrown or picked. And the pendulum swings or circles in answer to your question. The answer is then interpreted according to the book or chart that came with the tools.

Once you get the feel for your cards, runes, or ogham sticks, and have some understanding of their meanings as given in the literature, you will want to learn how your personal symbolism relates to these common meanings. This will add great depth and increase the accuracy of your readings.

Get a bound journal or a three-ring binder filled with paper. This will become your personal reference on the divination system. Decorate the outside as you like and find a safe place to keep it. Now pull one card from your deck (or

one rune or ogham stick). What images, thoughts, feelings, or memories pop into your head when you see it? Write them down. Now stay with this image and let your imagination flow. Write down any additional insights you have.

When nothing else is really coming up for

you, pick out a few words that seem to have a significant charge to them. Write one of them down in the center of a clean sheet of paper and free associate from it. What other words does this one give rise to? Write them down, drawing lines from the original word to the new words. If those secondary words give rise to other words, write them down too. You will find that you have created a web of personal associations that may or may not be reflected in the common meanings for that particular card, rune, or ogham. Continue to do this for the rest of your divination images.

Also use your reference book to record the readings that you do and the life situations they applied to. If possible, document your accuracy and the end result. Over time you will see patterns, and new meanings will arise.

Another wonderful way to use these systems in more depth is to take the image or images you receive into a meditation or shamanic journey. This adds a whole new level of potential guidance from the spirits and has a way of opening the lines of communication even more.

So how does all of this help you get to know your deities? Well, the better you get at interpreting your divination system, the better you will be able to understand the messages that come through from your deities. In this way, you can use divination to ask how you might best work with them or honor them. You can gain insight into why they have entered your life and what lessons they are bringing to you at any given time. After that, it is up to you to take action on the messages you get.

Deepening Your Relationship

At some point, most relationships get to the point where they are either clearly not going anywhere or you want to take it to another level. You are interested and comfortable enough that you want to get to know each other better. Of course, our deities have a pretty good idea of who we are, but we grow and change through deepening our relationships with them. In order to truly honor them and work with them most effectively, we need to find the best ways to do this.

Creativity

Creative forms have been used across the globe since the most ancient times to communicate with deities, to share direct experiences of the divine with fellow humans, and to merge our energies with those of patron spirits. Art and music bypass the rational mind and speak to our spirits, just as ritual and shamanic journeying do. When you create in honor of your gods, your personality is set aside, permitting the manifestation of your collaboration with your spirits.

Many people find that their connections to spirit guides are strengthened when they work with the energy of guides in a tangible manner. The creation of sacred art is a form of moving meditation. As you create, you embody your deities. They are able to work through you more effectively when your rational mind does not analyze away many of their messages. Through the use of artistic abstraction a powerfully symbolic creation can be born.

The first step in using creativity is to release all judgment, embarrassment, and fear you may have regarding your artistic ability. The goal is not the end result or the final creation—the goal is the process itself. If you have never worked with art before, it may take some experimentation to find the right form for you. Keep in mind that although traditional sacred art usually manifests as sculpture, painting, music, and the making of masks or musical instruments, your personal creative outlet may be body art, writing, gardening, or decorating. Some people connect with their deities through the crafting of power pouches, cloaks, and jewelry. Others find the connection flowing when they wrap smudge sticks or cook.

It is best to begin with something you feel drawn to, something that intrigues and excites you. The hardest part is making those first few steps: drawing the first lines, beginning to mold the clay, making the first cuts in a piece of wood or stone. Once you make that first step, you make another, then another, and before you know it you are creating.

Ritual

Ritual both catalyzes and marks change and transformation. With regard to deity connections, ritual can be used from your first introduction throughout your entire relationship. It is in a ritual setting that you meditate at your altar and dedicate your ritual tools, divination systems, or creative pursuits. In ritual, you may call the gods into you and share in this intimate and highly spiritual merging. And through ritual you may acknowledge the changing nature of your relationship.

Many people will perform a dedication ritual when they first accept the call from a deity. In sacred space, they ritually promise to follow the path of a priest or priestess of this deity. Regular rituals are then performed to honor that deity and work with him, her, or it for specific situations, such as healing, protection, or other magic. And your deities are always invited to share in general rituals that you participate in, unless you are doing a ritual specific to one deity alone.

In general, there are four major elements to any rite of passage. This is a very basic overview that can be as simple as described or much more involved and elaborate.

Preparation: Though not actually a part of the ceremony, the preparation is as important as the rite itself.

You need to ensure that you are ready for the magic that will be done. And you need to craft the right ritual for you and your purpose. Be certain that the complexity fits the ritual, that you include suitable ritual items, colors, incense, and symbols.

Opening: In the opening of a ritual, you enter your ritual space, create sacred space, invoke the appropriate deity or deities, and state the intent for your ritual.

Center: This is the core of the ritual and may include a meditation, rite of passage, healing, teaching, etc. In a dedication ritual, this is where you will anoint yourself with special water or oils and make vows to your deity.

Closing: As you close the ritual, you want to ground excess energy, open sacred space by giving thanks to spirits, unwind a circle if one was cast, and exit the ritual area.

Although these are all wonderful places to get started, your relationship with your deities will dictate how you connect with each of them. The methods of connection will reflect both of you as individuals as well as who you are in relationship with each other. As I said, this connection will change your life in beautiful, powerful ways you never imagined. So to really do it right, you need to trust yourself and the messages you receive from your deities. Listen to suggestions from others, but don't let that limit you. Your deities will guide you to the appropriate ways and, when you follow their lead, your connection will be exquisite and unbreakable.

Children and Ritual

by Laurel Reufner

Children are great participants in a ritual, as long as those rituals are aimed at having children present and participating. They bring an amazing sense of wonder and already have a built-in suspension of disbelief.

What follows are some suggestions in general for doing rituals with your children and then some rituals written for each of the seasonal holidays. Please, take these rituals, adapt them as you need, and use them with your own children.

There are some simple things to keep in mind when performing rituals with children. Most children are active, and sitting still for longer than ninety seconds is torture for them, especially when you want them to sit still. They need to be actively involved in what is happening. Also remember that children are fun and spontaneous: they will enjoy the ritual whether it goes exactly to plan or not, so relax and go with what is happening.

Here are some general guidelines to keep in mind. And if your particular path calls for something specific, let it override what I've written here.

When opening and closing the circle, let your child help. Either walk the circle with your child or let him cast the circle himself. He can either use a branch, wand, or a finger to "draw." Explain that he should "see" the circle in his mind, envisioning a pretty blue light coming from his wand to form the circle.

To close the circle, thank and dismiss the deities and then thank and dismiss the elements, beginning with the direction where the circle casting started. Walk the circle in reverse to open it, envisioning the line of blue light being erased.

Child-friendly Rituals

Elemental calling was written with the seasons firmly in mind. Calling the elements starts with the direction that seems appropriate for that ritual. As always, feel free to change how it's written, especially if your belief system requires starting in a different direction.

Remember to play it safe. Some of these rituals call for candles. If you don't feel your children are mindful enough around candles, either substitute something else, tuck them inside those lovely hurricane lamp–like covers you can find in many craft stores, or place them high enough to be safe. Always keep a container of water nearby, just in case. If those measures don't seem to be enough, adapt the rituals as needed.

Now, go have a fun, rewarding spiritual experience with your children. And remember, you can only plan so much, it doesn't have to be perfect, and yes, the gods do have a sense of humor.

Imbolc Pet Blessing

North: cheese
South: red candle
East: milk
West: spring-like incense
Spray bottle, lavender essential oil, tea tree oil, small loaf of bread, deity representations.

While we're still firmly in the grip of winter's cold, Imbolc serves to remind us of the coming warmth ahead, as well as the promise of new life. Many of us have pets, and children connect especially well with animals. This ritual should help strengthen those bonds.

Cast the circle and then summon the quarters. Beginning in the north, summon the powers of earth, which are beginning to stir after a long winter's sleep. In the east, welcome the powers of water, now beginning to flow and nourish the earth once more after months spent frozen. To the south welcome the powers of fire, which is once more warming the Earth as days grow longer. And to the west, welcome the powers of air, whose breezes bear the scent of coming spring and lush green.

The main part of this ritual involves making the protective spray for your animal companions. Fill a spray bottle with 1 pint of water, 10 drops of tea tree oil, and 20 drops of lavender oil. Shake well. Allow each child in turn to bless the bottle for their pet's safety. Lavender serves as an antiviral/antibacterial as does the tea tree oil. Furthermore, many of those little pests that enjoy tormenting our pets don't like either of those oils. Spray the potion where your pets like to sleep or lie. If your pet doesn't mind too much, you can also lightly spray them as well.

Share the cheese and milk. Perform a circle closing and the ritual is finished.

Ostara Spring Welcoming

North: eggs or spring flowers
South: oil lamp
East: spring water
West: feathers
Hard-boiled eggs for each person participating in ritual, egg decorating supplies, pots, potting soil, plants, small loaf of bread, deity representations, sparkling grape juice.

Cast the circle and then summon the quarters. Starting in the east, welcome the powers of water, quenching the thirst of Mother Earth as she awakens from her wintry sleep. In the south, welcome the powers of fire, warming the land once more. To the west welcome the powers of air, as its breezes lift our spirits with the energy of renewed life. In the north welcome the powers of earth as life is awakened after the cold winter months. After summoning the directions, invoke the deities if you wish.

The main part of this ritual is very simple. Bless the eggs, put some soil in the pots, put an egg in each pot, and then add

more soil and the plant. Eggs are a symbol of life, hence their inclusion in the pots. This is also a good time to introduce raising and directing personal energy, showing your children how to raise energy in their hands and then direct that energy toward the soil surrounding the plants. Enjoy the bread and juice. Perform a circle closing and it is done.

May Day Merriment

North: a plant
South: red hot candies or a red candle
East: honey
West: streamers on a wand or tied to a tree branch
Paper ribbon, silk flowers, ribbons, streamers, bread or cakes, sparkling grape juice, deity representations.

Cast the circle and then summon the quarters. Starting in the east, welcome the powers of water, which have brought new life to Mother Earth. In the south welcome the powers of fire, becoming warmer each day. To the west welcome the powers of air, carrying upon it the smells of greening life. In the north, welcome the powers of earth, covered in lush green.

Using the paper ribbon, make wreaths sized to fit each individual's head with just a little extra room. Then comes the fun

part! Each person gets to decorate his or her wreath with flowers, ribbons, streamers, and whatever else comes to mind. Put them on and have a show with a small parade around the ritual area. If you have the means and space, put up a May pole and dance to your heart's content. You could also skip the May pole and just dance! Share the bread/cakes and juice. Perform a circle closing to finish the ritual, and it is done.

Midsummer Fairy Shrine

North: flowers
South: red candies
East: milk or honey-sweetened tea
West: wind chimes or streamers
Streamers, bells, ribbons, and whatever else you can think of;
deity representations; milk or sweetened honey; cakes.

The main part of this ritual involves creating a fairy altar or shrine. Find a special spot, preferably outside, to create a space just for the fairy folk. Hang small bells and tie streamers on low branches, drape more ribbons and streamers from the altar itself, and add some special dishes for offerings of milk, honey, and cakes. You and your children could also write wishes on paper streamers and add those to the altar. This is a time for playfulness. Wear your wreaths from May Day. Add bells. Dance around. Honor the Fey with your fun and play. When finished, sit around the altar with your children enjoying the cakes and milk. Share a fairy story or two. Perform a circle closing and it is done.

Lammas Harvest Ritual

North: grain such as corn, wheat, or oats
South: spicy incense
East: grape juice
West: airy flowers, such as daisies
Hay and some wheat, twine, small loaf of bread, deity repre-
sentations, sparkling grape juice, branch to cast the circle,
drums and other noisemakers.

Before the ritual, construct a simple straw man from the hay or straw. Hide the loaf of bread in its body. Tuck some wheat inside to connect to both the harvest and the bread hiding inside.

Cast the circle and then summon the quarters. Starting in the south, help your child light the incense and welcome the powers of fire, which are still burning brightly upon the land. In the west, welcome the powers of air, helping cool us in the still, hot days. To the south welcome the powers of earth, laboring to give us food to enjoy now and to save for wintry months ahead. In the east welcome the powers of water, needed to nourish us all. After summoning the directions, invoke the deities if you wish.

The main part of this ritual involves dancing and drumming around the straw man. Dance until energy is raised and you feel it start to lower, then ground a bit, explaining to your children how it is done. Now comes the fun part. Let your kids pull apart the straw man, explaining how nature sacrifices her bounty (the harvest) to nourish the rest of her creation. From the grains we get flour and from flour we get bread. Enjoy the bread hidden within the straw man along with the sparkling grape juice, remembering to give offerings to the Earth and deities. After the ritual, the remaining hay or straw can be sprinkled around plants to serve as mulch. Perform a circle closing and it is done.

Mabon Harvest Visit

Gather your children and head out for some harvesting together at an orchard, pumpkin patch, or even the local farmer's market. Discuss on your way there what it is you are looking for and what you need for your seasonal altar. Look at what's available and take your time to mindfully select apples, pumpkins, gourds, ornamental corn, and whatever else is on your shopping list.

Show your children how to seek that inner stillness and then to listen to that little inner voice helping them choose which produce to select. Only take what speaks to you and remember to thank Mother Earth for providing for our needs.

Once you get home, bless your goodies for abundance in the coming months. Then use them to decorate your home as a reminder to be thankful in the coming months for what nature has provided. If possible, enjoy a meal of hearty vegetable soup, warm bread, and cider.

Samhain Remembrance Feast

This ritual is a bit different than the others as it celebrates a meal in honor of the dead. It can be part of a regular meal, or something special in the afternoon or evening. Gather everyone around the table for a feast celebrating the lives of those who have passed on. If possible, include some of the foods they would have enjoyed. Where you can, let your children help you with the meal's preparation. Set the table with a bowl of apples, the Celtic food of the dead. Include pomegranate seeds on the menu in memory of Persephone. If possible, eat in the family or living room around a low table, so all can sit on pillows on the floor or relax in chairs.

Once the food is ready, create sacred space by lighting incense and raising energy around the chosen dining room's perimeter. Light candles on the table. Sit down and enjoy your meal. Remember and share stories of family members and friends who have passed on to the Summerland. Remember family pets that are no longer with you. At the end, close the meal with a moment of reflective silence. Then lower the sacred space-defining energy and it is done. This ritual serves to not only remember the dead, but to reinforce family ties and stories.

Yule Snowflake Wishes

North: picture of a tree
South: picture of candles or fire
East: picture of water
West: picture of feathers or wind chimes
Paper squares, scissors, colored pencils or colored pens,
     holiday cookies, deity representations, hot chocolate.

Let your children draw and color the pictures for the elemental directions. Young ones especially will enjoy helping with the ritual preparations in such a manner.

Cast the circle and then summon the quarters. Starting in the north, welcome the powers of earth, slumbering deep in winter's frost. In the east, welcome the powers of water, running cold and waiting to usher in spring. To the south welcome the powers of fire, whose strength is increasing day by day. In the west welcome the powers of air, whose chill makes us appreciate the warmth of our homes. After summoning the directions, invoke the deities if you wish.

The main part of this ritual involves cutting paper snowflakes and then writing wishes for friends and loved ones upon them. If your children don't know how to fold and cut a paper snowflake, then show them. Remember that younger kids will have very different results than older ones. That's fine.

Cut out the paper snowflakes and then write a wish for a friend or family member on each one. Remember to make a wish for yourself on one of the snowflakes. When done, bless them with well wishes for all. Enjoy your hot cocoa and cookies (if you haven't already been munching on them). Perform a circle closing and it is done.

Banishing

by Elizabeth Genco

Some years ago when I first began exploring Wicca on my own, I struggled (as most of us do) to make sense of the myriad conflicting practices. Magical and ritual work had the most complications to sort out. Instructions in books would contradict each other, or I would get bogged down in the "how to" or in lists of obscure ingredients (where does one find mandrake and lodestones, anyway?), second-guessing myself every step of the way. It's a common problem, borne of a religion in which there are many paths to the same destination. Despite the fact that there was much that I didn't understand about magic, a few things came easily—almost instinctively. These intuitive workings included a series of powerful banishings, performed when I was an absolute beginner (more or less).

Sound odd? I suppose it was. After all, "banishing" is one of those loaded words that (pardon the pun) conjures up images of old hags at the crossroads, burying foul remnants of sympathetic magic, muttering curses at the poor fool who made the unfortunate misstep of crossing her. There is as much archetypal baggage associated with the act of banishing as there is, well, with the word "Witch." To many, "banishing" and "Witch" are inextricably linked, and intrinsically negative.

So what business did I have mucking around with banishing back then? Indeed, what is a modern magical practitioner to do with it now?

Like all magic, the key to banishing lies in its purpose and the object of the working, which brings us directly to ethics. A discussion of Wicca's main ethical tenant, "harm none," is outside of the scope of this article; ultimately, each practitioner will have to come to grips with its implications, and the line of what constitutes "harm" will be different for each. When I did accept formal training, it was with a group that explicitly prohibits workings that interfere with the free will of another; in fact, my tradition puts its money where its mouth is and requires an oath to that effect. Among the Wiccans I know, "harm none" is serious business, and a banishing that impedes with another's free will in *any* way is out of the question.

Fortunately, my use of banishing doesn't conflict with my oaths, and never did. Though it has always had a reputation as manipulative magic, and, indeed, can be put to ill use, baneful banishing is only a small part of the story (you know, like the images of green-faced hags passed off as Witches in the popular consciousness). My banishings, then and now, are designed to help me deal with those things *inside myself* that hinder my personal growth. Such workings are moving, cathartic experiences. A personally designed, carefully crafted banishing can be one of the most affirming tools in a modern Witch's toolbox.

At its most basic level, "banishing" is simply another word for a cleansing. A ritual clearing of magical space or objects before a rite could be called a banishing, as could a clearing of a dwelling after a negative event. When used for personal growth, a banishing is a cleansing of the self, designed to sever ties with those things within us that no longer serve us. The implications of the magic are powerful: by clearing our internal garden, we make room for something new and better to take root and grow.

What sorts of internal baggage might you want to banish? Maybe you've been plagued by a bad habit for years, such as smoking, drinking, or overeating; a banishing can help you begin or continue your road to recovery. Maybe you've just gone through some kind of personal upheaval, such as a layoff or an eviction, and have been left with lingering feelings of self-doubt and disempowerment; a banishing can help you work through these emotions and move on. If it's really necessary, a banishing can help you put an end to something inconsequential but still annoying, such as biting your nails or saying "y'know?" too many times in a day. Personally, I have used banishing to get rid of self-doubts and put an end to the negative chattering voices in my head. Just about anything can be adopted to a personal-growth banishing, as long as it is about *you*. The focus on you is important, not only because of the ethical and karmic issues, but because personal magic is the most effective.

Once you've pinpointed a problem and have decided to take action, you might be tempted to skip straight to a working. Resist that urge. Take some time to meditate on exactly what you are banishing, and why. By performing a banishing, you relinquish a part of yourself forever. It's a big step, and thus merits extra consideration. You might wish to enlist the aid of a divinatory tool, too. Here are some questions to ask yourself before performing a banishing:

What, exactly, do I wish to banish? Clearly articulating what you wish to be rid of will establish important boundaries.

Why do I wish to banish this? There should be a clear motive behind your working.

What purpose has it served in my life up until now? All of our behaviors serve a certain purpose—even so-called bad behaviors. What purpose does the behavior in question serve now? The behavior you wish to banish may indeed be draining you, but by asking this question, you are making sure that it does not still help you in some way. And even though you will be asking a part of yourself to move on, it is still a part of you, and its contributions to your well-being should be acknowledged.

How is what I wish to banish preventing me from moving forward? The flip side to the previous question.

What do I hope to gain from this banishing?

Am I prepared to deal with any unforeseen consequences of this banishing? All magic sets into motion forces that we cannot stop. Once the cork is out of the bottle, so to speak, we are no longer fully in control. You won't be able to foresee all possible outcomes of your working. Considering ahead of time what results other than what you intended that might arise is also helpful.

Though personal-growth banishing is a positive step, it is permanent, and not to be taken lightly. Be sure that it's what you really need to do.

Some magical practitioners will tell you that magic should be performed, then "forgotten"; that is to say, put out of one's mind so that the work can take hold. Certain kinds of banishing, however, should be backed up with action in the mundane world. For example, it would be unrealistic to expect to stop smoking without a concentrated, regular conscious effort. In cases where you're fighting some serious demons, consider creating an action plan consisting of magical and mundane steps designed to maximize your success.

Petition Magic

Petition work is among my favorite flavors of magic. Its effectiveness comes from its simplicity; namely, it relies on the power of the written word to give tangible form to that which you want to eliminate, and the cleansing energy of fire to clear it away.

Simple Banishing

This spell can be used for something small, or if you're just getting used to the idea of banishing. It can be used for "the big stuff," too, and can be repeated as needed.

You'll need a slip of clean white paper, a pen (I prefer black ink, but use whatever color suits), tweezers, a lighter or lit candle, a small cauldron or some other fire-proof dish, and sea salt.

To prepare, gather all of your materials at your altar or chosen working area. Place a little sea salt in the bottom of the cauldron. The salt will create an uneven surface, which will allow for the flow of oxygen around the paper and will result in a better flame.

Create sacred space in whatever way you'd like. When you're ready, take the pen and write that which you'd like to banish on the slip of paper. Fold the paper and hold it with the tweezers. With an image of what you're banishing firmly in your mind, light the paper.

As the paper burns down, imagine yourself free of whatever you banish. As the flame engulfs the paper, drop it into the cauldron.

After your ritual, scatter the ashes outside or flush them down the toilet, continuing your visualization.

Witch Bottle Spell

This spell is a bit more involved, and can be used for more than one banishment at a time, or to go deeper with a particular banishment. It evokes some of the old stereotypes of Witches and banishing, but turns them on their head to create a positive, personal experience.

You'll need a small glass bottle (with cork, stopper, or some other means of closure), a candle in an appropriate color (your choice), slips of white paper, and a pen. You can also include other small objects relating to your banishment if you wish.

Gather your materials and create sacred space in your usual manner. When you're ready, begin to write that which you want to banish on the slip(s) of paper. If your intention is made of a few different parts, or you wish to banish more than one thing, write each one on a separate slip of paper. As you finish writing down each banishment, drop each slip into the bottle. Visualize that part of you falling into the bottle along with the paper. If you have other objects relating to your banishment, add those now.

When you have finished, top the bottle with its cork or stopper. Light the candle and drip wax over the top of the bottle to seal.

Next, dispose of the bottle in some manner you feel is appropriate. Burying the bottle works well, as does tossing it in a large body of water. These aren't my favorite methods, however, since they aren't environmentally friendly. We live in a modern age; as such, I prefer a ceremonial disposal in the trash!

As you dispose of the bottle, visualize your banishments breaking away from you. Bid them a gentle, thankful farewell, for they have served a certain purpose in your life, and, until now, you needed them in some way. Send them on with light and love.

Ritual Housecleaning

Sometimes we have distinct physical manifestations of that which we're trying to get rid of in our home or other environments. Clean house with this simple but effective procedure. (This one is particularly good for dieters—you can get rid of all those unhealthy snacks in the kitchen!)

Going from room to room, gather up any and all objects that you'd like to get rid of that pertain to your banishment intention. When you have them all, bring them to your working area and create sacred space.

Visualize that which you'd like to banish gently falling away from you. Acknowledge that the objects before you are physical representations of parts of you that served you well at one point in your life, but are no longer needed. Give thanks for what these banishments have given you in the past, then state your intention to move on. Take as much time as you need, then close your ritual. Dispose of all objects gathered immediately.

The First Thing a Spell Changes Is You

by Paniteowl

Whether it's a simple spell to find a parking place or a major working to change your life, the very fact that you are concentrating on a specific issue heightens your awareness of the world around you. But preparing to be magical is often overlooked in our haste to *do* magic, and then we wonder why our spells don't work out exactly as we planned.

A good spell crafter incorporates the mundane into magical workings. Why? Because it is the mundane world we attempt to change, or affect, when working spells. Preparing the environment for change is a basic part of our craft—one that many overlook in their zealous attempts to control the world.

As a follower of an Earth-based religion, I take the hints that the Earth gives me when doing spell work. For instance, if I want to grow vegetables, I need more than the seeds. First, I must prepare the soil by tilling a garden patch. I need to dig the rows to receive the seeds. I need to know how deep or shallow I must plant those seeds, and then I have to water the seeds to help them grow. I also know that certain seeds will not grow in my climate, so I'll choose seeds that are hardy for my planting zone. Then I'll weed the garden and fertilize as needed. Will I be rewarded with a great crop? Maybe—if I've also paid attention to the environment, and taken steps to fence in the garden so that the deer, rabbits, woodchucks, and other critters don't think that I've just decided to provide them with fresh veggies for the season.

Formulating a spell and gathering the necessary ingredients is much like preparing to plant a garden. Selecting the right seeds depends a great deal upon the mundane cnvironment. Selecting the right spell also depends upon the mundane environment. What we have to remember in spell working is that we are the fertile soil that must be prepared to nurture a spell. If you remember nothing else from this article, please remember this: the first thing a spell changes is you.

Every spell working teaches us something. Maybe it's nothing more than how *not* to do something, or even to *never try that again.* I'm not saying that random magic doesn't work. Often, it's the only thing that does work in a specific situation. Most of us have been in a car and narrowly avoided an accident by our own willpower alone. We've looked back at the circumstances and shaken our heads in wonder at our good fortune, or pure luck. But what we seldom take credit for is the fact that we have imposed our will on a situation that was out of our control for a fraction of a second, and in that time our subconscious use of magic has gotten us out of a nasty situation. However, it's probably a good thing that we don't recognize that as a magical occurrence, for if we did, we would probably put ourselves back in a dangerous situation and trust that our magic would take care of us—but it doesn't work that way. What does happen is that we're allowed to look at our mistakes, or our foolhardiness, and adjust the way we do things in order to avoid getting ourselves into a mess in the first place.

When working a spell, we are attempting to overcome an obstacle or adjust a situation to our advantage. We become responsible for the spell working, and must respect the ways in which we should operate to have an effective outcome. We must prepare ourselves first, and be very clear as to the goal of the spell working. We are responsible for learning as much as we can about a situation before we attempt to change it.

I have a dear friend who created the "perfect" spell to find the love of her life. She thought about it for some time, and wrote down exactly what she would like in a mate. She specified hair color and style, eye color, personality, attitude—

and most importantly, that he would be totally devoted to her. And so she cast her spell . . . and it was answered quickly! She was given a beautiful puppy, with long dark hair, big brown eyes, and a great personality—and it's totally devoted to her! She got exactly what she requested. Too bad she forgot to include the species she was looking for. The moral of this story is to never forget that the deities have a sense of humor, and it may be a bit warped at times.

Try this great spell for attracting love instead: Use four candles: two white, and two red. Light them and place them on the four corners of your bathtub. Fill the tub with warm spring water and add thirteen drops of essential oil. (I'd suggest lavender, patchouli, or dragon's blood.) Immerse yourself in the sacred waters. Relax and picture yourself as attractive and interesting. While in the water, use a soft cloth to massage your skin from head to toe. Step out of the water and look at yourself in a mirror. Smile at yourself; you are beautiful. Brush your teeth, dry and style your hair, put on some deodorant, and get dressed. Now call a friend, and go out. Treat yourself to dinner and find a nightspot where you can dance and sing and have a good time—and maybe even meet someone who has also been bathing, and brushing his or her teeth, and making an effort to be attractive. See: you'd have something in common right away!

OK, the above spell may give you a laugh, but the bottom line is that you are responsible for your own casting. If you want a good job, prepare yourself by studying, attending classes, and learning that job. Go to job interviews ready to present yourself in the best light possible. Take a course on interviewing techniques. Look through magazines to learn how to dress appropriately. Take a course in public speaking. Making a good impression is a skill, and developing your own style is an art. Be a skillful artist when it comes to knowing who you are. When you are ready, cast your spell to give you confidence that all your work will be appreciated and recognized by the person who will interview you.

When you are prepared, the magic comes easily. When you want something bad enough you will adapt and change and create the person you want to be. Magic is a tool, and having the right tool for the right job is as important in spell casting as it is in building a house or fixing a car. I may have a great socket set, but that doesn't mean I can fix my car when the transmission fails. And I know my mechanic has a kitchen in his home, but that doesn't mean he can prepare a decent meal. We all have different areas of interest and expertise. Use what you know best when devising a spell, and know your limitations.

Magic by the Stars

by K. D. Spitzer

Timing is very important in magic, and it depends upon the influences of the stars. "As above, so below," the saying goes. Without putting in years of study, you can just follow some simple astrological rules to harness planetary forces to achieve your goals. Understand the themes of each sign and planet, but pay particular attention to the Moon and Mercury. They whiz through the sky so quickly that they offer a guide for timing that is very useful in spellwork.

The Moon

The Moon is our closest neighbor, and the most easily observable. It moves through the zodiac completely in twenty-nine and a half days, staying in each sign about two and a half days and taking on the flavor, mood, and meaning of that particular sign. It's like she's changing costumes. When she moves through Scorpio, her dress reveals her to be very mysterious, very feminine, and very sensual for two and a half days. Then she moves into Sagittarius and puts on her running shoes and grabs her bow and arrows, tent, and soap box as she flies out the door.

Surely you've noticed by now that the Moon is measured by her relationship to the Sun. When she's close to the Sun, and thus in the same zodiac sign, we can't see her. She hides under the Sun's beams. This is the Dark Moon which, within a day or two, begins to move into the New Moon phase. A week later she shows up on any calendar in her first-quarter phase. Astrologically, this is the fourth zodiac sign from where she started; she has just "quartered" her cycle.

From the New Moon to the Full Moon, she is considered to be waxing. The Full Moon is halfway around the zodiac from where she started, so she must be in the sign opposite the sign the Sun is in. It's important to know that the very minute the Moon is full, she starts to wane.

Look at the calendar for the symbol for the fourth or last quarter. It appears seven or eight days after the Full Moon, just another "quarter" or ninety degrees farther around the zodiac. If you look at the sky at night, you will have noticed that the waxing Moon always has a full, curving belly on the right-hand side (☽) and the waning Moon has a curve on the left (☾). Symbolically, the Moon is always drawn as a waxing Moon.

So now you have a bare outline of what you need to know about the Moon to begin to set up a spell. It's also helpful to know that Monday is the Moon's day, and the first hour after dawn that day is the Moon's hour. That timing gives added pizzazz to a spell or psychic studies. Planetary hours give a real boost to your workings and are worth investigating for their added punch.

There are other considerations as well, such as how the phase of the Moon can determine the best hour to cast a spell. For example, the New Moon gets up with the Sun at dawn. The Sun hogs all the light while keeping the Moon close. Then they both go to bed at sunset. The power hour of the New Moon is noontime, which is the highest point she reaches at this time. In a couple of days, as soon as the Moon starts pulling away from the Sun, the power hour shifts to the halfway point in the cycle. So the Full Moon, which rises at sunset and sets at dawn, has the power hour at midnight. The power hour is always the best time to cast your spell.

As the Moon moves through a particular zodiac sign, you can apply the energy of that sign to your magical workings—but of course it's not quite as simple as that. As the Moon does her work, she comes into contact with the other planets. This contact is called an aspect and is a mathematical relationship first described by Ptolemy, a famous Greek astrologer who lived two thousand years ago.

When the Moon is in a particular sign and has finished making aspects to all the other planets, she can remain in that sign, just hanging out with nothing to do until she moves into the next sign. This is called void-of-course Moon time, and it can vary as the Moon moves through each sign. Often she can be void for just minutes, but sometimes she can be rudderless for a couple of days before moving on.

For magical purposes, when the Moon is void of course, her energy can no long be harnessed; indeed it can work against whatever you are trying to accomplish with your spell. It is important to remember in astrology that, with the exception of the New Moon, if you have missed an aspect or timing, it is gone, done, over! Ya blew it! Time to move on and reschedule.

Check the calendar or almanac carefully to see the window of opportunity you have for your spell. If you are starting a new business and want to access Capricorn business energy, then cast your spell before the Moon has her last aspect and becomes void of course in Capricorn—hopefully when she is waxing.

Learn to flow with the lunar cycle. This is a natural cycle that can help you organize your time, reduce stress, and generally perform better. This is the cycle of the Goddess, and learning to work with it is crucial for spiritual, physical, and mental well-being. If the Moon is a key player in your chart because it rules your Sun (Cancer) or your Ascendant, then it is doubly important to observe and value her rhythms.

However, it's also important not to micromanage your life using astrology. You can't just take to your bed every other day or so while the Moon is void of course, and you certainly can't pull the covers over your head three or four times a year for the weeks when Mercury is retrograde. But it is important to use the planetary energies available when you are trying to accomplish something considerably meaningful.

For example, research by astrologer Debbi Kempton-Smith revealed that in every one of the presidential elections from 1900 to 1972 the losing candidate was nominated by his party during a void-of-course Moon. Jimmy Carter's second-term nomination in 1980, Al Gore's in 2000, and John Kerry's in 2004 were all done during a Moon that was void of course. (Makes you think the Democrats ought to keep an astrologer on retainer.)

Research has also shown that our judgment is slightly skewed during these minutes and hours, and decisions may result in false starts or errors. Delays can bring frustration. Activities with important consequences like job interviews or surgery or spell casting should never be scheduled during a void-of-course Moon. What you accomplish then may need major adjusting later.

Because a void-of-course Moon often disrupts communication, it's just as easy to bypass this time in spell work, rescheduling for later. Or, you can make it work for you. Estelle Daniels, whose book *Astrological Magick* belongs in every Witch's cupboard, swears that Ronald Reagan, who did have an astrologer on retainer, always scheduled his speeches to deliver excuses or unpleasant news during a void-of-course Moon. The public didn't pay attention to or acknowledge these manipulations and it explains how he evolved into the "Teflon® president."

Mercury

Communication is also the theme of Mercury. By now, word has reached the general public about this speedy little planet, and his reputation is often maligned. Without a clear understanding of what's actually going on, people blame Mercury for everything unpleasant that happens in their lives, whether he is retrograde or not. This excuse is used even by people who say that astrology doesn't work!

Mercury is the planet closest to the Sun, moving quickly to revolve around it every eighty-eight days. The Earth moves slightly more deliberately, but inexorably. We creep up on Mercury in our orbit, coming alongside to overtake it. For a while it looks as though we are neck and neck and then it seems as though, intimidated, Mercury loses speed and reverses direction. It's really an optical illusion, though, because the Earth has just pulled ahead, leaving Mercury in the cosmic dust.

Once Mercury starts falling behind in relation to the Earth, it is considered to be retrograde. The word comes from Latin and means "to go back." Its symbol is much like the symbol for a prescription: a capital *R* with a cross through the tail. (℞). An astrological calendar will indicate this time with R which means retrograde—the planet has stopped and is reversing course back through the zodiac. At the moment it starts moving forward again, you will see *D* (Direct) on the calendar.

This will happen about three times a year (sometimes four, in certain years). Mercury rests for about three weeks each time. Some will say that there *is* no rest with Mercury the Coyote, the Trickster. Annoyed to be thwarted in his duties, he plays havoc with all communication devices: hard drives crash, software melts, the phone develops static, our cars develop engine trouble, our luggage goes awry at the terminal, and we have major blowups with our families. We don't want to leave on a journey, sign a contract, or make a major decision. Certainly, we need to drive defensively.

People who have Gemini or Virgo strong in their charts, with either of those two signs ruling the Sun, Moon, or Ascendant, should move cautiously during these times. Mercury plays a major role in their lives. Avoid signing contracts—especially a marriage contract—keep a grip on your budget and an eye on your car, computer, and household appliances. We don't want to *re*do projects, *re*open negotiations or *re*pair our cars.

Mercury retrograde is not a good time for spell working. If you must do a spell, write down all the words you are going to speak and then review them. You want to say the words correctly so that the spell doesn't boomerang. Take care not to spread yourself too thin. You could easily do two things at once, and that may not be a good thing during an important ritual. Plan all ceremonies carefully. Some say that if you must do a spell during a retrograde period, avoid doing it on Wednesday, which is Mercury's day. Certainly wear Mercury colors of blue and yellow and burn a light and airy incense.

The retrograde periods this year are February 13 to March 7, June 15 to July 9, and October 12 to November 1.

In the Moment:
Practicing Everyday Magic

by Dallas Jennifer Cobb

As Pagans, we practice many types of magic. We work with our circle or coven; some of us are solitary practitioners; we weave magic in community; we use herbs, spells, incantations, and trance. But the realm of magic is expanding beyond those who identify as Pagan or Wiccan as the world becomes more aware of everyday magic. Recent research is revealing that we engage in a form of everyday magic regularly. We tap into intuition, use our psychic abilities, divine outcomes, and predict the future. And most of us do this without even knowing it.

Whether it is in a crisis situation or a mundane matter, we all rely on a variety of instinctive skills to provide us with the information needed to make quick, effective decisions. First responses—our quickest instincts and their resultant reactions—prove to be sound judgments. It has led many researchers to delve deeper into the factors that influence these decisions, and they are finding that our propensity for instinctive knowing has some incredibly deep roots. Linked with intuition, first responses are based primarily on naturally occurring factors. And while they are mysterious and seemingly magical, these first responses are natural and everyday.

This article will look at rapid cognition, face reading, and intuition, and the factors that inform our first responses. It will suggest everyday practices to facilitate the development of good instinctive responses, and aid you in recognizing your latent abilities and honing your intuitive skills.

Rapid Cognition

The first two seconds of a job interview are said to be the most important. In those two seconds your prospective employer sizes you up. The data she amasses in those two seconds includes her visual observation of you, emotional and cognitive responses she experienced in response to your presence, and perhaps her like or dislike of the feel of your hand and the sound of your voice.

Rapid cognition happens in a blink of an eye. Within those two seconds data is compiled and a series of conclusions are formed. These conclusions are powerful, important, and for most people quite accurate.

The term *rapid cognition* applies to this situation more closely than the term *intuition* because these sort of decisions are made without direct historical experience of that person. The process is a rational one. It is high-speed thinking. Because it is such rapid cognition, we are often unaware of the series of thoughts that went into the cognitive process, and when we find ourselves jumping to a conclusion we are surprised by it. The conclusion itself seems mysterious: Where did it come from? But there really is nothing so mysterious here. Rapid cognition simply feels different from our usual sort of thinking wherein we ponder or deliberate something, but it is still thinking.

Rapid cognition, like that which happens in the first two seconds of encountering someone, is a quick-thinking method of acquiring data, analyzing it, and making conclusions based on the analysis. While the context of meeting a person is a new situation, our memory banks are filled with the data of our experiences—our perspective. We draw upon this when we engage in rapid cognition. While we may experience an instantaneous impression of a person, this impression is based on the analysis of the data accumulated from all of our past experiences.

Intuition

While the word *intuition* is often used in opposition to the word *rational*, intuition *is* a rational cognitive process. Intuition comes from the German word *Anschauung*, meaning a perspective or a point of view. In English intuition is defined as receiving or assimilating knowledge by direct perception or comprehension. Because we all have a point of view, we all have intuition. Simply put, intuition is a feeling or understanding based on past experience. It's a perspective acquired through experience and learning.

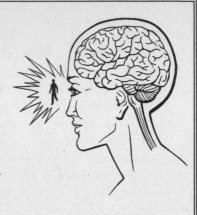

We have a variety of kinds of intuition, which are always active within us to some extent. If we don't pay close enough attention to our intuition, we don't notice its existence. The closer attention we pay to our intuition, the more aware we are of it and its efficacy.

Where Is Intuition?

While many would argue that intuition is primarily a cognitive function that occurs in the brain, as a result of stored memories being accessed for perspective, it can also be felt in the body. When we become aware of the physical signs, and note their occurrences, we can become more attuned to our intuition and first-response system.

Intuition can be felt in the solar plexus area of the body. This is often what people refer to as a gut instinct. It is a feeling of foresight that is communicated not in words but in a bodily feeling. A tightening of muscles, a nauseous wave, a fluttering tummy.

While the gut instinct is one way of physically being in touch with your intuition, many of us find that with practice we can identify other physical signs within our body indicative of intuition. Whether it is a chill up the spine, a prickling of the skin on the back of the neck, or a tingling of the scalp, each of us has a tangible connection to our own intuitive knowing.

Everyday Ways to Strengthen Intuition

You can develop your intuition. Like practicing magic, there are some steps that may help you. Ground yourself first, and be aware of your desire and commitment to be in touch with your intuition. Center yourself on the process, and take a moment to release any blocks that you may be feeling physically, mentally, or spiritually. Usually this requires you to let go of your doubts. Affirm that intuition is natural and normal to all humans. Align yourself with your own intuition by tuning in to your gut instincts. Let your mind wander and your energy feel expansive. Ask the question you are concerned about, or call to mind the person, place, or thing you are trying to become clear on. Listen within your body, mind, and spirit for the answers. These answers will not necessarily be words. They may be physical sensations or emotions which will require your interpretation.

Like an athlete who trains for the task that he performs, it is important to strengthen your intuition before relying heavily on it in a critical or important situation. Experiment with everyday practices in order to tune in to, be aware of, and improve your intuition. Consider some of the everyday occurrences that you could use to exercise your intuition.

How many times have you picked up the telephone and heard who was calling only to say: "I just thought of you." Telephones are great intuition workout devices. Forget Caller ID: when the telephone rings, take a moment to consider who might be calling; then answer the phone and find out. If you are someone who receives many calls a day, this might be more difficult, but for those of us who enjoy a limited number of callers, we can often use rapid cognition to make an educated guess about who is calling, determining his or her identity before picking up the phone. There are no real secrets to this.

The organic computer, our brain, boots up and quickly consults historical data files, analyzing and comparing, looking for similarities of circumstance. Based on the available data, we then make an educated guess about the identity of the caller.

For example, if my telephone were to ring now, my organic computer might go through a series of thoughts to help determine the identity of the caller. They'd be something like this: My husband usually phones from work mid-morning, but I already heard from him earlier, so chances are he won't be calling again. My mother usually calls in the early morning or afternoon. My friend usually calls just after lunch when she is stumped in the writing of her thesis. It's too early for her; she's probably writing away or editing yesterday's work. My daughter is at preschool, but she is rarely sick, and was well when I dropped her off this morning. Her preschool session is only three hours, and there're about forty-five minutes remaining before I pick her up. So unless an emergency has occurred, it is not the preschool. I left a message yesterday for the duct-cleaning service, and if they started work at nine then they might just be getting to the messages on their machine now. Oh. I bet that's who it is.

For every phone call the data that is processed and analyzed is different. And while it seems like a lot of data, this can all happen in an instant. Between one ring and the next is usually long enough for me to figure out who might be calling.

Being Fully Present

How many of us drive across town in rush hour traffic thinking about the problems we left behind at the office, or planning the dinner that we need to make at home? How often have we tuned out what someone was saying to us, even for a split second, because we were listening to our own thoughts or judg-

ments? How often have we "glazed over" at work due to fatigue or boredom?

Being fully present in the moment involves the engagement of our senses, feelings and thoughts in the task at hand. It is a focused awareness that enables us to fully absorb all the data that a situation offers, allowing these multiple perspectives to inform our rapid cognition and decision making.

While many people have found that meditation helps

284

them to learn a singular focus of mind, senses, and spirit, we can also cultivate our natural abilities. We can learn to limit the busy-ness of our mind, clear ourselves emotionally, and practice a cultivated awareness of our surroundings.

Whether you use journaling to clear your mind and untangle problems, therapy to resolve emotional blockages, or prayer to connect with a higher power, each of these can help you be more present in the moment. This presence enables us to be aware of and identify the data coming in.

Harnessing Our Higher Powers

In addition to practicing and strengthening our intuitive abilities, we can learn to use tools that help us focus our attention in the moment, and help us make sound decisions.

Sometimes called divination, there are many ways to use a tool to focus our intention and intuition. Common divination tools are the pendulum, divining rod, scrying mirror, and water bowl. Each of these tools requires you to form a relationship with it, tuning in to and understanding your own specific responses as they manifest through, and with, the tool. Many books have been written on each of these subjects, and are widely available through Llewellyn Worldwide if you wish to pursue the use of a divination tool.

Through regular awareness of your rapid-cognition process and regular exercise of your intuitive abilities, you can allow this higher power to be a part of your decision-making process. No longer limited to just thinking or puzzling out a problem, we can come to trust more in our quick responses, our gut instincts, and our flashes of brilliance. Because they are grounded in everything we have ever learned and known, these instantaneous responses are well researched, and may actually stretch even further than our history, connecting us to some of the stored collective memories of our evolutionary process.

So let yourself be fully present in the moment, give yourself permission to tap into those amazing abilities, and let the everyday magic begin.

Chaos for Creativity:
Spells to Unblock Your Inspiration

by Elizabeth Barrette

The tide rises, the tide falls. The Moon waxes and wanes. Summer gives way to autumn's drifting leaves and winter's desolation. All things in nature have their cycles, their peaks and ebbs of energy. The same holds true for personal energy and inspiration.

It doesn't matter whether you are a writer, an artist, a musician, a handicrafter, or a hobbyist: all creative people have something in common. They have an inner muse who inspires them to create beautiful or terrifying things, who whispers ideas to them, who fills them with creative energy—and who sometimes goes on vacation at inopportune times. Here are some practical and magical techniques for coping with creative blocks.

Causes of Creative Blocks

It can feel like a wall, something you pound your head against but can't break through. It can feel like a vast, enveloping fog that makes it impossible to find your way. It can feel like you've gone to the well only to find it dry. Whatever the subjective experience, creative blocks tend to stem from a few basic causes.

1. You're not ready to create. This is one of the most common problems, and, happily, the easiest to fix. Maybe you don't have an idea yet. Maybe you have an idea, but no groundwork. Inadequate preparation can stall any project. All you need to do is finish your research: read the source books, find the right pattern, study that new artistic style, lay out your materials. If you just need a place to start, try writing down your resource list first.

2. You're afraid to create. Fear can take the wind right out of your sails, whether you're afraid of success or of failure. Another frequent obstacle is the fear of messing up an important project. Energy work can often help you get past your fear.

3. You're trying to create entirely inside your head. Your head is where you incubate ideas. It takes your hands to manifest them. It's easy to get stuck trying to move from one to the other, so aim for forward momentum; even a little progress will help get the project into the material world where you can refine it as needed.

4. You feel too crowded to create. It's hard to produce a masterpiece with the phone ringing, the kids crying, and supper boiling over on the stove. You need time and space free of interruptions. Consider working outside your home at a park or library or coffeehouse—or you might get up or stay up an hour earlier or later than everyone else. Magically, work on your shields to protect you from unwanted outside pressure.

5. You started in the wrong place or from the wrong angle. Back up and start over. You may be able to reuse what you've already done, or you may have to discard it and begin from scratch. Regardless, you won't make useful progress down a wrong path. A fresh start should revive your enthusiasm.

How Magic Can Help

Although practical concerns can contribute to the problem, creative block is fundamentally a metaphysical affliction. It is easier to affect mundane things through material means, and ephemeral things through mystical means. Because it works on the same plane of reality, magic readily influences creativity and offers many possibilities for handling creative blocks.

First, consider your personal energy. You should be free of negative impulses from outside, and you should have enough energy to work comfortably. Experiment to see if your inspiration flows better when you are more or less grounded, with your magical shields up or down—but you should always center yourself before you begin.

Next, consider your workspace. A warded room is best, to keep out unwanted energetic interruptions. Purify the space periodically with a sprinkle of salted water or with sage smoke. To attract positive energy, hang wind chimes, spinners, or crystal prisms in the window; keep a potted plant or small aquarium on your desk. This is also an ideal place for your muse shrine (see below).

When you work, pay careful attention to the magical implications. For writers and painters, sometimes a blank page or canvas can act as a subtle energy barrier. You can break this "surface tension" much the same way you'd cut a door in a circle: by touching it with the tip of your athame. Those of you working in malleable media such as yarn, fabric, or clay may find it useful to play with the materials before beginning serious work. Composers and musicians benefit from communing with their instruments at the beginning of a session, warming up with favorite tunes according to mood, and so forth.

Finally, spellcraft provides a more methodical means of restoring and maintaining your inspiration. The following spells deal with different aspects of creativity. Each relates to one of the five causes of creative block, as described at the beginning of this article.

Divination for Creativity

To avoid running out of ideas, and to always have a place to turn for fresh inspiration when you want to begin a new project, you can make a simple divinatory set to give you a random selection of concepts. Writers, teachers, and other people whose creative outlet involves language may want a collection of words, such as a jar of tiles from a "Magnetic Poetry" set. Painters, graphic designers, and other visual artists may prefer a set of pictures, such as loose magazine clippings. Knitters, scrapbookers, and other handicrafters should have luck with a box of miscellaneous supplies (balls of yarn, paper squares, etc.) that can suggest a color or style. Musicians and miscellaneous creative folks can find any of the above options useful.

For this spell, you will need your creative divination tool, an incense burner and lighter, and a stick of incense. Inspiring scents include neroli, sandalwood, clove, ginger, or any blend named something like "Creativity." Light the incense and waft your divination set through the smoke three times. Each time, say: "I charge this tool as a container for my creativity." Then hold the tool and concentrate on its energy and potential. Let the incense burn out on its own.

Whenever you need ideas, draw three objects from the set and combine their concepts in a project. You might wind up writing a poem about flowers, bridges, and juggling; or sculpting a candle-holder featuring dogs and children. You can do this ritual twice, and then combine two or more divinatory sets—for instance, words and colors. Draw one or two items from each set. In this case, you could compose a tune inspired by lightning and the color violet.

Confronting Your Fear

Doubt, hesitation, worry, trepidation, stage fright, timidity, panic—by any other name, fear remains one of our most formidable obstacles. We can feel it, yet we can't touch it. Part of its formidability comes from its very formlessness. So one of the best ways to disempower fear is to give it a material form.

For this spell, you'll be making a physical manifestation of your fears. (This is best done away from your home or other primary workspace.) Use any symbol of something that holds you back. If you're a writer, you might make a papier-mâché figure out of rejection slips. If you're a sculptor, you might build a sandcastle to represent your self-doubts. A good option for anyone is to write or draw your worries on a scroll, roll it up, and tie it with a black ribbon for binding. As you create this object, concentrate on pouring all your fears into it.

Sit for a while with your symbol, and acknowledge the effect that fear has had on your life in general and your creativity in particular. Then destroy the object. You could burn it and scatter the ashes, if it's made of paper. The tide will naturally come in and dissolve a sandcastle built on a beach, and so forth. Imagine your fears magically disintegrating along with the object. Feel them lose their power over you, leaving you free to create. Watch until the symbol is completely destroyed, tidy up the area and dispose of any garbage in an appropriate receptacle, then walk away without looking back.

Honoring Your Muse

Inside every creative person lives a divine spark of inspiration. This muse gives us ideas and guides us as we bring things from the realm of mind into the realm of matter. This same energy can help when you get stuck at that juncture. It helps to have a special place for invoking your muse.

Start by creating a shrine for your muse. A small table, shelf, or corner of a counter is ideal. Cover it with an altar cloth of gold (for revelation), blue (for communication), red (for creative power), silver (for dreams and inspiration), black (for receptivity), or other colors with special meaning for you. Add symbols of your creative success: copies of your work, letters of acceptance, contracts, sales slips, thank-you notes from satisfied customers, compliments from people who have admired your material, pictures of yourself creating, etc. You could even include an image of the nine Muses from ancient Greece. Leave room at the front and center of your space.

For the spell itself, you'll need nine white candles (tea lights work well) and holders, a lighter, and a vase full of colorful flowers. Begin by putting the flowers in the vase as an offering. Light the first candle and say, "I give thanks to my muse for bringing creativity into my life." Light the second candle and make a request or wish, such as, "I ask for the energy to complete my new project by this Friday." Light the third candle and give thanks again. Continue alternating thanks with requests. Light the ninth candle and close with thanks, saying, "I give thanks for all that I have created in the past, and all that I will create in the future."

Spend a few minutes meditating on your muse. Allow the candles to burn out on their own, if practical, or extinguish them when you're done meditating.

You Can Do It in Your Sleep

Creativity springs from the subconscious, and one of the best ways to access it is through dreaming. Your sleeping mind roams free of constraints that could block your creativity in waking space. I've been using my dreams for inspiration for many years, and more than once I've awakened with an entire poem or story in my head ready to be written down.

For this spell, decorate your altar (or your muse shrine) in deep, dreamy colors such as blue or violet or silver. If you can find a star-spangled altar cloth, so much the better. You will also need a Moon-shaped candle; if you can't find one, a regular candle in a Moon-themed candleholder will also work. The most important part of this spell is the item you use for your dream focus. A dreamcatcher is one good choice. Find a blue or violet one with turquoise, amethyst, or jade beads; a quartz point is another ideal decoration. (You can dab a dreamcatcher with a drop of jasmine or peppermint oil for visionary dreams.) Alternatively, you could use a dreampillow; these are often made from celestial-themed fabrics, stuffed with rice or buckwheat hulls and herbs such as bay (inspiration and wise dreams), mugwort (visions), mullein (repels nightmares), rose (happy or clairvoyant dreams), and white sage (attunement to the spirit world).

Work this spell after dark, shortly before you go to bed, when the Moon is waxing. Light the Moon candle and say, "My inspiration waxes like the Moon. As the moonlight fills the night, so creativity fills my dreams." Take hold of your dream focus. Feel its shape, smell its scent. Let your subconscious mind learn to recognize it. Imagine this object guiding you to new and exciting ideas. Fill it with your power. Say to your dream focus, "I give thanks to my muse for my creativity. With this dream focus, I summon refreshing sleep full of splendid visions and inspiration." Meditate on this idea for a few minutes, and then extinguish the candle. Hang a dreamcatcher over your bed or take a dreampillow to bed with you when you go to sleep.

Three Impossible Things before Breakfast

Sometimes you just get stuck in a rut. When that happens, you need to get unstuck—you need something to jolt yourself out of the rut. In Zen meditation, the master may whack the student with a bamboo stick to startle him out of his ordinary thought patterns. But you don't need to get hit with a bamboo stick; you just need to do something slightly outrageous.

For this spell, you will need three beads, large enough (eight millimeters or half an inch, or bigger) to handle easily. Choose either clear quartz, which can be "programmed" for any magical purpose, or glass in whimsical shapes that you find inspiring. You will also need a tassel and some colored cord or ribbon—wild neon, rainbow, gold, or silver are good choices. String the beads one at a time onto your cord, knotting it between each bead. Then tie the cord closed with the tassel hanging at the end. You may size it as you wish: keychain, bracelet, and necklace sizes are all effective.

This spell works best when performed in the morning before you eat; food is a grounding influence, so avoiding it for a little while helps access your intuitive mind. But if, like me, you're *really* not a morning person, you can do the spell later in the day.

Put the beads in your pocket and go out. Do three outlandish (but not dangerous) things. Make them things you would ordinarily never do. Visit an art museum or listen to music of a style you usually avoid. Pretend you don't speak English (or whatever the local language is) and try to order coffee. Wear all your clothes inside out or backwards. Go into an ethnic restaurant or pastry shop and eat things you don't recognize. Use your imagination! (If your imagination refuses to wake up and play, try asking for suggestions from the first five-year-old you see.) For each outrageous thing you do, touch one of the beads. Infuse the bead with the energy of that moment when you experience something totally unexpected, that sudden jolt of sensation when you leave behind what you knew for what is new. Remember to eat breakfast after you finish charging the beads, if you didn't work it into the charging process.

Next, take your fully energized beads to your creative workplace. Lay out your supplies. Think about how "stuck" your inspiration has been, like a car in a rut. You know how you get a car unstuck, by rocking it back and forth? Rub your fingers over the beads like that—forward one bead, back one bead, forward two, back two, forward all three—gathering the energy as you go.

Magic Wands & Wizard's Staffs

by Lynn Smythe

So Moses and Aaron went to see Pharaoh, and they performed the miracle just as the Lord had told them. Aaron threw down his staff before Pharaoh and his court, and it became a snake. Then Pharaoh called in his wise men and magicians, and they did the same thing with their secret arts. Their staffs became snakes, too!

—Exodus 7:10–12

Wands and staffs are special tools used in certain magical rituals. Although certain traditions assign the wand and staff to either the element of air or the element of fire, the majority of practitioners utilize these tools as a general aid to their magic rituals. Wands and staffs are used to collect, store, direct, and release energy to and from a certain point. Some practitioners may own only one wand or staff for conducting their magic while others may have a collection of wands and staffs—one for each type of magic ritual they perform. Although wood is traditionally used, wands and staffs may also be created from a variety of materials including glass, clay, gemstone, or metal. This article primarily deals with wands and staffs made of wood.

Ancient healers would often use a wand-like tool, such as a twig or small branch, to help them cast out evil spirits from the bodies of their patients. These evil spirits were thought to be the cause of disease. Once the evil spirits were cast out, the healer could continue to heal their patients using a variety of herbal remedies.

According to folklorists and authors Ernst and Johanna Lehner, the use of magical wands can be traced back to the bible: "In the Dark and Middle Ages, when the professional sorcerers usurped every bit of mythological belief and religious legend of miracles for their own use, they choose the rod of Aaron as the symbol of the magician's efficacy. The rod became the magic wand for magicians of all times and all peoples."

Asclepius, a Greek god of medicine renowned for his great healing powers, was knowledgeable in the use of medicinal herbs. He also knew various magical incantations and had the power to bring the dead back to life. One of his symbols, which is known as Asclepius's rod, was a long staff made from a rough-hewn cedar branch with a single snake entwined around it. The caduceus, a symbol of the Greek messenger god Hermes, is a wand or rod often made from a short piece of olive branch with a pair of snakes entwined around it, and topped by a pair of wings.

Hermes, who was known as Mercury in the Roman pantheon, used his magic wand to conduct the souls of the dead to the underworld. The caduceus is a powerful symbol: the snakes represent immortality and wisdom, the wings represent spirituality and imagination, and the rod represents authority and power. A serpent-encircled wand was a symbol often associated with herbalists and healers during the early Middle Ages. The serpent, which periodically sheds its skin to renew itself, is a symbol of immortality and renewed life. Both

Asclepius's rod and the caduceus are symbols used in the modern age by various medical organizations.

Blasting Rods

A more sinister version of the magic wand and staff was the blasting rod. This was a magical tool referenced in certain ancient grimoires such as *The Key of Solomon the King*, translated by S. L. MacGreggor Mathers in 1888, and *The Book of Ceremonial Magic*, written by A. E. White in 1913. Both MacGreggor's and White's publications were based on earlier medieval grimoires. A grimoire is a book containing symbols, spells, and charms, and instructions for using them in various magic rituals.

The blasting rod or wand was to be cut from a branch of hazel from a virgin tree—that is, a tree of less than one year's growth. The branch was to be cut on the day of Mercury (Wednesday) at sunrise, with the finished length being approximately nineteen inches long. Certain magical symbols and sigils were to be carved upon the rod. (The magician's staff was to be created in a similar manner as the rod but cut from either cane or elder wood.) The blasting rod or staff could be used either to invoke the aid of spirits or to send a summoned spirit back to the underworld after the magician was done questioning it. The blasting rod later came to be associated with a wand or staff made out of any material that was hard enough to make an effective weapon. Blackthorn was one material often used to make blasting rods.

Wand and Staff Materials

Magicians and wizards were often seen traveling with a long rod or staff, which could double as a walking stick, to aid them on their journeys. These staffs, which were usually crafted to be the same height as the user, also doubled as an effective weapon against potential thieves. The wood from which a wand or staff is made represents the power and energy associated with the type of tree from which they are created. The branches of the blackthorn tree (*Prunus spinosa*) was one of the types of wood used to create walking sticks. Magical wands made from wood are often cut to the length of the user's forearm, either as measured from the inner elbow to the end of the finger tips or from the inner elbow to the base of the palm. Some traditions use a predetermined length of twenty-one inches for all magical wands. Modern-day wands, made popular by the *Harry Potter* series of books written by J. K. Rowling, are typically ten to fourteen inches long. Wizards staffs are commonly made between fifty and sixty inches tall. Since wizards staffs double as walking sticks, the length is determined by the height of the wizard using it.

Magical Properties of Trees

These magical wands and staffs can be made from a variety of materials. In addition to blackthorn, a variety of other trees are traditionally used to make magic wands. I have listed the magical properties of only a few trees in this article. See Lily Gardner's article "The Nine Sacred Trees" in Llewellyn's *2006 Magical Almanac* for the magical properties associated with birch, rowan, ash, alder, willow, hawthorn, oak, hazel, and holly. You may want to choose one of these woods as the basis for you own magic wand or wizard's staff.

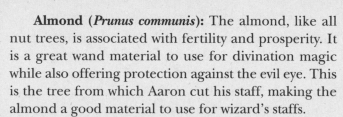

Almond (*Prunus communis*): The almond, like all nut trees, is associated with fertility and prosperity. It is a great wand material to use for divination magic while also offering protection against the evil eye. This is the tree from which Aaron cut his staff, making the almond a good material to use for wizard's staffs.

Apple (*Pyrus Malus*): This tree is associated with eternal youth, fertility magic, love spells, ancient knowledge, strength, healing, and wisdom. The apple tree is also known as the fruit of the underworld. The goddess Freya is associated with this tree, making an apple wand a good choice to use for goddess-based magic.

Cedar (*Cedrus libani*): The magical properties associated with cedar include consecration, immortality, prophecy, prosperity, protection, and purification. Use a staff made of cedar to help you with any magical workings on the astral plane and in any dream-based magic. Cedar was the tree used to create Asclepius's rod.

Elder (*Sambucus nigra*): The elder tree was supposed to provide protection from Witches in addition to granting great healing powers to whomever possessed it. Wands made from this material could also be used to summon up storms, as it was believed that lightning would never strike an elder tree. Elder is also a tree of regeneration and fulfillment. Fairies are said to have a fondness for this wood. Old English folklore says you must ask the spirit of the elder tree for permission before cutting down any of its wood:

> *Old woman, old woman*
> *Give me some of your wood*
> *And I will give you some of mine*
> *When I grow into a tree.*

Elm (*Ulmus* spp.): The wood from this tree was supposedly the material of choice for medieval magicians. Elm is a tree of strength, intuition, and meditation, and is another wood that offers protection from lightning. Elm is also a good wood to utilize when working any kind of love spell or charm.

Maple (*Acer* spp.): Maple is a tree of love, harmony, peace, and prosperity. Maple will help to bring balance and harmony to yin-yang energies. It is a popular wand material and helps to awaken one's intuition and creativity.

Walnut (*Juglans regia*): A tree of fertility, prosperity, and wisdom. Use wands and staffs made of walnut to help awaken your inner wisdom. This is also a good material to use for initiation rituals.

Yew (*Taxus baccata*): Yew is a powerful magical material which has associations with both life and death. This is another tree that can be used in magic rituals that focus on honoring one's ancestors and recently deceased loved ones.

Making Wands and Staffs

Making your own wands and staffs, or any magical tool for that matter, will give you a greater understanding of that tool while attuning yourself to your own natural powers and abilities. Naturally fallen branches and tree limbs should be used when creating your own magic wands and staffs whenever possible. Take a walk in the woods, especially after a storm, to look for fallen tree branches. The tree spirits, sometimes referred to as devas, may become resentful if you cut down a living branch. If you must cut down a branch from a living tree, first make sure the tree is on your own property or that you have the permission of the land owner. Then, visit the tree and meditate on how you are going to shape the limb into a wand or staff for use in your magic work. Then ask permission of the tree spirits and thank them for their gift.

A variety of decorations can be incorporated into your wands to imbue them with extra magical energy. Copper wire is often wrapped around a wand, as this metal is an excellent conductor of energy. A variety of decorative items can be added to the copper wire before it is wrapped around the wand, such as beads, buttons, feathers, and small gemstone beads. In addition, silver wire can be used to represent goddess energy, while gold wire can be used to represent god energy.

A special stone or crystal can be added to one or both ends of the wand if desired. Embellishing the top of the wand with a crystal is thought to represent male and god energy. Embellishing the bottom of the wand by carving a hole or cutting a slit in it is thought to represent female and goddess energy.

Wand and Staff Dedication

Raise your wand or staff to the sky to collect the energy from the Sun or the Moon depending on the time of day you are conducting your magic work. The Moon's energy can be collected any time at night while the Moon is visible. Midnight is a particularly potent time to collect the Moon's energy. The power of the Moon can also be captured during certain phases of the Moon depending on the type of magic you wish to perform. New Moon, First Quarter, Full Moon, and Last

Quarter are all powerful times during which to collect the Moon's energy. Moon magic also corresponds to goddess energy, creativity, psychic powers, fertility, and the element of water.

Moon Power Dedication Charm

Recite this charm three times while holding your wand in your healing hand. Your healing hand, which is also referred to as your power hand, is the hand you use when writing.

> *Magical wand of mine,*
> *I dedicate you to the magic of the Moon.*
> *May the goddesses aid and protect me*
> *While performing my rituals, spells, and charms.*

Sun Power Dedication Charm

Recite this charm three times while holding your wand in your healing hand. The Sun's energy can be collected any time during the day when the Sun is visible. Sunrise, noon, and the few moments just before sunset are particularly potent times to harvest the Sun's energy. Sun magic also corresponds to god energy, spontaneity, power, vitality, and the element of fire.

> *Magical wand of mine,*
> *I dedicate you to the magic of the Sun.*
> *May the gods aid and protect me*
> *While performing my rituals, spells, and charms.*

Sigils & Signs

by Sorita D'Este

A sigil is a pictographic representation of your intent. When you make a sigil, you are creating a focus for your will, so you can achieve a particular purpose—usually a spell. Sigils are one of the easiest forms of spells, and can be created very quickly and easily. There are many popular sigils used today, which have gained a lot of power through repeated use. These sigils, which include the pentagram, the Goddess and God symbols, and the elemental symbols, can all add power and focus to your spells.

Sigils are all around us. Look at the logos for big companies and see how many of them have sigils, and use appropriate magical colors. They are used to create identities and to encourage people to "go with the brand" and be loyal customers. And because they are a very simple and effective form of magic, they work very well.

Let us consider some of the most popular sigils used today, which can be included in your own sigils. The pentagram represents balance and the perfection of the self. The five points represent the five elements of air, earth, fire, water, and spirit, with spirit on the top point. The pentacle also represents man, with the five points representing the five senses and five "limbs" (two arms, two legs, and head) of man.

Pentagrams are used as a symbol of protection and blessing, and for consecrations and invocations. They also act as doorways for the elemental powers, to bring their energy into your sacred space. The famous French magician Eliphas Levi said of the pentagram, "The empire of will over the Astral Light, which is the physical soul of the four elements, is represented in Magic by the Pentagram."

The Goddess symbol represents the triple aspect of Maiden, Mother, and Crone. The crescents of the waxing (Maiden) and waning (Crone) Moon surround the circle representing the Full Moon (Mother) in the center. The circle also represents the totality of the Goddess as the whole universe, as expressed by Isis in her words, "I am all that is and was and ever shall be."

The God symbol is the same as the astrological symbol for Taurus—a crescent on its side, atop a circle. The crescent represents the horns that symbolise the power of the God, and the circle represents the Sun as his fertilizing energy. The God symbol emphasizes the life, death, and rebirth cycle that the God goes through each year.

The Goddess and God symbols, like the pentagram, can be used as symbols of blessing and protection, and may be included with other sigils to emphasize the divine influence and the divine energy you bring into your spell.

The elemental symbols are all drawn from the hexagram (a symbol of the universe). The upward pointing triangle of fire and downward pointing triangle of water, when combined, produce the hexagram. The air symbol is produced by combining the upward-pointing triangle with the base of the downward-pointing triangle, and the earth symbol is created by combining the downward-pointing triangle with the base of the upward-pointing triangle. Thus the four elemental symbols are all contained in the hexagram, showing that the universe is made up of the four elements.

The elemental symbols can be included individually or together in sigils to bring in the energies and qualities of the elements you feel are appropriate to the nature of your spell.

It is very easy to create your own personal sigils for use on candles, magical tools, amulets and talismans, charm bags, or just about any use you can think of. Sigils are very versatile and the only limit is your imagination. There are two common methods of sigilization, both of which are very easy to use.

The first form of sigilization is called reduction sigilization. All you need to do is write down a word or sentence that represents your intent. You then remove all the duplicate letters and make a sigil with the remaining letters. This is so the sigil can act on your unconscious mind and tap into all the latent power there, encouraging your energy to be focused and directed towards achieving the desired result of your intent.

Here is an example to show how easy this technique is. This is for a house protection sigil. The intent is verbalized as, "My house will be safe." So first remove the duplicate letters in that phrase, and you are left with $M Y H O E W I L B S A F$. Now draw a sigil that uses those letters. You can combine letters: the I can be written as part of the L, the E as part of the B, etc. Also remember the letters can be written upside down, back to front, on their sides, and in different sizes. How you put the letters together is completely up to you; let yourself be creative and inventive when you create a reduction sigil.

Reduction sigils are commonly drawn using capital letters, as these are easier to combine. Remember also to use an appropriately colored pen for the planetary or elemental energy you wish to focus with your sigil.

You can start your sigil with any of the letters; for this example I have started by combining the *H*, *A*, and *W*. The *W* will also represent the *M* upside-down. This also makes the *Y* at the right of the sigil.

Adding the *E* on the side includes the *F*, *I*, and *L* within it.

By looping the *E*, the *B* is formed, and the *S* is drawn into this as well. Finally the *O* is drawn large around the whole thing to represent a protective magic circle.

When you have made your sigil, you place it somewhere where you will frequently see it, such as on a door, for a set period of time—often a lunar month. Every time you see the sigil you reinforce the intent that has been programmed into your unconscious mind at its creation.

If you are using a sigil for something permanent, such as marking a tool or creating a house protection, the sigil can be kept forever. For spells where you set a fixed time for the result, you should destroy the sigil at the end of the spell when it has worked. In these instances you should make your sigil on paper or inscribe it on a candle or some other perishable medium that can be easily destroyed.

A second technique is to draw your sigil on a magic-number square (also called a *kamea*). A magic-number square is a square of numbers where each horizontal, vertical, and diagonal line add up to the same number. The squares are attributed to the classical planets, and work with planetary energies. Each square has sides the length of the planetary number, so the Saturn square is 3 x 3, Jupiter is 4 x 4, etc.

When using magic squares to form a sigil, you should formulate a word or very short phrase to represent your desired intent. Each letter of the alphabet has a number in the range one through nine attributed to it, the same as in numerology. Your word will thus convert to a list of single-digit numbers.

1	2	3	4	5	6	7	8	9
A	B	C	D	E	F	G	H	I
J	K	L	M	N	O	P	Q	R
S	T	U	V	W	X	Y	Z	

If your intent was "good health," you would get the following sequence of numbers: 7, 6, 6, 4, 8, 5, 1, 3, 2, 8

The first letter is chosen as the starting point on the appropriate planetary kamea, marked with a small circle and a straight line drawn to the next number on the square, on to the next, and so on until the last letter is reached. A small bar line is drawn to mark the end of the line. If two consecutive letters have the same number, a small loop is drawn. For three or more consecutive letters with the same number, add another loop for each extra occurrence.

The figure then represents the word as a sigil, to be drawn on a talisman chosen for the appropriate planetary energy. For this sigil you might choose Jupiter or Mercury as appropriate to good health.

The Jupiter Square

4	14	15	1
9	7	6	12
5	11	10	8
16	2	3	13

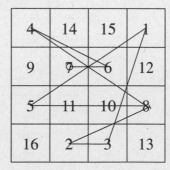

The magic squares are given below so you can use whichever one you choose for creating your sigils. You will notice that you only use the numbers from one through nine in making your sigil. The rest are ignored for this purpose; in this context they provide the spaces between which the numbers one through nine are placed.

The first time you draw the sigil, it is a good idea to use a background with the appropriate magic square on it, so you can draw a mock-up of your sigil easily. When you draw or carve the sigil for real, you should copy it free-hand from the mock-up you have already made.

By drawing the same word on different squares you will get very different sigils, showing how the different planetary energies have different effects and produce different results.

Saturn

4	9	2
3	5	7
8	1	6

Mars

11	24	7	20	3
4	12	25	8	16
17	5	13	21	9
10	18	1	14	22
23	6	19	2	15

Venus

22	47	16	41	10	35	4
5	23	48	17	42	11	29
30	6	24	49	18	36	12
13	31	7	25	43	19	37
38	14	32	1	26	44	20
21	39	8	33	2	27	45
46	15	40	9	34	3	28

Mercury

8	58	59	5	4	62	63	1
49	15	14	52	53	11	10	56
41	23	22	44	48	19	18	45
32	34	35	29	25	38	39	28
40	26	27	37	36	30	31	33
17	47	46	20	21	43	42	24
9	55	54	12	13	51	50	16
64	2	3	61	60	6	7	57

Sun

6	32	3	34	35	1
7	11	27	28	8	30
19	14	16	15	23	24
18	20	22	21	17	13
25	29	10	9	26	12
36	5	33	4	2	31

Moon

37	78	29	70	21	62	13	54	5
6	38	79	30	71	22	63	14	46
47	7	39	80	31	72	23	55	15
16	48	8	40	81	32	64	24	56
57	17	49	9	41	73	33	65	25
26	58	18	50	1	42	74	34	66
67	27	59	10	51	2	43	75	35
36	68	19	60	11	52	3	44	76
77	28	69	20	61	12	53	4	45

Summer Magic

by Lily Gardner

Summer and the smell of barbecues waft over neighbors' fences. The country is flooded with bird song and parks are filled with children and their parents. Even those of us not fortunate enough to have a garden often nurture pots of geraniums or tomato plants. We camp and go to the beach. With the Sun at its most glorious, summer is a perfect time for magic.

The pagan summer begins on Beltane, May 1. For centuries, young people went "a-Maying" in the nearby woods to gather hawthorn blossoms for the Beltane festival. Often, May Day brought a pregnancy, thus proving the girl was fertile and therefore marriageable. Huge Beltane bonfires burned to worship the return of the Sun's heat. Beltane festivities are emblematic of summer's magic. Summer is the season of fire, frivolity, fertility, and sexuality.

Season of Fire

Archeologists have lately determined that *Homo erectus* used hearth fires at least 790,000 years ago, although there is no evidence that our earliest ancestors cooked their food until 30,000 to 10,000 BC. These earliest hearth fires were for warmth, naturally, but fire's magic is self-evident. According to Joseph Campbell, the hearth was the first shrine, and within the hearth burned the earliest embodiment of the divinity. Fire worship is the oldest religion. Even today, with our furnaces and light bulbs, the customs of hearths and fires continues. Many of our fire spells for purification, protection and divination incorporate these ancient customs.

A sacred fire is a fire built with intention. When you have gathered together the paper, kindling, and wood for the fire, but before you light it, face the south and meditate, focusing on your breath and allowing your mundane thoughts to fall away. When you feel ready, invite the spirit of fire into your space as you put match to tinder.

The sacred fire can be used to purify magical tools, amulets, or symbols for spell work. Build your fire with the intention of consecrating your objects. When the fire is burning, pass the objects through the smoke and ask the spirit of the fire to purify them.

Our ancestors passed their children through the smoke of a sacred fire and drove their livestock through its dying flames to keep them healthy and safe. To protect your home, burn nine laurel leaves, nine ash leaves, and a handful of frankincense in your fireplace or cauldron. As the fire burns, say:

> *Spirits of the fire,*
> *Protect this home and all who live here.*
> *Fill my abode with happiness, good health,*
> *And abundance.*
> *Blessed be!*

To banish bad habits, throw symbols of your habits into a sacred fire, built on a night of the waning Moon. As the fire consumes those symbols of unwanted feelings or addictions, feel the urges within you burn away.

During the summer, develop your divination skills by looking into the fire with an unfocused gaze. A wealth of fire lore interprets the burning patterns of fire.

If a fire burns badly, someone in your family is in a bad temper. If the fire burns hollow (meaning a large cavity in the center of the fire), it foretells a parting. If a fire burns brightly after a woman has stirred it, she has an ardent lover. If the fire burns only on one side, it means that change is in the air. Let your mind see patterns and shapes in the flames. The most profound meanings come from your own intuition.

Candles have been used for fire magic for centuries. By lighting a candle, we are releasing energy into our magical circle. This summer, burn candles in all your castings. To make wishes, burn a candle on the night of a Sabbat or a Full Moon. Make a wish and jump over the candle. To bring a new love into your life, cast this candle spell on the first Friday of the June waxing Moon. Anoint a new red candle with honey and essence of rose. Say:

Lover, lover, come to me,
By the rose and honey bee,
Passion bright as dancing flame,
Truest heart be mine to claim.

Storytelling and history first developed around a communal fire. Sit with friends and family around a campfire and tell stories. A wonderful game to play is for one person to begin a story—the more fantastic the better. After five minutes, the first storyteller hands off the story to the next person, and the second storyteller continues, adding new plot twists before handing it off to the next storyteller. This is a great way to stretch your imagination. On a deeper level, it connects you with the chain of humanity that extends back to prehistoric times, when we first told stories around the fire.

The suit of wands in the tarot is the suit of fire and summer energies. Wands depict how our inner fire or drive manifests in the outer world. Wands are about change and movement. Wands also demonstrate the negative forces of fire—bringing life but also destroying it.

During the summer, choose a tarot card from the suit of wands for each week. Note how each card in the suit of wands reflects the attributes of fire. Without consulting a book for the meanings of the card, free-associate with what the image brings to mind. If you are lucky enough to have more than one deck of tarot cards, use the various images of the particular wand card you are working with. How do the images differ from deck to deck? Do the different cards offer fresh insights? On the final day of the week, research what others have written about the card. Does their interpretation deepen your understanding?

The Art of Play

Frivolity is another aspect of summer's magic. How many of us get caught in the adult world of work and don't allow ourselves the release of play? Dottie Ward-Wimmer, in her paper "The Healing Potential of Adults in Play," writes: "Play, joy and spontaneity are rooted in all our hearts." Playtime is as valuable as work to the human heart. Adult play can take many forms. It can be an after-work soccer game, tap dancing lessons, turning semi-precious stones into necklaces or bracelets, flying kites on the beach, or playing board games. In order for it to really count as play, these criteria must be met:

1. The point of the play is pleasure and not outcome.

2. You must use your imagination in some way.

3. The activity must be something you truly wish to do.

Remember, moving our bodies invites release, while cultivating the imagination leads to a deeper integration of mind and heart. Make a vow to yourself to spend one evening or afternoon a week at play this summer.

Out in Mother Nature

Being outdoors is the gift of summer, whether it is sunning on a beach, a stroll during your lunch break, reading a book on the porch swing, or dinner in the backyard. For those of us who live

in the north, it's shedding layers of clothing and baring arms and legs to the warm summer air. Summer is the season when we can hold our rituals outdoors in comfort. It is also the easiest time to commune with nature.

While you're outdoors, take the time to learn more about the trees, wildflowers, wild animals, and geology that comprise our environment. This summer, become expert on one facet of the natural world. By knowing the names of the wild plants and animals, we forge a deeper bond with our environment.

If you decide to work toward a deeper understanding of trees or plants, I would suggest keeping a special notebook as a reference for this purpose. Collect leaves from each tree you identify or a sample of the flower and leaf (assuming they're not rare) of herbs and wildflowers you find.

A fun project is to make inked prints of the various leaves you've discovered over the summer. All you need is a pane of glass, a table knife, a ball of cotton wrapped in a small square of silk, and printer's ink, which can be found in shops selling stationery products or rubber-stamping supplies.

Begin by spreading the ink as evenly as possible over the surface of the glass. Press the silk covered cotton ball lightly over the glass surface, lifting and pressing, so as to distribute the ink uniformly. Select a leaf and place it facedown on the inked glass. Lift it and check that it is completely covered with ink, making sure that it isn't saturated. Now carefully press the leaf on a white sheet of paper. Cover with waxed paper and press the leaf into the white paper. Peel off the waxed paper and lift the leaf off the sheet. With a little practice, you will have marvelous imprints of leaves.

Next to the print, in your journal, log the tree or wildflower, including its botanical name and where you identified it. Research the magical properties of the plant. Are there teas or tonics that can be used from the plants or can you use the leaves in your spell work? These journals are guaranteed to become keepsakes.

Creativity

Beltane's sexual frolics herald the summer season. Our sexuality is the profound and mysterious energy that leads us to make connections with other people. Summer is an excellent time to cast love spells and do sex magic.

I would like to make a case that this mysterious sexual drive is the same drive that urges us to create. "Create" comes from the root word *ker*, the same root word that forms the name of Ceres, the Roman goddess of agriculture. It means "to cause to exist, bring into being." The creative spark resides in all of us, and being human affords us the ability not only to procreate but to create.

Expand your understanding of creativity to encompass everything you make, be it an omelet, a radio you built from scratch, a knitted sweater, or a vegetable garden. For many of us, the more creative we are the happier and more fulfilled we feel. Try to challenge yourself to "think outside the box" with every project you do this summer.

Try a spell to deepen your creativity. This spell invokes Ceres, the spirits of fire, and the totem energies of the fox. The fox is Ceres's animal. He is known for his resourcefulness and his ability to shapeshift. In the Apache myth of creation, it was Fox who first stole fire from the gods and gave it to man. The fox is associated with sexuality and freeing the creative force in all of us.

On the New Moon crescent, build a fire—in your fireplace or, preferably, outdoors. You will need an image of a fox, the tools you use for your creative endeavors, and a bowl of grains, berries, and grasses as an offering to Ceres and the fox. A nice touch would be to include a vase of poppies, Ceres's flower, as a special offering. Cast your magic circle, beginning in the south, and call in the elements of fire, water, earth, and air. Ignite your fire. Once the fire is blazing, sit before it and breathe deeply. Focus on your breath, releasing stray thoughts as they race across your mind. Allow your eyes to half open and gaze upon the fire. Meditate in this way for at least twenty minutes. Slowly stand and cast grains and grass into the fire. Invite Ceres and the fox to join you in sacred space. Say:

> I am a child of Ceres.
> Creativity is Ceres's gift to me.
> Using my creativity is my gift to Ceres.
> I open myself to exploring my creativity.

Say these words slowly and let their resonance burn within you. As you feed more wood into the fire, think about what feeds

your creativity. Now pass your tools for creativity through the smoke of your sacred fire. Ask the fox to bless your endeavors. Close the spell as you would any ritual.

Food Magic

What do you like best about summer? "The food!" is the answer I most often hear. Vine-ripened tomatoes, corn on the cob, fresh berries, rhubarb pie, gazpacho, fruit salads—summer brings a wealth of sweet fruits and vegetables.

Why not try using food in your spell work this summer? For a wonderful compendium of food magic, I recommend Scott Cunningham's *Wicca in the Kitchen*. Before you begin your food spell, light a new red candle on the kitchen table and invoke Vesta, the ancient hearth goddess, to bless your efforts. Here are a few ideas to get you started:

Love Potion Cordial

Use strawberries or cherries. Clean and measure 4 cups of fruit into a bowl, leaving them as whole as possible. As you clean the fruit, visualize its qualities of beauty and sweetness. Add 1 cup sugar. Say:

> *Sweetness of these plants and trees*
> *Release your loving energies.*

Place in a jar and cover with 120-proof vodka. The vodka's essence is fire, and fire ignites the earth energies of the fruit and sugar. Imagine passion imbuing your potion.

Cover the jar and let stand for 6 weeks on your kitchen counter near a window, allowing the sun to saturate your love cordial. Shake it once a day and visualize your heart's desire. Strain the cordial through two thicknesses of cheesecloth. Squeeze all the juice from the berries and strain again. Bottle your love potion in a red or pink glass bottle.

Drink a sip or two as you cast a love spell or have a small glass as you take a candlelit bubble bath. This cordial is for you alone. It may be shared with your lover as long as he or she is aware that the drink is a love potion.

Protective Blueberry Vinegar

Both blueberries and vinegar are well known for their protective qualities. As you prepare this vinegar, think of the sweet berries melding with the tart vinegar to provide you with a powerful tonic.

Wash 1 gallon of blueberries and lightly mash. Add ½ cup sugar and cover with rice vinegar. Stir and leave covered for 48 hours. Strain the vinegar and discard the berries. Pour the strained vinegar over a fresh gallon of mashed blueberries. Add ⅛ cup sugar. Cover and let stand 48 hours. Strain the vinegar again and discard the second batch of blueberries. Bottle and refrigerate. This wonderful protective vinegar can be used as a salad dressing. And it's fat free!

The long hours of daylight, the heat, the flowers and fruits all make summer a time of richness and beauty. I hope these ideas for summer magic will make this season even richer. Blessed be.

Water Magic

Water Magic

by Chandra Moira Beal

Water is the essence of life. We are, in fact, mostly water. As a fertilized egg we are 96 percent water; our adult bodies consist of more than 70 percent water. Amniotic fluid has a similar make up to seawater, and the fetus in the womb echoes our evolution from the ocean. Seventy percent of the Earth is covered by water. We are born in water and all life depends on it.

Water can take the form of a liquid, a solid, and a vapor. It is colorless but it enables us to see the colors of a rainbow. Water has no form, but gives form to everything. Water is billions of years old but can constantly rejuvenate itself.

Water is at the heart of many of life's rituals, from baptism at birth to the ceremonial washing of a body at death. There are water rituals for almost any event in life. Ensuring an easy birth, recovering from illness, succeeding in an examination or new job, attracting more money or peace or wisdom—all can be encouraged by the ritual use of water.

Immersing yourself in a river is perhaps the most intimate contact you can have with a deity, and this symbolic consummation of the man-god relationship may be the origin of the earliest water rituals. Shrines were often built in places of natural beauty where there was a river, a spring, or a waterfall. Today's "shrines" have a more urban slant, and can be as mundane as the kitchen sink. Your bathtub, washing machine, swimming pool, or any other fixture of modern life can all be used for water rituals.

Water rituals include bathing, baptizing, cleansing, and purification. Even perfumes are an example of a small water ritual. Other rituals include having a home sprinkled with blessed water, spraying yourself with charged water to restore energy vibrations, and soaking in a charged bath to draw in or release energy. Even the simple act of drinking a glass of water can be a ritual if you want it to be.

Ritual water works in two ways: it gives energy and it takes away energy. Water gives health, wealth, and wisdom because of its sacred origins or its blessed condition. It takes away evil, bad luck, or the spiritual grime of daily life by virtue of its purity and simple cleansing properties.

Water and Emotion

Water is the element of emotions and feelings. Qualities such as intuition, compassion, empathy, sympathy, devotion, aspiration, intention, appreciation, integrity, harmony, beauty, balance, serenity, fluidity, grief, apathy, joy, and love all have a different kind of watery feel. Think of the different ways water moves. It can be like the tumultuous tumbling of a waterfall or the stillness of a stagnant pond. The magic of water is involved with pleasure, friendship, marriage, fertility, happiness, healing, sleep, dreaming, psychic acts, and purification. If you are facing any sort of life problem in any of these areas, working with water can help.

Just the same as water itself, emotions are best dealt with if they are allowed to simply flow on their own. When you call upon water in your rituals, you will find that it has a smooth, calming effect. Its energy is crisp, cool, and refreshing. Water tends to have an initial impact, and then it slowly dissipates. It has a ripple vibration that means its effects are lasting but can have a few waves here and there.

If you are using water to work with relationships, remember that it is a receptive element and is governed by the female aspect. Water is also a giving element, and it usually gives unconditionally. Any gift of love should come with no strings attached. Water teaches us to feel on an inner level, and this is why water is usually associated to intuition. Using this inner intuition almost always leads to success.

Drinking Water Ritual

You can do this easy ritual with your children, family members and friends. Place a glass of water on a table in your kitchen or dining room. Gently say to the water, "I love you," and "thank you." At the same time, visualize all the waters on Earth connecting with each other. Your love and thanks will be sent out to all the water on Earth through the water in the glass.

Place small notes or stickers saying "thank you" near your faucets and sources of water to remind you of the importance of expressing your gratitude to water. Each time you have a drink, bathe, water plants, wash laundry, or do anything involving water, give thanks for its availability and usefulness.

The water element can help you manifest what you want in life. Think of how water can help things pick up speed and flow. Before drinking a glass of water, write down a word that embodies something you are trying to manifest in your life, such as "success." Tape the word to the glass and focus intently on it, then drink the glass of water, imagining it filling you with the qualities of the word.

Household Water Ritual

While you are doing the dishes, washing vegetables before cooking, or washing your clothes in a sink, imagine your love and gratitude for water overflowing from your heart through your chest, shoulders, and arms, and going out through your hands into the water going down the drain pipe. Your vibration will go through the flow of water very easily into the drain, into the nearby rivers, and finally into the ocean. The vapor from the ocean will build clouds and then the water will fall down as rain onto various parts of the world. In this way, the energy of love and gratitude that originated from your heart will be transmitted all over the world through the water network. This is an easy ritual that you can do every day and every time you use water.

Group Water Blessings

Host a gathering of friends and family around a pond or a lake, or along a river or the seashore. Stand in a circle, holding hands, and say simple expressions of gratitude for the water. Remember that the power of prayer is proportional to the square of the number of people. What you give out, you will receive back. This is a great ritual to do for local bodies of water that need healing, but can also be extended to other places in need.

How about sending love and gratitude to the Jordan River to raise the vibration of water there? Many Israeli and Palestinian people are living along the river's banks. There is no border in the path of flowing water. People on both sides certainly drink the water originating from this river, and their bodies will be filled with the vibration of love and peace that you send.

Other areas of the world where wars and conflicts are continuing, such as the United States and Iraq, India and Pakistan, Afghanistan, nations in Africa, and so on, can all benefit from healing water prayers. Send love to the water where people are suffering from pain and sorrow. It will change into healing water, and everything and everybody will be filled with a vibration of love and harmony.

Alone or in a group, visualize that the vibration of love and gratitude is transmitting into the world's water as golden or silver light. Imagine that all of the waters of the world are clean, clear, and sparkling, making the whole planet shine brilliantly. When filled with the highest vibration of light, everything is healed and harmonized. Visualize the faces of all the people on Earth smiling. Then visualize the vibration overflowing like an endless fountain, reaching every part of the globe and healing the whole world.

Bathing Rituals

Water is the element of purification and can be a highly useful element to work with in solving everyday problems. If you've had a stressful day or you have pain in your body, you can use the water element to literally wash your pain and stress away. Just stand in the shower for several minutes and imagine all the pain, tension, anxiety, and strain leaving your body, and see the water carrying it all down the drain. The heat from warm water will also help melt away muscle tension.

Soaking in a bath can either help you purify and cleanse your aura or help draw in certain energies. For a purification bath, start with a clean tub. Fill it with warm water and add about two cups of sea salt. Swirl the water around counter-clockwise with your hand to dissolve the salt. If there is a particular issue you want to be freed of, focus on this while you imagine it dissipating and dissolving away with the salts. Soak in the tub for about twenty minutes, then pull the plug out. Stay in the tub while the water drains away completely, taking with it any negativity.

If you are trying to attract a mate or want to make yourself more beautiful, take a copper scrubber (often used in the kitchen) and rub down your body with it gently in circular motions while you are in the shower. Copper is the metal of Venus and is said to change your vibration so you can attract a lover.

Water Elements

You may also wish to call upon water's elementals and spirits in your rituals, or use its associations to enhance their effect.

Although water is technically clear, it is associated with shades of blue. Medium blue represents water used for healing physical conditions, such as increasing hydration. Deep blue is more attuned to mental and emotional aspects of water. Water that is blue-black has to do with spiritual matters, and is usually associated with the subconscious. Water can also take on shades of green, gray, or indigo, depending on your purpose. Use different colored glasses or pitchers, such as cobalt blue, to lend different moods to your water.

Any sort of receptacle can represent water, such as a chalice, cup, goblet, or cauldron. Mirrors, too, can represent water's reflective surface. But don't limit yourself to the usual household objects. Sinks, buckets, puddles, silver spoons, birdbaths, umbrellas, washing machines, garden hoses . . . anything associated with water can be turned into a magical tool. The sea, fog, or rain can all be used to perform water magic, too.

Many flora and fauna can be symbolically used to represent water. Exotic flowers such as water lilies, jasmine, gardenias, and roses, and the herbs yarrow, Irish moss, and sandalwood all complement water rituals. And of course the graceful willow is always found growing near water sources. All animals that live in the sea, including fish, whales, and dolphins, are obvious choices for water magic, but don't forget mythical creatures such as dragons, mermaids, naiads, and nymphs.

The zodiac signs of Scorpio, Cancer, and Pisces are all water signs, so conducting rituals during their months could add an extra boost to your desired effects.

Using stones such as aquamarine and amethyst, or the metals of mercury, silver, and copper (particularly in the form of an instrument such as a resonant bell) are all excellent choices for use in water magic.

Many water-magic rituals involve an object being tossed or placed in or on a body of water, like a penny in a fountain for a wish. The surrounding waters can charge up an object, such as a crystal placed in a bowl of water under the Full Moon, or can help to purify an object with a symbolic pouring away of the water afterwards.

How you use these elements is entirely up to you. You may choose to surround yourself with pictures of the flora or fauna, add food coloring to your bath, pour a glass of water from a silver pitcher, or any number of things to honor the role of water in your daily life. When your cup is full, have a drink in honor of life.

The Comfort of Ritual

by Cerridwen Iris Shea

Comfort. In the past few years, our definition of the word has changed. "Comfort" used to be most often found on the physical plane—300-thread-count sheets, designer clothes, things, things, things. In the aftermath of 9/11, the tsunami, the London bombings on 7/7, and Hurricane Katrina, comfort relies far more on emotional solace than physical.

We want and need to know that we matter. Not just to our immediate circle, but in the larger context of the world. Ritual helps us find that peace, that comfort, in ways that can last longer than the actual ritual itself. And in ways that allow us to take the comfort we achieve in ritual and enhance the world around us, thereby increasing the comfort of those around us.

The act of performing a ritual means that one takes specific and familiar steps in a considered sequence to achieve a desired result. Rituals gain meaning through repetition. Rituals that evoke specific emotions or feelings start triggering these feelings as the ritual starts, giving us a sense of security and place in the world. While one does not want the movements and words to ever become simple "muscle memory," the repetition of rites allows them to gain power over a period of time. No matter how many times the ritual is performed, rendering it mindfully is of vital importance to its success. The comfort found in the repetition adds to the mindfulness. The feeling of pleasure, serenity, and familiarity in the rite feeds its power.

Does that mean that you must craft a set of rituals and never deviate? Of course not. Because our lives and our spirits are in constant evolution, our rituals must grow and change along with them. Although that sounds like a contradiction of the previous paragraphs, it's not.

Traditions are set up to support rituals. Rituals fit in with specific paths. Even an eclectic practitioner has specific ways to cast a circle, call in the elements, and perform ritual. Experimenting with different types of ritual will allow you to find what works best for you. In your private, personal ritual work, you don't need to be defined by anyone else's ordinances. Even if you work with a group, you can create specific and personal rituals for your private work that answer to nothing but your own spirit.

In order to find what works for you, you need to read everything you possibly can, and experiment. Finding rituals that give you comfort takes time. There will be some ceremonies you try that won't feel right. They won't give you that inner sense of knowing that means you've found the ritual best matched to your spirit. The knowing starts in your gut, at the solar plexus chakra, and it radiates both up and down, filling you. It's an experience you can read about a hundred times, but it won't make any sense until you experience it.

Once you experience it, you'll want to write out the details of the ritual (hopefully, you've taken notes during all your explorations), so you can recreate it. Be aware that you will never recreate exactly that first experience. Because rituals are live, each one is unique, even if all the same steps are taken. You will find the rhythm of the right ritual, but nothing ever matches, exactly, the first time a particular ritual touches your soul. But within the context of the familiar, you will continue to make new discoveries. That's yet another comfort of ritual—a safe space in which to explore your spiritual goals.

Creating a book of rituals for esbats, sabbats, and specific needs will help in your growth. It gives you a touchstone, a place of sanctuary, and a foundation for your future work. As the world grows and changes, and as you grow and change, you will create more rituals to meet specific needs.

For instance, at the time of this writing, the devastation caused by Hurricane Katrina has created specific needs—not just for those immediately left bereft of home and family, but for everyone who watched while the government tried and failed to mount an adequate response. Creating rituals specific to this tragedy—to encompass humanity, healing, and, most importantly, actions for positive change so this type of aftermath never happens again in the wake of any other disaster—is vital to our survival as a species. The rituals created at the time of this writing will continue to grow and evolve and still be relevant by the time the article is published, and beyond. Finding comfort in ritual gives us the strength and courage to continue with our lives. Living in a state of fear and anger after a tragedy will eat you alive. You need to seek respite, to recharge, to step back and mull over creative and positive solutions, to do your part in making sure the tragedy is not repeated. By creating and performing specific rituals and garnering the comfort derived from them, you regain your sense of purpose and your strength. Then and only then can you take the action needed to create positive change.

Ritual gives you the time and place to connect specifically with the spirits that work most closely with you. It's not about kowtowing to them or begging them. It's about interaction, an exchange of energy. You are perfectly within your rights to question the fates, to question the angels, to ask for explanations. Ritual gives you a place of sanctuary to explore the myriad feelings that tangle you up and can trip you up—whether it's a tragedy on a global scale, or a tragedy on a personal one. And the personal pains are just as real and just as relevant as the global ones. Rituals don't need to be elaborate. The way you light a candle, the way you prepare a specific type of tea that you drink before meditation, the way you prepare yourself in the morning to meet the day—all of these actions can be ritualized, and utilized in a way to give you comfort. Comfort, in the spiritual sense, creates strength, and only with humane strength can we save and improve our planet. It is also a place to express gratitude, to give thanks for what does work, and to promote joy and love. The energy flows both ways. It's not about payment to spirit, it's about partnership with spirit.

The firmer your foundation, the more comfort you give and receive in the ritual process, the more strength you gain, and the more positive impact you can have on the world.

Emotional Wreck–
Or Empath?

by Edain McCoy

I remember with detailed clarity the winter night when I could no longer ignore the bothersome barrage of emotions I'd felt coming from other people every day of my life. Often these intruders were strangers, as was this elderly man who boarded our bus just before midnight on a cold night in Harlem.

In the memory I'm just seventeen, sitting in the back of a crosstown bus with some friends, on the first leg of our way back to a place in midtown where we could crash for the night. And as soon as this unknown gentleman sits down on one of the side-facing seats in the middle of the bus, the memory consists only of him. If I were an artist I could draw a picture of him, and the background of the bus, and the night-darkened neighborhood where he boarded.

He wore a white jacket, unzipped. It appeared thin, but underneath I could see a green-and-blue plaid flannel shirt and the evidence of a thermal undershirt at the collar. He carried a gun-metal gray lunch box, darkened and dinged from years of use.

What overwhelmed me most were the emotions I felt. They entered me, became part of me, and I could feel everything he was feeling. Emotions come to an empath in layers, just as if they are sprayed from a bottle of perfume. The top note was despair and resignation. Beneath that was resentment and a strong sense of loyalty. The bottom note was composed of the dead desires of youth and anger long since released.

Perhaps this old gentleman was depressed, knowing that he was again going to a job he hated, knowing he had no choice, and knowing that at this point in his life there would be no other choices. Did he have a wife? Grandchildren to spoil? Would he retire soon? Could he afford to retire? Or would he continue to work until his death?

Long-lost dreams hovered within, veiled by a consciousness that tried hard to suppress those plans and hopes of his youth. At seventeen I understood poverty, and I was aware of the decades of deep prejudice this African-American man had endured.

He sat with his eyes cast down at the floor under the empty side seat opposite him. I don't think he was aware of my fixed stare, but I could not disconnect from

the emotions bombarding me, and my eyes were part of how I read the messages he sent. If he did notice my intense gaze he was polite enough not to remark on my apparent rudeness. Then again, perhaps he was conditioned during the decades of Jim Crow not to raise his eyes to meet those of a strange white girl.

When the man got off at his stop I felt as if I breathed for the first time since I saw him. The source of the sorrowful feelings was out of my presence, but the power of his emotions had merged with mine so thoroughly that when my friends and I were back in midtown Manhattan, at a crowded coffee shop, my preoccupation was remarked upon by everyone. So I pretended to listen, laugh, and join in the conversation, but I was still emotionally bound to that elderly African-American man. To this day I wonder what happened during the remainder of his life.

From my earliest memories such emotions plagued me. I assumed they were normal and never understood why no one talked about them or, even stranger to me, why no one ever acted upon them. I could never be mean to the new kid in school, and to hear about a hurt or abused animal would haunt me for weeks. I couldn't understand why other people didn't immediately react when reading the emotional messages people sent. When I was as young as seven I could feel the effect of words on a third person, and cringed at things others said. Often I tried to smooth over situations where I knew words were escalating negative emotions, but the person doing the talking always seemed as clueless to my attempts as I was to his lack of empathy.

I was almost thirty before my Craft teacher and mentor asked me if I'd considered that I might be an empath. I knew what empathy was, but thought empaths were the creation of science fiction. Wrong! There are empathic people everywhere, and, my teacher told me, she believed that as people opened themselves to the awareness of other realities as they studied Paganism or New Age practices, they also opened their emotional centers. She told me I was a classic case. I was born with an empathic predilection. I'd carried it through to adulthood, and then Pagan practices had kept this channel open, perhaps even expanding it.

If she was correct, it would answer lots of old riddles.

She said only I could say for sure what I was and was not. She asked me a series of questions to consider instead of slapping a label on my forehead. I didn't have to think about them very long. They made it clear to me that I was an unshielded empath. Since that revelation twenty years ago I have developed a self-examination for my students to consider if they think they might be empaths. There are no right or wrong answers, but if you notice that your inner turmoil seems to come from other living beings and not fictional character and events, and not as much from objects (sensing emotions from objects is called psychometry, and this is another topic completely), then you may be able to pinpoint where you fall on the empath continuum.

1. Does a sad movie or television show stay with you emotionally all night?

2. Does a sad true story stay with you emotionally all night, or perhaps longer?

3. Do you feel you require more solitude than others to remain healthy and balanced?

4. Do you prefer nighttime to daytime?

5. Do you work with the public on a regular basis and, if so, how do you handle upset, angry, or frightened customers?

6. Are you comfortable in old homes or antique stores?

7. Does the way you feel about a person influence the way you feel about any gift he or she may give you?

8. Do you feel as if you're being watched even when others say you're imagining things or call you paranoid?

9. Do you act on feelings of fear, regardless of what others do, only to discover you were correct because you were sensing the emotions of someone out to do harm?

10. Do friends and family members trust your instincts about who, what, and where is safe?

11. How long does it take you to "shake off the day" when you finish working?

12. Do you have a history of making friends with the annoying person no one else wants around?

13. Do you find it hard to say "no" when people or organizations ask for extra help, even when you are struggling to carry your own load?

If you're an empath, the answers to these questions probably came with ease and perhaps specific examples. Empaths feel no fear from most objects, but will pick up on dangerous intentions in other people. They often prefer nighttime to daytime because there are fewer people awake and about to bombard the unprotected empath with emotional chaos. Solitude is a necessity so the empath can ground and reenergize. They find it hard to say no to anyone or anything, and always feel sorry for the "odd person out." They will end up adopting the friendless because they can't stand to feel the pain from someone else's loneliness. Sad movies or television shows affect them as they would anyone else—after all, it's only fiction—but the true stories of atrocities wrought on other living creatures is a negative energy that works its way into the solar plexus and begins to feast on the emotional pain.

So how does an empath ward himself from this daily bombardment of random emotions without warding out his compassion?

Start by identifying your hot spots—the times when you feel that kick in the solar plexus or in the stomach. These are two of the body's most earthy and emotion-centered chakras, energy centers on the body that allow specific energies to move in and out of us. The term "kick in the gut" has a telling history.

Once you identify your hot spots, you can prepare for them ahead of time, and protect your own emotional health and well being without losing your compassion or your ability to read emotions. You must find a way of controlling them rather than allowing them to spin your life out of control when they hit. For empaths these hits are daily and multiple kicks in the gut.

The seven major chakra centers on the body can be controlled by your will and visualization. You may have to begin doing this in a meditative state of mind, but with practice you can raise your shields as soon as you know you need them. When you feel the emotional bombardment, visualize the chaos being channeled upward into the throat, third eye (center of forehead), or crown chakra. These chakras—the latter two in particular—are connected to spirit, thought, and reason. Pulling the emotional turmoil upward will allow you to sort through these feelings rationally. This puts you in a position to apply rational objectivity rather than knee-jerk subjectivity to your emotional reactions to other's emotional chaos. This is an excellent technique if you're not sure what to focus on and what to let go.

Chakras can also be closed, open, or somewhere in between. While prevailing opinion is that they should be more open than closed, and all in equal proportions, this is not good advice for an empath. (If you have someone do a chakra balancing for you, be sure to let that person know you're empathic.) The empath needs the solar plexus and navel area chakras more closed than open. You want to be able to feel and remain a person of compassion, but you also want to filter out the overload.

You may also need to clear your home and work areas of clutter. Some people thrive in an environment of knickknacks and family photos, others feel jittery. Just the sight of all these things causes an emotional overload.

The same advice applies to the people in your life. If you have a person who is always living from crisis to crisis, and always comes to you for help, you must wean this person away from dependence on you. Some people love to live this way, some for the attention, others because they need some intervention to get them on a normal life-track.

The mental image of a battle shield, an egg of light, a multifaceted mirror ball, or a warning ax or blade are also images you can employ in your defense. These are good techniques for those who work daily with the public and are the scapegoat for other's anger, verbal abuse, frustration, and need to bully someone.

To avoid taking home any of the emotional mess you have collected during the work day, use each step as you walk to your car, bus, or train as a method of grounding. As each foot hits the pavement, visualize the unwanted emotions of the day sinking into the ground where Mother Earth will cleanse them and keep them far away from you.

Wearing protective jewelry is another popular method of blocking or collecting unwanted energies from others. A clean quartz crystal worn around your neck and settled against your heart center can be empowered as an emotion catcher. Allow it to take the brunt of the negative emotions each day and cleanse it again at night by running it under cool water and visualizing the negative energies being cleared and drained away.

As you experiment with what works best for you in the emotional warding department, you'll eventually stumble upon a method or combination of methods that works for you. Best of all, you'll notice yourself feeling healthier and more energetic as time goes by and you gain expertise in dodging or blocking both the random and the focused emotional debris of others.

Coping with Grief and Loss

by Chandra Moira Beal

The loss of a friend or loved one is among the most traumatic events that a person can experience. The emotions of grief and the grieving process are painful, but they are natural, expected, and necessary parts of healing and recovery. There is no one way and no right or wrong way to grieve, and there is no schedule or deadline for the resolution of and recovery from loss. Everybody grieves and incorporates the experience of a loss in his or her own way. Nevertheless, many bereaved persons share some common feelings and reactions.

The Grieving Process

Grief has long been broken down into stages. One cycle made famous by psychiatrist Elizabeth Kübler-Ross, author of *On Death and Dying*, uses the stages of denial, anger, bargaining, depression, and acceptance. But modern researchers have shown that specific stages don't always apply to the grief process. Some people suffer interminable grief, while others show no distress at all.

The recovery period can also vary widely—particularly for those who suffered an abrupt loss. When a person dies suddenly, the mourner learns the reality of her loss by having the need for the loved one repeatedly frustrated. These people may enter a state of shock that delays recovery, often for extended lengths of time.

When confronted with death, many people at first feel shocked and numb and can't quite believe what has happened. This is often followed by protest. Many times this manifests as anger, but it can be continued denial and refusal to accept the reality of the situation. This brings with it the risk of taking quick, inappropriate action.

Our lives may feel completely disrupted following a death. We might retreat to less mature behavior, or feel more dependent on others. Concentration is disrupted while memory suffers, and this makes the routine tasks of daily living difficult.

When acceptance eventually comes, life slowly returns to normal, but it is a "new normal" and may require a long period of adjustment.

It is important to understand that the resulting confusion and all of the feelings that appear after suffering a loss—sadness, anger, fear, or frustration—are normal and expected. Acknowledging this fact is helpful because it enables us to talk to others about our distress, and talking stimulates the healing process.

Grief is not a linear process, but is often experienced in cycles. It may help to think of it as a spiral movement: while some people move through different phases one after the other, others seem to take one step forward and two steps back, or experience a multitude of feelings simultaneously. They may feel relief one moment, and denial and anger the next, for example.

Men and women grieve differently, too. While women tend to talk and cry, men will react by thinking and acting. For example, men often mourn the death of their fathers by taking action, such as taking up a skill that their fathers practiced or embarking on a project to memorialize them.

It is important to remember that grief doesn't necessarily have to come from physical death. Loss can be experienced when family members leave home, with a change in neighborhoods, when retiring or being laid off from a job, from becoming disabled, with changes in financial states, or with divorce or separation. Sometimes we do not realize that grief comes from loss in our lives related to many things.

Factors That May Complicate Grieving

Sometimes other circumstances affect the grieving process and the responses of the bereaved. These include the age of the deceased and the circumstances of death, whether the loss was sudden or expected, and the cause of death—particularly if violence was involved (e.g. suicide, disaster, crime, etc.).

The nature and quality of the relationship between the deceased and the bereaved person is important, too. Earlier unresolved losses, whether occurring through death, parental divorce, or broken relationships, for example, may also complicate an individual's recovery. Death is often a time when old, unresolved interpersonal conflicts resurface, but death also offers a blessed opportunity for healing rifts and seeking forgiveness.

Taking Care of Yourself

Be sure you seek the support of others. Gathering and using social support is essential to recovery. It reduces the feelings of isolation and loneliness and increases one's sense of security, safety, and attachment. Talk to friends openly about your loss. Learn about the grieving process so you understand the phases you are going through.

Participate in rituals to say goodbye. Ceremonies and rituals help us to make the "unreal" more real and to move toward accepting and integrating our loss. Attend the funeral or memorial service. Mark important anniversaries in ways that are meaningful to you.

Care for yourself physically. Make sure you get adequate rest, nutrition, and exercise. Indulge in comfort foods. Go for a walk in nature and get some fresh air.

Care for yourself emotionally. Give yourself permission to grieve. Allow quiet time alone to reflect and to explore and experience your thoughts and feelings. Allow time to heal without setting unrealistic goals and deadlines. Delay making major decisions or changes in your life.

Express your feelings. Allow opportunities to express the full range of your emotions, such as journaling or drawing pictures. You may express sadness, but perhaps also fear, guilt, anger, resentment, and relief. Avoiding your emotions through excessive activity, denial, or abuse of controlled substances only complicates and prolongs the pain of loss.

Consider seeking professional help. Most communities offer free individual counseling, support groups and workshops on grief. Look in your local telephone book or public library for resources.

Helping Others Grieve

Most people feel at a loss as to what to say to a friend who's recently lost someone to death. You can simply invite him to talk if he wants. He may need to tell the death story over and over; it is a tool for him to process the loss. If it is appropriate and he will allow it, try gently touching or holding him, because touch helps to reaffirm that we are alive.

The time of a loved one's dying is not the time to advance your own spiritual agenda—or any other kind of agenda, for that matter. Keep in mind that everyone suffers the pain of loss in his own way. It is of utmost importance that we respect the feelings and faith traditions of everyone involved in a death. Don't force your method of grieving on the other person. Respect what the person wants.

Remember that grief has no timetable, and avoid minimizing the loss. It is unkind to say to someone in mourning, "It's been a year now; it's time for you to stop crying and get on with your life." Never tell someone to "get over it" or offer false cheer. And if anyone says such a thing to you, disregard it. Grief is an individual process that takes as long as it takes. Our grief should be respected, and each of us should be allowed time to experience and process our loss.

Be a good listener. Allow the bereaved person to vent her feelings, knowing that you can't solve the problem. Don't judge the person's thoughts or feelings, or feel you need to offer advice. Listening in itself is very powerful.

Be present. Simply make yourself available to the mourner. Call, stop by to talk, share a meal. Your companionship is important.

Take some action. Send a card, write a note, call. This is important not just immediately after the loss, but especially later, when grief is still intense but when others have resumed their daily lives and support for the bereaved may dwindle.

Encourage self care. Remind your friend to care for herself physically, emotionally, and socially. Encourage her to seek out support or professional help, if appropriate.

Accept your own limitations. You cannot eliminate the pain your friend is experiencing. Grief is a natural, expected response to loss and each person must work through it in her own way and at her own pace.

Ways to Memorialize Loved Ones

Build an Altar

One ritual in which survivors can usually collaborate, with the potential for solace to all, is to build an altar in memory of the deceased. Using photographs of the loved one, his or her jewelry or other belongings, favorite flowers or plants, favorite foods, and your collective creativity, survivors can honor and celebrate the life of the person whose loss you all mourn.

Tell Stories

Another way to include all mourners of any faith tradition in the rites in your loved one's honor is to provide the opportunity for everyone who wishes to share personal stories about the beloved. Try using the "talking stick" method where you pass around an object that belonged to the deceased, such as a trowel if she had been a gardener in life, a baseball mitt if he played baseball, a wooden spoon if your deceased loved to cook, or even a lock of her hair.

To give everyone an opportunity to speak, explain the process and suggest a time limit. Have plenty of tissues available, as these intimate stories often elicit tears. Another way to do this is to open the dais, pulpit, or speaker's stand to people who may come up as they are moved to speak. Because those close to the deceased often don't remember what has been said at a ceremony, providing a book where people can write down their memories can bring comfort to others later.

Samhain

October 31 is Samhain, the night when the veil that divides our world from the netherworld is thinnest. Since ancient times, Halloween has represented the turning of the yearly cycle from death to rebirth. The dead could, if they wished, return to the land of the living for this one night, to celebrate with their families. This offers yet another opportunity to mourn the dead—this time collectively rather than individually.

Rituals for Moon and Earth

by Lily Gardner

In a time of date planners, multi-tasking, and countless habits for effective people, Pagans around the country are taking a deep breath and turning to the Moon, mankind's oldest timekeeper. Moon worship is the celebration of the lunar phases of decline and growth, of rest and hard work, and of shedding and initiating.

The Four Quarters of the Moon

The first phase of the Moon is the Dark Moon, the three days between the waxing and waning Moon where she remains hidden from us. The middle day of the Dark Moon is technically when the New Moon rises. Meditation and divination are especially powerful during the Dark Moon.

When the New Moon rises, state your intention for the month. This can be based on your heart's desire or on what was revealed to you through divination. Make a prayer tie by cutting a small square of silver cloth. Place in the cloth an offering to the Triple Goddess and a slip of paper with your written intention. Fold the cloth into a small bundle and tie with a silver ribbon. Your prayer tie can rest on your altar or hang on a tree branch.

Make sure to note in your journal the night you first glimpse the New Moon crescent. You should be able to spot it just before it sets in the west the night following the New Moon. Persephone, embodying the maiden energy, rules from the waxing crescent Moon to the Full Moon. Use her vitality to empower your intentions. Intellectually and emotionally, this is a time of growth. Make a point to take a moonlight walk on the night of the first-quarter Moon and write a lunar haiku.

The Full Moon energy traditionally extends for three nights: the night before, the night of and the night after the Full Moon. The Full Moon rises just after sunset in the astrological sign opposite the sun. Demeter, the mother, reigns during the Full Moon. The mother energy is that of fulfillment. The night of the Full Moon is the most magical night of the month. Cast spells, write a Moon poem, drink, dance, and make love. It is said that wishes made

on the Full Moon come true. The Full Moon is the time to consecrate waters used for ritual, to cleanse magical tools, and to empower crystals used for healing and divination. It is an excellent time to throw a tarot spread or to scry. Use your Moon mirror, a crystal ball, or a cauldron filled with spring water.

Hecate, the crone goddess, governs activities during the waning Moon. The waning Moon energies are a powerful time of the month to cast spells of protection and to rid yourself of everything no longer useful, be they bad habits, outworn ways of thinking, or the physical clutter that clogs many of our lives.

Hecate is called the queen of the Witches. Many believe that she is the most powerful of all the goddesses. This is to say that the powers of the waning Moon are as transformational as those of the waxing and Full Moon. The energies we employ to clean our psychic house will have much to do with the success of all our other magical workings. The waning Moon is when gardeners plant their trees and perennials because the energies of the waning Moon go into the roots of the plant. This is the time in our workings to concentrate on long-term plans and to attend to the foundations of our magical practice. Honor Hecate on the night of the fourth-quarter Moon. This Moon rises at midnight. If you hear the sound of dogs barking, she has answered your prayers.

Use these energies of waxing and waning as you cycle around the Wheel of the Year.

Spring

Spring is a time of great fertility and energy, a time to ask blessing for your seeds, a time to plant early vegetables and flowers, to clean closets, to take long walks and write poetry.

Spring is the domain of the element of air. Incense, feathers, bubbles, kites, and origami birds are all objects that you can use in spring rituals. As it relates to the Witches' pyramid, spring is the time of knowing. The ability to visualize is tantamount in magical workings of any kind.

Meditate for at least half an hour during the Dark Moon. Focus on your breath. When thoughts arise, let them slip away and return to your breath. At the end of your meditation, scry into your sacred bowl of water or your crystal ball. Write in your Moon book any impressions that you received during this time.

Greet the Moon on the night of the New Moon crescent. Stand in her pale light and absorb the lunar energies. At this powerful time of the month, what thoughts or feelings arise as you gaze at her? What do you wish to manifest this year? Is it a new business, a thriving garden, or a new love affair? Burn a pale yellow candle to honor Persephone. On a sheet of fine white paper, write down your desire in the form of an affirmation. The act of writing is bringing your desire from the realm of thought into the world of action. Writing affirmations is a powerful form of air magic. Affirmations are positive "present tense" statements. An example would be: "My new business has a positive cash flow." Write this statement over and over until it becomes a mantra for you. Repeat this ritual on the night of the waxing Moon.

The Full Moons in spring are February's Snow Moon, March's Hare Moon and April's Seed Moon.

On the day of the Full Moon, take your written affirmations to the top of a building, a hill, or

a mountain. Fold them in the shape of paper air-
planes and sail them off into the air. On the night
of the Full Moon, as the energies turn from maiden
to mother, burn a red candle to honor Demeter.
Be sure to walk in the moonlight and once again
write your impressions and feelings in the form of a
poem. Bow to the Moon and make a wish.

As the spring Moon wanes, burn a black candle
to acknowledge Hecate, the crone. Write down in
your Moon book the negative habits or thought patterns that obstruct your stated desire. Write three
affirmations that change your negative habits into
positive traits. Visualize yourself with these new positive traits. How can you act on this change?

The waning Moon is the perfect time to clear
your house of outworn clothing, furnishings, and
paperwork. Use the waning spring Moons to perform house blessings.

Summer

Summer is a time of great sexual energy. Birds and
animals bear their young, bees pollinate the blossoms,
people shed their clothes and bathe in the sunshine.
Play is another important component of summer. It is
the best way we over-worked adults can love ourselves.

Summer dwells within the element of fire. The
summer months are best for love magic and for creativity spells. Use symbols that correspond with what
you wish to manifest in these areas. If possible, conduct your summer rituals outdoors. Build a small
fire. Hold seeds in your dominant hand and state
your need. Toss the seed into the fire and watch your
desires transformed by the flames. Fire is the catalyst
for transformation. As it relates to the Witches' pyra-

mid, summer is the place of will. Will is the force that brings thought into being.

The summer Full Moons are May's Pink Moon, the Strawberry Moon in June, and the Mead Moon in July. Take a Full Moon walk and write down your impressions. Take a red candle outdoors, make your wish, and jump the candle. Please be cautious when using fire magic so you don't burn yourself.

Have you given yourself time to recreate? Play opens up a clear channel to creativity.

Autumn

Sunlight diminishes, and the leaves turn gold and scarlet and fall to the earth. Apples, nuts, and vegetables ripen and are harvested. Autumn is a time of harvest, gratitude, ripeness, and, finally, decline.

Autumn is ruled by the element of water. Seashells, mirrors, coral, pearls, fish, and water plants represent the element. This is the time of daring in the Witches' pyramid. Water rules our emotions. The Moon's influence over us during this season is especially potent.

In the early evening, you will notice the first Moon crescent setting in the west. Note how your feelings differ from the spring and summer months. The autumn is an especially emotional time. Some people experience excitement at the visible change, while others experience depression as they observe nature in decline. How do you experience this change? Write a haiku that explores your feelings.

Burn a pale blue candle to honor Persephone, who has descended to the underworld. This is a time of thanksgiving. The practice of gratitude and its twin, generosity, is often overlooked in our daily

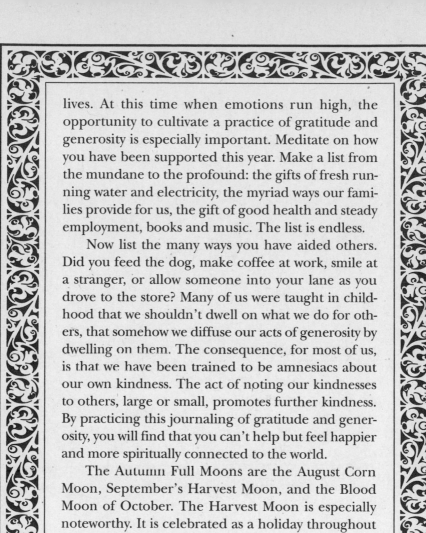

lives. At this time when emotions run high, the opportunity to cultivate a practice of gratitude and generosity is especially important. Meditate on how you have been supported this year. Make a list from the mundane to the profound: the gifts of fresh running water and electricity, the myriad ways our families provide for us, the gift of good health and steady employment, books and music. The list is endless.

Now list the many ways you have aided others. Did you feed the dog, make coffee at work, smile at a stranger, or allow someone into your lane as you drove to the store? Many of us were taught in childhood that we shouldn't dwell on what we do for others, that somehow we diffuse our acts of generosity by dwelling on them. The consequence, for most of us, is that we have been trained to be amnesiacs about our own kindness. The act of noting our kindnesses to others, large or small, promotes further kindness. By practicing this journaling of gratitude and generosity, you will find that you can't help but feel happier and more spiritually connected to the world.

The Autumn Full Moons are the August Corn Moon, September's Harvest Moon, and the Blood Moon of October. The Harvest Moon is especially noteworthy. It is celebrated as a holiday throughout Asia with Full Moon parties, special Moon cakes, and lunar poetry.

On the nights of the Full Moons, burn a red candle to honor Demeter. This is a special time to give her thanks for the bounty you have received through the year. Has your garden thrived, has your business done well, have you found a lover or completed courses of study? In ancient times, people brought loaves of bread and jars of wine and beer to their altars to give thanks. Use this same principle when you decorate your altar for Thanksgiving.

During the waning Moon, write those habits you wish to rid yourself of on leaves and float them down the river. This is also the perfect time to clean your house of the clutter that no longer serves you. Bless all that you wish to give away so that its new owners will find it useful.

Winter

Winter is a time of rest and dreaming. It's a good time to read, make soups, and burn candles. Earth is winter's element. Earth energies are those of the physical plane: soil, fields, mountains, deserts, and everything that grows. Many say that earth magic is the most potent of all because it manifests those things we wish to bring into the world. This is the time of silence, the fourth corner of the Witches' pyramid.

During the Dark Moons of winter, give yourself extra time to meditate. These months of winter are the time to review the last year. There is much to consider: have the needs you felt so strongly last year been met and are they still important to you? What do you envision for the New Year? Use the tarot as a tool to help you determine areas of your life that you wish to change. Make your prayer ties based on your findings.

Light a pale green candle on the night of the winter crescent Moon. Use Persephone's maiden energies while you dream of new beginnings. Write winter poems to the waxing Moon on the nights of the crescent New Moon and the waxing half Moon. Begin a new lunar journal on the night of the January New Moon.

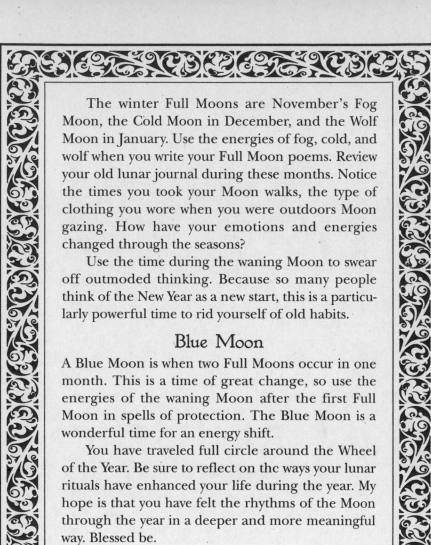

The winter Full Moons are November's Fog Moon, the Cold Moon in December, and the Wolf Moon in January. Use the energies of fog, cold, and wolf when you write your Full Moon poems. Review your old lunar journal during these months. Notice the times you took your Moon walks, the type of clothing you wore when you were outdoors Moon gazing. How have your emotions and energies changed through the seasons?

Use the time during the waning Moon to swear off outmoded thinking. Because so many people think of the New Year as a new start, this is a particularly powerful time to rid yourself of old habits.

Blue Moon

A Blue Moon is when two Full Moons occur in one month. This is a time of great change, so use the energies of the waning Moon after the first Full Moon in spells of protection. The Blue Moon is a wonderful time for an energy shift.

You have traveled full circle around the Wheel of the Year. Be sure to reflect on the ways your lunar rituals have enhanced your life during the year. My hope is that you have felt the rhythms of the Moon through the year in a deeper and more meaningful way. Blessed be.

Magical Baths

by ilspeth

While working in a little botanical shop several years ago, I learned from the owner as he prepared magical baths and bottled them for his customers. Being predisposed to "Kitchen Witchcraftikin," as my husband calls it, I was making my own in no time.

Magical baths can be used alone or with a spell. When used alone, the bath becomes the work, while in spellwork, a ritual bath will prepare you physically and spiritually for your spell. I usually prepare my baths at night—I find it easier to focus that way, and it makes for an enjoyable evening of magic.

For the four methods I recommend, you'll need a slow cooker or large pot (preferably ceramic or glass), a large bowl (or two bowls, depending on your method), a lid, a knife, cheesecloth or a fine strainer, twine, herbs selected for your goal, and the purest water available. Cleanse your tools with sea salt before beginning your work.

Sun Method

Fill your container half full of water and add the herbs, breaking or cutting them to the appropriate size. Cover the herbs with more water and cover the container with a glass lid. Place the container in a sunny area for the better part of a day.

Stovetop Method 1

Fill your pot half full of water and add the herbs. Add more water to fill the pot, cover with a lid, and heat to near boiling. As soon as the water begins to bubble, remove the pot from the heat and let the contents steep for several hours.

Stovetop Method 2

Place your herbs into a ceramic bowl. Pour boiling water over the herbs and cover the bowl with a glass lid. Leave this to steep for several hours.

Slow Cooker Method

This is the method I use most often. Fill the ceramic insert half full of water. Add your herbs and cover with more water. Place the lid on top of the cooker and turn the heat to the lowest setting. Leave the cooker to slowly steep the herbs most of the day.

If you are working indoors, your home will fill with the aroma. This is one of my favorite parts of the process. Light candles and listen to music, read a book that corresponds with your goal, or even write out your spell on parchment. Everything you do during the creation of your bath can become part of the magic itself, if only you decide.

When the herbal water has turned a deep, dark color like a strong tea, it is ready. The next step is to strain the herbs from the water. Stretch cheesecloth over a large bowl and secure it with twine, or use a strainer fitted across the top of the bowl. Carefully pour your infusion into the bowl through the cheesecloth or strainer.

When I use a cloth, I untie it from the bowl after straining the herbs and squeeze out every drop of liquid I can before burying the herbs in the yard. (If you do not have a yard, you can bury them in a flowerpot.) Nothing negative is being created here, so burying the herbs in a flowerpot or garden will just give them magical compost. Please don't toss them into the trash. To me, that shows disrespect for the herbs and the properties you obtained from them. You can store your infusion in the refrigerator for a few days, but it will sour quickly.

Using Your Magical Bath

Prepare a sacred space in your bathroom before you take your bath. (If you do not have a bathtub, you can pour the herbal water over your head in the shower.) Be sure to have a clean and tidy environment, so scour that tub and clean the floor. A cozy robe and a fluffy towel are also recommended.

Place candles wherever you desire, and perhaps set up a small altar on a table beside the tub. Music is usually a good thing, so if you won't be able to hear your stereo while you're in the bath, consider bringing a CD player into the bathroom to help set the mood. Burn a smudge stick in the room to cleanse out all negativity, and seal the room. This might mean that you are restricted to having your ritual bath at night after everyone is asleep, but many times that is best anyway.

Take a shower or a bath to become physically clean. Drain the tub and rinse it out. Next, fill your tub with comfortably hot water and settle in. Pour the magical bath into the tub, making sure to warm it first if it has been in the refrigerator—the last thing you want is the shock of chilly liquid poured into your bath! Swoosh the water around, blending it well with the herbal infusion. Visualize your goal and see it in everything you do. Know that the properties in this bath are assisting you in your outcome.

If your goal is spiritual cleansing of negativity or physical healing, visualize the bath drawing out impurities and rendering them benign. The longer you soak, the more you remove. It is important that you submerge your head at least once. If this is not possible, use the bowl that contained the concentrated bath to pour the water over your head. Lay back, relax, and enjoy your sacred space. This is an ideal time for meditation.

When your work is finished, pull the plug and stay in the tub as the water drains. The heaviness that you feel as the water drains away is the perfect, relaxing peace that results from a successful endeavor. If it is difficult to force yourself to get out of the bathtub, then stay for a while! Enjoy your sacred space until you are ready to leave.

After your bath is complete, dry with your fluffy towel and don your cozy robe. Leave any ritual candles to burn out or remove them to another sacred space if they will take more than the evening to finish. You skin will be scented with the herbs, and this is another way the bath reinforces any work. The scent becomes another element of your work as it helps you to retain focus.

If the bath was your work in whole, clear your sacred space and have a wonderful night's rest. Vivid dreams are common afterward, so you may want to keep a dream journal beside your bed. If you have used your bath in preparation for a larger work, you can proceed with the rejuvenation and empowerment obtained from the simple magical bath.

Spiritually Social:
A Guide For Sticky Situations

by Tammy Sullivan

We've all been there. Someone at a party tells an off-color joke, and as everyone around us laughs, we are horrified. At times like this it can seem like the rest of the world just doesn't quite "get it." The joke offends all of our sensibilities—due in no small part to our spiritual path. As practicing Witches, we understand the world on a deeper level. We work hard to eliminate such cruelties and disrespectful practices from our world. We purposely rip ourselves to shreds in order to reach deep down inside and remove all hints of such barbarism. It can be shocking to encounter hostility disguised as a joke.

How best to respond to such a situation? Is there a solution that will not embarrass ourselves, or our host, and yet will allow others to see that we are firmly against this sort of talk? Yes, but keep in mind that the solutions presented here are simple and polite ways of dealing with sticky social situations. Your mileage may vary.

When faced with the obscene joke you can simply cast your eyes down and lower your head. Allow your expression to show that you are hurt and disappointed by the remarks. Do not laugh politely or even smile. You may notice that those who did laugh will be quickly embarrassed by it once they see your bowed head. Good. Maybe next time they will think twice. There is nothing funny about prejudice, cruelty, or hatred.

While the sort of passive response suggested might not be your usual reaction to such a joke, when you are a guest you must make every effort to remember your host. The four key words of etiquette are respect, kindness, consideration, and honesty. You should uphold these responsibilities not only for the host, but also for the person who told the joke, for yourself, and for the unfortunate soul who served as the punch line.

What if you personally are a target due to your spiritual practice? Perhaps you are at a perfectly lovely cocktail party and overhear someone talking about asking you to turn someone else into a toad. What then? Well, a lighthearted laugh can go a long way when you are targeted personally. Combine it with an off-hand remark like, "Oh, I think the world has quite enough toads. Don't you?" Don't forget to dazzle them with a smile. Clearly, they were exceptionally rude to tease someone as wonderful as you. Believe me, your host will thank you for your tolerance and polite responses. But there is a fine line between being polite and being a doormat: don't just ignore disrespectful remarks; respond carefully, but respond nonetheless.

Others are always interested in our religion. There is so much misinformation bandied about that people are frequently confused about what our practice actually entails. Educating even one of them is a task worthy of reward, but best avoided at a social gathering. Emotions run hot when it comes to religious debate and to avoid such a potentially heated discussion, abide by the "golden rule" of etiquette: no discussions of religion or politics.

If you are asked directly about your religion, it's best to keep your responses short. A simple statement of "I am Wiccan" is perfect. There is no need to go into detail unless asked, and then answer only if you choose to do so. The statement of your faith alone can draw stares from non-Pagans, as if you had just announced something grotesque or highly personal. Instead of squirming in embarrassment when you find all eyes on you, simply smile.

You do not ever have to provide others with personal information. It is a social faux pas to ask personal questions, not to refuse to answer them. A girl I know had an odd situation in which a relative tried to "out" her during a coffee klatch. Luckily, the other person present was familiar with the concepts of Wicca and everything turned out okay. She never asked the relative her intentions, but from reading her tone of voice and body language she felt the point was an attempt to belittle her. How best to handle this type of situation if it happens to you? With humor, of course. Laugh and say, "Oh, I have a better one to tell about you!" and then proceed to tell a funny incident. There is no definite right way to handle it when someone tries to out you, but humor is a sure-fire way to get off the topic.

Unfortunately, at social gatherings you may also run into the type who feels it is his moral obligation to "save" you. This is a very sticky situation. It can easily put you in a defensive mode, which usually leads to a nasty outcome. The key to handling this type of conversation with grace is to keep in mind that often the other person's religion teaches that "saving" people is his duty. He is not necessarily trying to be obstinate, rather it is his fervent belief. Try a light smile and a response like, "I can see you mean what you say and I admire that you embrace your beliefs so tightly. Perhaps we should save this conversation for another time. It isn't appropriate right now." Do not excuse yourself right away; give the other person a chance to change the topic. If he continues with the religious talk, then excuse yourself as politely as you can. Keep in mind that most sticky situations come about because of one person talking too much. Don't be that person. Remember the verse "speak little, listen much" and let the other guy make the mistakes.

Particularly caring hosts will often invite other friends that share your faith in an effort to make you both feel more comfortable. Unfortunately, the Know-It-All Witch can be even harder to handle than the fundamentalist non-Pagan. Yes, she may have walked the path for decades, but it was her path. Unless you follow a strict tradition, you must walk your path. Spoon-fed religion can be smothering. We have to mold our philosophy to fit us personally in order for everything to make sense. Someone else's opinion should be regarded only as a jumping-off point to form your own—not as the absolute truth.

In a social setting, it's best to keep the conversation light. However, some Know-It-All Witches prefer to test your knowledge and will drill you with question after question. Worse, most times your answer won't suit them and you end up embarrassed and feeling the fool. Don't play this game. If you think you may have met a Know-It-All Witch and the questions start to fly, you can always excuse yourself. Clearing your throat and commenting on the hostess's beautiful new drapes will work, too. Remind yourself that your hostess meant well by caring enough to invite others with common interests. Refusing to get caught up in a test can be the only chance you have of obtaining the Know-It-All Witch's respect. It shows you are strong enough to put others first, and it takes quite a bit of strength not to argue.

What if you meet someone who expresses a genuine interest in the Craft at a party? Someone who pens you in a corner for hours with questions because he is sincerely weighing Wicca as an option for himself? Be polite, but firm, and respond that you can "talk shop" some other time, because tonight is a celebration. Suggest a particular book, and if he is truly interested he will read it. Remember that Wicca seeks no one—people seek Wicca. We are not out to convert anyone.

Remembering our host or hostess, friends, and family is critical to enjoying one's social life. If you concentrate only on pleasing yourself, before you know it you won't be invited anywhere. We may consider ourselves to be the enlightened ones, but we can't sit back and expect others to do as we do. It's like being the only vegetarian at a barbecue: you can't expect the other guests to go without ribs just because you only eat potato salad. Even the most eloquent of speeches about the positive points of vegetarianism won't keep barbecue sauce off those smiling faces. More than likely they won't understand what you are talking about and will think you are nuts for passing on such a feast.

Also, don't get hung up on discussing occult-related topics to the exclusion of all else at social gatherings. Chances are that you know much more about the topic than the other guests do. Not everyone is interested in ghosts, crystals, or herbal healing, and you will only

freak out the straights if you go on and on about the vibes of your new bloodstone or how you channeled a new spirit the other day. I'm not telling you not to be yourself, only that you choose wisely how much of yourself to share with those of different paths.

Another potentially sticky situation is prayer before meals at friendly dinner parties. Suppose your boss invites you to Thanksgiving dinner and a decidedly Christian atmosphere pervades. When everyone gathers at the table they hold hands and bow their heads. Your brain yells, "No! I pray when I choose and to whom I choose!"—but to say anything that may disrupt the prayer would be the height of rudeness, and this is your boss, after all.

The right to prayer is absolute. We never have to do it, and certainly not at anyone else's command. But we do have an obligation of silence and respect for others' beliefs. You do not have to bow your head or close your eyes. It is a good idea to participate in the handholding, though, out of respect for the act of prayer in general.

The final sticky situation is one I experienced with a member of my own family. A female relative of mine had never heard of Wicca before, and over the course of conversation one day my religious beliefs came up. When I said I was a Witch she told me she "didn't believe in Witches." I was stunned. She may as well have said she didn't believe in blondes (and I'm that, too). My natural response was, "Well, I'm sitting right here and I am one." She was not sure how to take that and excused herself. I could have handled that with a bit more grace and decorum. In all fairness, she had no idea that it was such an offensive statement because the only Witches she knew of were from the movies. It's important to keep your sense of humor when staring in the face of ignorance.

Love Magic and the Waning Moon

by Muse

In any type of magic, the phase of the Moon influences the energy. The Moon phase should be taken into consideration in the timing of your spells and rituals. Love magic is especially affected by the Moon. Love and the emotional, feminine energy of the Moon work together—or can work against each other if the intent of the spell and the phase of the Moon do not coincide.

During the waxing Moon, the Moon is growing from New to Full, increasing in size. This phase is the best time to do magic to draw energy, do a spell for growth, or begin new projects. The Full Moon is the end of this cycle, and is a very powerful time for positive/increasing magic. The energy of the Full Moon lasts three days—the day before, day of, and day after the technical Full Moon. However, the most powerful time is at the exact time of the Full Moon.

During the waning Moon, the Moon is going from Full to New, decreasing in size. This is the best phase to do magic for banishment, removal of obstacles, lessening of illnesses, and removing harm. The New Moon is at the end of this cycle and is the ideal time for banishing and removal spells.

So what is a Witch to do when the Moon is waning and she's in need of a little boost to her love life? Options abound! With a little creativity, a Witch cannot be held back from her work by inauspicious astrology.

Waning Moon Spells

The answer to casting a love spell during a waning Moon is often in a Witch's intentions. She must change the way she thinks about the focus of her spell to combat the potentially antagonistic Moon. Instead of focusing on drawing love, focus on banishing loneliness. The following is a spell you can use during the waning Moon to amplify your love life.

Banishing Loneliness

You'll need two candles—one red and one black. Get comfortable in your normal spellcasting environment, whether it be a full circle or a simple altar.

On your altar or in front of you in your circle, place the red candle on the left and the black candle on the right and light them. Close your eyes and meditate for a few minutes on your intention of banishing loneliness. When you feel your intentions are fully focused, open your eyes and raise your hands—left hand palm open to the red candle, and right hand palm open to the black candle.

Imagine you are drawing love in with your left hand from the red candle, and pushing your loneliness out with your right hand into the black candle. Repeat these words:

Loneliness leaves me
Loneliness is replaced by love
Love banishes my loneliness
Love brings me joy

Lower your hands, close your eyes, and meditate once again on your intention to banish loneliness.

Catching the Tail of the Full Moon

For the two nights surrounding the Full Moon, the energy of the Moon is not waning and not waxing. If you catch the Moon in this timeframe, you can cast a spell that would work best in the waxing phase and still draw the right energy from the Moon. The following is a spell that can be done at this time:

Candle Spell

You'll need one red taper or tall votive candle, rose oil, jasmine oil, and Dragon's blood oil (optional). To draw in the energy of love, anoint the red candle with the rose and jasmine oil from the tip and bottom inward toward the center:

I personally like to use a bit of dragon's blood oil as well. It acts as a catalyst, speeding up the spell.

At night before going to bed, light this candle. Sit in front of the candle after you have lit the wick, concentrate on finding love, and say this seven times:

As this candle burns
My heart yearns for love
Let the flame be a beacon
And let love find me here

Love Perfume

I love essential oils. I will wear an essential oil instead of perfume any day. It lasts longer, smells prettier, and carries with it a magic that is unique and irreplaceable. And the most wonderful thing about essential oil blends is you can wear them every day for every intention—they do not need the Moon's power to work; the plants from which the oils were derived have an energy all their own. However, keep in mind that if they are created during the waxing or Full Moon, they will have extra oomph. It would be a good idea to create these oils during the next waxing or Full Moon and keep them stored for later use. But again, the plants that these oils are derived from do have an energy all their own and will still draw the energy of love even if they are created during the waning Moon.

To make a sweet love oil, combine two parts rose oil, two parts jasmine oil, and one part vanilla oil. To make a passionate love oil, combine two parts rose oil with two parts strawberry oil and one part clove oil.

Charm Bags

Charm bags are another easy way to draw love energy during any phase of the Moon. As with oils, a waxing or Full Moon does give extra bang to these pouches if they are created during that time, but the waning Moon phase will not harm the intention or the energy of the items within.

I have had the most success using red or pink cloth pouches for this spell. You can buy one from your local new age supply store, or make one yourself using squares of pink or red cloth tied with a string. Keep these bags on you at all times during the day—around your neck or in your pocket is perfect.

Charm bag 1 (best for pink pouch)

Dried rose petals
One vanilla bean
A piece of rose quartz

Charm bag 2 (best for red pouch)

A piece of wax from a red candle
A piece of dried apple peel
A clear quartz crystal

Although these pouches have worked well for me, feel free to combine, mix, and match to create the pouch that works best for you. All ingredients blend well together.

Bouquets

There's nothing more delightful than a fresh bouquet of flowers in your home. But why wait for someone to buy them for you? This is just another opportunity to draw love no matter the phase of the Moon. Flowers are an ancient sign of love. Each flower has its own energy, and when brought into the home draws loving energy for several days.

Go to your local florist and put together your own bouquet from the recipes below, or use this section as a guide to find pre-made bouquets that have the intention you're after.

Love Bouquet

Roses
Daisies
Baby's breath

Love Bouquet 2

Lilies
Waxflowers

Passion Bouquet

Snapdragons
Irises
Asters

Happy Being Single Bouquet

Sunflowers

Baby's breath

Love is probably the number-one goal of magic. There are more books and websites dedicated to love magic than there are on almost every other subject. Love is important to each and every one of us, our entire lives. So it is no wonder that through the ages witches have found ways to circumvent the decreasing energy of the waning Moon in order to complete this very important magic. With the tools in this article, you should be able to get through the two weeks of the waning Moon with ease and draw love when your heart needs it most.

Word of caution: You must be careful when you do a love spell not to try to control the desires of another. It is easy to cross the line between drawing love and controlling another human being. When you focus on your goal of love during these spells, please focus only on your OWN love, and drawing an appropriate partner to fulfill your spiritual and emotional needs. Please do not focus on a specific man or woman! This crosses into the realm of controlling magic and breaks the "do as thou wilt, but harm none" rule. Remember, everything comes back to you three fold . . .

Good Night Anointing Oil

by Sybil Fogg

The night can be frightening for those youngest among us. It's filled with shadows, silence, and darkness. This combination has its way with children's minds until the silence is filled with whispers, shadows move with awkward gestures, and darkness hangs heavy overhead. Our imaginations can get carried away, especially after reading a horror novel or watching a suspenseful thriller. Children have the most potent minds of us all, and the slightest shift in the seasons brings darkness ever closer. Thus, nightmares are created.

One way to ease our little ones to sleep at night is with the aid of an anointing oil that will open up the mind's eye and fill the night with pleasant dreams. Using a blend of essential oils chosen for their sleep and protective properties in conjunction with magic words soothes a child's troubled dreamscape by chasing away scary images. They will see that, in fact, it is the part of the day when the Goddess is at her full strength. The same whispers become incantations, the movements we catch out of the corner of our eyes are entities from other realms come to assist our casting, and the darkness holds the secrets of the Goddess's womb. For the most effective results, the intended recipient should participate in the manufacture of the anointing oil.

Any combination of essential oils will work if the intention is there, but thought should be put into correspondences and into the number of different scents you combine. It is best to choose no more than three, so as not to create a blend that is working on too many levels and has lost its singular notes.

A peaceful sleep inducer that also works well in chasing away nightmares is a combination of amber, rose, and sandalwood. To protect the sleeper, combine juniper, pine, and sweet clover. For prophetic dreams try anise and honeysuckle. And if the intention is to settle an infant beset by colic or to soothe a stubborn toddler, a mixture of chamomile and lavender works wonders for the exhausted parent. Or better yet, bring out a collection of different oils that have been gathered according to their correspondences and allow the child to pick from them to make a truly individualized concoction. It is always useful to make a study of essential oils or keep a reference book handy because some can cause an allergic skin reaction—as I learned when my youngest daughter anointed herself with cinnamon and broke out in a blotchy rash that persisted for a few uncomfortable days.

Once the oils are chosen, think about the container that stores the potion. It is important to get the child's input if he or she is old enough. Any color bottle will work, but if the recipient wants a clear bottle, remember to keep the potion in a dark cabinet. Blue works well for its natural darkness as well as its sacredness to the Goddess. If the child in need is fond of faeries, green works well in all faerie magic. Amber colored-glass is good for grounding and earth energy. Keep in mind that the bottle should be glass, as many plastics let off pollutants when exposed to acidic liquids. It is unknown what effect this may have on the sleep potion, but as in all cases, it is best to not take any chances of contaminating the magic.

Glass bottles can be purchased at new age stores, most health-food markets, antique shops, flea markets, yard sales—pretty much anywhere. Interestingly designed bottles can also be found at the local dump or even occasionally stumbled upon during hikes and city walks. No matter where or how the bottle is acquired, it needs to be cleaned thoroughly and blessed with the four elements. One way to do this is by sprinkling the bottle with charged water and salt and then passing it through a candle flame and incense smoke. This is best done during a ritual designed specifically for this purpose, at the time when the oils are added. The best day for this is usually a Monday during a New Moon, because the intent is to create restful nights for everyone in the household. The Moon should be in Cancer, as this is the Moon's sign, and the Moon governs the night.

As you add each oil, speak words referring to the intent of the scent. These will have more potency if written and spoken by the child. If she is too young to do so, she can charge the bottle by either holding or touching it. The words need not be extravagant—simple one-sentence utterances will do, such as:

> *Amber give me love, comfort, and happiness while I sleep.*
> *Rose fill this room with love and blessings to ease my fears.*
> *Sandalwood take from me all negativity that haunts my night's journey and remind me that I walk not alone.*

Once the oils have been added, cap the bottle and store it until nighttime use. If the bottle is a dark color, tie a ribbon around the neck in the child's favorite color or choose one with an appropriate correspondence such as silver, white, or blue (all sacred to the Moon and the Goddess), green (to have the faeries watch over the child), pink (to draw love), or purple (for divinatory dreams). This way the potion can be hung from the bed for added protection each night. This should only be done if the child is old enough to not break the bottle or open it and ingest the contents.

If the family does not have a bedtime ritual, this would be a good time to construct one. Everyone will feel more unified if all partake in the creation of such a ritual, but it's not necessary. I started ours when my oldest was a baby and have carried it through for each of my children. It consists of bedtime stories, singing seasonal or holiday songs, and then tucking my little ones into bed and kissing them, stopping to snuggle for a few moments. After everyone is settled, dab the potion on your finger and anoint the child's third eye (the center of the forehead). This is a perfect time to say a spell that will be spoken every night. Again, these words will hold more strength if created with help from the child. If that's not possible, keep in mind that eventually he or she will be speaking with you, so keep the words simple enough to memorize. An easy rhyme helps.

Nighttime can be scary even for children being raised among those who walk the path of the Goddess. Educating our children about the importance of shadows, silence, and darkness is the best way to show them the opportunities the night holds. And for those who have nightmares or concerns when the lights are dimmed, a goodnight anointing oil will help them get the rest they need to carry them through their Sun-filled days, especially one created specifically for them and with their help.

> *Mother Goddess in the sky*
> *Please protect me where I lie.*
> *Father Sun, please use your light*
> *To safeguard my dreams tonight.*

Potions, Oils,
and Useful Brews

by Diana Rajchel

I often tell this story about my first love potion: While attending a microscopic college in Wisconsin, I lived in an 8 x 10 dorm room. At the time, the school offered no kitchen facilities in that dormitory, forcing me to improvise on my cooking and storage options. Between the rural isolation and my lack of transportation, I was often forced to stay in on weekends and find ways to entertain myself. One dull Saturday night I gathered a few things off my storage shelves and brewed a love potion in my hot pot. Lacking a better option, I stored the result in a used Dr. Pepper bottle.

I stashed this bottle in my fridge and forgot it for a week. The next weekend, as I was watching TV, I opened the fridge and grabbed a bottle without looking. I got a mouthful of my own potion. I swallowed it quickly (there was no sink to spit it out in and the whole point of lazing was not to move), made a face and got a proper bottle of soda to wash the horrendous taste from my mouth. Twenty minutes later, the person I had the most interest in at the time knocked on my door—shirt off, loopy as all get out, and trailing Twizzlers wherever he went. I insist my favorite part was the Twizzlers.

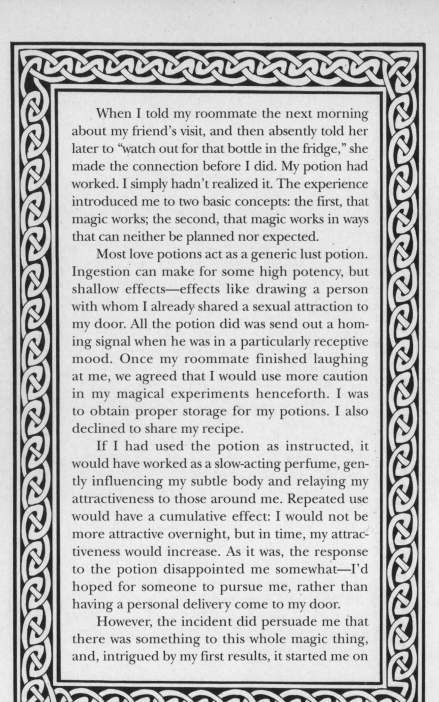

When I told my roommate the next morning about my friend's visit, and then absently told her later to "watch out for that bottle in the fridge," she made the connection before I did. My potion had worked. I simply hadn't realized it. The experience introduced me to two basic concepts: the first, that magic works; the second, that magic works in ways that can neither be planned nor expected.

Most love potions act as a generic lust potion. Ingestion can make for some high potency, but shallow effects—effects like drawing a person with whom I already shared a sexual attraction to my door. All the potion did was send out a homing signal when he was in a particularly receptive mood. Once my roommate finished laughing at me, we agreed that I would use more caution in my magical experiments henceforth. I was to obtain proper storage for my potions. I also declined to share my recipe.

If I had used the potion as instructed, it would have worked as a slow-acting perfume, gently influencing my subtle body and relaying my attractiveness to those around me. Repeated use would have a cumulative effect: I would not be more attractive overnight, but in time, my attractiveness would increase. As it was, the response to the potion disappointed me somewhat—I'd hoped for someone to pursue me, rather than having a personal delivery come to my door.

However, the incident did persuade me that there was something to this whole magic thing, and, intrigued by my first results, it started me on a path that I've been on for ten years. In those ten years, I was able to incorporate at long last my love of herbs and my never-ending curiosity about scents, mixes, and the possibilities of the human spirit. Suddenly water, oil, and cups of tea meant so much more.

Potions

Potions, like the one I mixed in my hot pot, are water-based herbal mixtures. Most are used as either libations or beverages. Potions may also be added to a bath, or can be worn as a perfume/body wash. A potion must be used very quickly from the time it is made: herbs mold easily, and even refrigeration and alcohol cannot stem the tide of bacterial growth. On more than one maddening occasion I brewed and bottled something wonderful, only to get a bottle of grey fuzz for my efforts. I certainly haven't perfected the art of potion-making, but I have learned a few tricks to reduce its potential as a sixth-grade science project.

First, when making a potion, always include a preservative in the mix. I prefer cheap vodka or gin. However, lots of people have reason not to use alcohol as a preservative. In that case, adding a fixative herb to the mix like benzoin or myrrh can head off bacterial growth. If you want to avoid any bitterness, honey also works well as an antiseptic and preservative.

Potions are always based in water, intended for quick or even immediate effect, and should be used in totality. Because most potions are applied to healing, they are ideally composed of edible material. The water-based nature also gives potions a homeopathic effect. A small amount, ingested or applied to the skin, has a big effect, whereas a large amount can eventually cancel itself out.

Potions blend the characteristics of select herbs into the medium of water. Water itself has its own magical associations, drawing upon depth, intuition, and emotion. By placing herbs with specific characteristics into water and then washing in it or drinking it, it acts upon the physical and subtle body together. Because of the subtlety, and because water flushes from the body so easily, potions act in the short term but do little in long-term magic.

But never mind that. Some of you readers want to know what that potion was that I used that got me my personal delivery. I won't lecture you on the ins and outs of love magic, but I still won't give you that. It's someone else's recipe to give away. I can, however, give you other recipes that have worked for me in other areas of my life, categorized by use and with ingredients you can find in a local occult shop or in your grocery store.

Teas

Teas are meant for drinking. Where possible, I proportioned herbs that taste good with those that, on their own, taste less than good. For instance, only the intrepid or the nerve damaged can really handle mullein by itself. Mullein in particular can have a potent sedative effect, and by itself it's very bitter. I recommend that you do NOT plan on going anywhere after taking this tea. You may also want to flavor it with plenty of honey or sugar.

To Calm

2 parts mugwort
1 part lavender
1 part mullein

For Clarity

2 parts peppermint
1 part citrus
1 part ginger

Serve hot or cold.

For the Common Cold

1 part rosehips, boil in water first
1 part coltsfoot
1 part sage
1 part mullein
1 part goldenseal
For flavor, add fennel or anise

Eat roast garlic at some point during treatment. If the roast garlic flavor bothers you, try garlic capsules, available at most grocery stores.

Bath Additives

Potions for the bath are generally mixed in a water base and then further diluted by pouring them into the bathwater. However, some prefer a stronger potency and will add enough herbs and sufficient time for the bath water to be the base for the potion. I am not so patient, and I generally can't afford enough herb to result in a tubful, so I resort to the water-based additive mix.

For Purification

1 part baking soda
1 part sea salt
A handful of lavender, peppermint, or rosemary

For a Romantic Evening

Add in equal parts: jasmine, rose, and hibiscus. Also add a pinch of sea salt, to carry the charge from your thoughts. Soak in the tub, and if possible submerge completely for a few seconds while thinking erotically about the evening to come.

Perfumes and Washes

Floor washes are potions to add to your usual mop water. Mop as normal—the solution should not interfere with your floor's general cleanliness, and it influences the energy of your apartment.

Anti-jinxing

¼ cup vinegar
One clove garlic
A piece of lemongrass
Juice of one lime

Let the garlic and lemongrass sit in the vinegar for one day. The following day, add it to your mopping water along with the juice of one lime.

Happy Home

A handful of rose petals
A pinch of sea salt
A handful of lavender
A handful of mint

Boil this as a tea (decoction). This promotes a feeling of calm throughout the home. If allergies interfere with any part of this, simply omit the offending ingredient.

Perfume To Draw Friends

Dilute some lemon juice into a pot of boiling water. Add to it one cardamom pod and a pinch of cinnamon. Bottle this in a glass bottle (allow it to cool before you cap it). Wash all your exposed skin in this before you go to a social occasion.

For Luck in Financial Transactions

Use this as a handwash before you go to the bank: Boil a High John the Conqueror root in a pot of water. Allow to cool, and bottle the water (bury the root). Wash your hands in the solution before you shake upon a new deal.

Offerings and Libations

Sometimes it's a good idea to make an offering to the fairy folk if you ever want to see your car keys again. When they make themselves known and I'm not able to access good mead, I've gone ahead and made up the following. While it's no replacement for quality honey-wine, it does in a pinch—but I'd better offer that mead as soon as I get it!

1 cup water
½ cup honey
A handful of violets
A handful of Queen of the Meadow
  leaf

Sprinkle a little in the corners, doorways, and windowsills of your home and finish by pouring the remainder across your doorstep. If you live in an apartment, sneak out some quiet evening and pour it in front of the entrance to your building.

A Potion for Tree Spirits

Once in a while, I've come across a tree that's been bled—meaning someone cut into it rather than tapping it properly, causing the sap to leak. Just like an unstaunched wound on a human being, if you cut a tree this way it will drain the life right out of it, and without proper treatment the tree will get an infection. I've mixed up the following when I've encountered such a crime:

In a pot of water, mix up the following: 1 part juniper berries, 1 part vervain, 3 bay leaves and, if possible, a few pine needles. Allow the mixture to cool to room temperature, then take the potion to the tree, and pour it over the injured part of the tree and pour the remainder on its roots. If you believe in the sentience of the plants, talking to the tree and reminding it of its nature will help (an old working partner once called it "remembering your roots"). Even if you don't believe in plant sentience, you might have trees and may find this handy for keeping them healthy.

Oils

Oils usually blend essential oils and, because of the preservative qualities of oil, can contain pieces of herbs with less (but still some) potential for the possibility of molding. Your chances of a moldy oil increase when you use herbs: if you have any moisture on your hands or in the herbs, those microorganisms will go to town on your oils as though they're a smorgasboard on Labor Day. Make sure your hands are clean and dry, and ensure that your plants have been dried or dehydrated thoroughly. If you can pinch the leaves between your fingers and you hear a satisfying "crunch" then you have dried it enough.

Oils are so much more than the molecular opposite to potions. Oils to me have so much more glamour, and frankly I find them the right tool to use far more often than I do potions. Oils rarely go bad (though they can) because the oil itself can act as a preservative; their scent lasts longer than that of a potion and can be diluted easily to attain the appropriate amount of subtlety. Oils, being of a thicker molecular structure, also carry magical charges much more aptly than potions. This makes them useful for long-running spells such as home warding or for quicker, stronger "charges" of effect.

Common uses of oils include bath additives, perfumes, anointing rubs for candles and other magical objects, and as invisible inks to trace symbols. They can be used like potions, but have a more lasting effect and a more insistent presence.

Oil offerings have a long rich history, from the anointing of kings to use as preservatives when preparing bodies. While waters and potions recycle quickly into the stream of ocean and cloud, oils last and must degrade with the earth. Oils are the anchor in the changes that spells effect, while waters are the flow and change.

An Offering to Hecate

Hecate is the quintessential Witches' goddess, keeper of the keys to Olympus, guardian of the crossroads, and the Crone (waning) phase of the Moon. During the weeks between fall and winter, soak some marigolds in olive oil—sneak out at the dark of night (*dark* dark, like 3 am dark) to a crossroads, and pour the oil as a libation on the north corner of the road.

An Offering to Kwan Yin

Blend together three parts jasmine, one part myrrh, and one part amber in a light oil base, such as safflower oil. Put a few drops in an oil burner and say a quiet prayer to Kwan Yin for peace in your home.

Banishing

Infuse together lilacs, Solomon Seal, and a drop of myrrh in a safflower base. Rub this on a black or white candle to take something out of your life, such as a persistent illness or a general feeling of malaise.

Practical Magic: Moon Lore

by Lily Gardner

Over the centuries, every culture has worshipped the Moon, our Lady of the Night. By closely observing her phases, our ancestors have planted crops, predicted storms and fair weather, noted when livestock thrived and when they perished, and determined which days were propitious or ill-fated. These old beliefs were discounted initially by the Christians and later by the children of the Industrial Age, but more and more, science is validating ancient lore.

The Moon influences the element of water. The link between the Moon and tides has been known for centuries. Tides follow the same cycle as the Moon—twenty-four hours and fifty minutes—and are strongest during the New and Full Moons. Together with the oceans, the level of water rises and falls in this same tidal rhythm in lakes and rivers. And there is a verifiable link between the Moon and rainfall. Lunar gardeners understand that the Moon's gravitational pull on the tides affects plant growth. Because not only plants but all living beings are mostly water, the Moon influences us as well. Animal cycles of mating, birth, and migration are tied to the Moon, and statisticians have noted changes in human emotional behavior during the Full Moon. By having a general knowledge of Moon lore, we can align ourselves with lunar energies for a more magical life.

The Dark Moon

Disappearing from our sight, the Moon is invisible to us because it rises and sets with the Sun. Our ancestors feared this absence of the Moon and considered it a time for evil deeds.

No Moon, No Man

The old wisdom circled around the belief that the three days of the Dark Moon were perilous. Many people carried a rabbit totem (rabbits being a lunar animal) to protect themselves.

Even with the benefit of artificial light, we still see this dark transition as a time of mystery. The Dark Moon is a period of rest and gestation. Because the Moon and Sun are in the same sign, the

New Moon is an excellent time for making prayers and wishes, for throwing a tarot spread, and for meditation.

The Waxing Moon

The lunar period between the New Moon and the Full is called the waxing Moon. The waxing crescent Moon rises in the east with the Sun and can be seen as a thin sliver in the western sky as it sets. In ancient lore, the young crescent was often called the New Moon and even in modern times its sighting continues to be a joyous event. Think of the New Moon as a seed ripening to fullness. It is a time of great creativity—and the root word for "create" is the same as for "crescent." It is a time to begin new projects, start a business, or begin a self-improvement program.

> *O Lady Moon, your horns*
> *Point to the east*
> *Shine, be increased.*

Money and knowledge spells are most effective during this period. Upon seeing the New Moon, bow to her and turn over all your silver coins to bring luck in all your affairs. Another Moon charm cautions the seeker to remain silent when making the wish to insure its success. An ancient blessing said at the time of the New Moon crescent is:

> *I see the Moon,*
> *And the Moon sees me.*
> *Luna bless the Moon*
> *And Luna bless me.*

Another common practice for luck and prosperity is to bow or curtsey to the crescent New Moon. If all is going well in your life, bow to the crescent Moon and say:

> *O Moon, leave us as well as you found us.*

The best time to get married or to move to new housing is during the waxing Moon.

View the crescent Moon over the right shoulder for luck, and if you see a star near the crescent it means good fortune. When a crescent New Moon rises on a Monday (Moon-day), it's a sign of good weather and good luck. And if, in spring, a crescent Moon

hangs like a cradle in the sky, the summer will be dry.

Love spells are best done during a waxing Moon. I find charms that have been practiced for centuries especially powerful. Not only are we aligning ourselves with the rhythms of the skies, but we are stepping in our ancestors' footprints. These three charms go back before Shakespeare's time. As such, they assume the seeker is a woman and, of course, they're preoccupied with marriage. It seems perfectly reasonable to me to change the sex of the seeker or to simply inquire as to whether your new lover is sincere.

Braid your hair or a cord while saying:

I braid this knot, this knot I braid,
To know the thing I know not yet
That while I sleep I plain may see
The woman (man) that shall my wife (husband) be.

Another age-old method of divining your future love-life is to pick yarrow by the light of the New Moon crescent. Place it under your pillow and say:

Good night fair yarrow
Thrice good night to thee.
I hope before tomorrow's dawn
My true love I shall see.

New Moon dreams are further defined in this ancient charm:

New Moon, true Moon, tell unto me
If [name], my true love, he will marry me.
If he marry me in haste
Let me see his bonny face.
If he marry me betide
Let me see his bonny side
If he will not marry me
Turn his back and walk away.

If you want your hair to grow quickly and luxuriantly, cut it during the first quarter Moon. And what Witch would be without a good wart removal spell? Take a slice of apple in the light of the crescent New Moon. Rub it on the troublesome warts and say:

What I see is growing.
What I rub is going.

Bury the apple. As it rots in the earth, your warts should disappear.

If your focus is more agricultural, remember to prune your fruit trees during a waxing Moon for good fruit yield. Shearing sheep, slaughtering pigs, and gelding animals are all done in the period of the waxing Moon. Mushrooms should only be harvested when the Moon is waxing. Plant annual flowers and vegetables that grow above ground during a waxing Moon.

Full Moon

The Full Moon rises at sunset. In every culture, since before written language, people have admired and worshipped the Full Moon. Just as the New Moon is the seed, the Full Moon is maturity. The Full Moon is the culmination of spells begun during the waxing Moon and a time to reaffirm projects begun at the New Moon. It is the best time to do magic because it brings great power to all workings. Bless your ritual water by having it soak up the light of a Full Moon. Rub mugwort over your crystal ball in the light of a Full Moon and its psychic powers will be increased.

Pray to the Moon when she is round,
Luck with you will then abound,
What you seek for shall be found
On the sea or solid ground.

Long ago, it was believed that too much time spent outdoors in the moonlight brought on madness. Our words "lunatic" and "loony" come from the same root word as "lunar," and although we realize how silly that belief was, it is true that more arsons, murders, and other acts of violence occur during Full Moons. Admissions to psychiatric hospitals increase.

Doctors report that they treat more people suffering from epileptic seizures and bleeding ulcers during the Full Moon. Statistics are beginning to verify the link between the Moon, water and our emotions. The Full Moon affects animals as well. Many species of animal mate or migrate during the Full Moon period. If the Full Moon is clear, the weather will be fair; if you see the man in the Moon, rain will follow; and if the Full Moon is ruddy in appearance, high winds are expected. On a metaphysical level, interpret fair weather as status quo, rain as a time of great creativity, and winds as change.

Harvest your seeds during a Full Moon. Some farmers claim that crops will come in a month earlier if planted during a Full Moon, but others insist that planting during a waxing Moon is more effective. In either case, they agree that the Full Moon gives all plants a boost in growth and water absorption. In times of drought, it's best to plant your vegetables closer to the Full Moon. Pick your tomatoes during a Full Moon and they will ripen most satisfactorily. Wine grapes retain the best flavor if they're harvested during a Full Moon.

Wishes come true on the Full Moon. The Gaelic word for fortune is "that which denotes a Full Moon." It is said that those born on a Full Moon will lead a lucky life.

The Full Moon is the heavenly mirror and as such all mirrors represent the Moon. Take a mirror that has been properly cleansed, or better yet, set aside for scrying purposes. Let the light of a Full Moon fall on its surface. Any vision you have will be connected with your future.

In the light of the first Full Moon of the year, say:

Moon, Moon, tell me
When my true love I shall see
What fine clothes am I to wear
How many children shall I bear?

At any time of the year, look over your right shoulder at the Full Moon. Take three steps backward. Say:

If I have a lover, let me dream of him tonight.
If I am to marry far, let me hear a bird cry.
If I am to marry near, let me hear a cow low.
If I am to marry never, let me hear a hammer knock.

It is considered bad luck to view a Full Moon through a pane of glass. It's also bad luck if the Full Moon rises on Christmas Day.

It's best not to boat down the path of Moonlight (called the Moon-line) but if you cross the Moon-line, make a wish. It will come true.

Waning Moon

The waning Moon rules between the Full Moon and the New Moon. The waning half Moon rises at midnight.

O Lady Moon, your horns point towards the west
Wane, be at rest.

When you want to banish old habits or negative energy, the best time to achieve your purpose is during the waning Moon. It is a wonderful time to begin a weight-loss program or to give up smoking. Finish your projects during the waning Moon.

Just as the waxing Moon is called the "right-handed Moon," the waning Moon is the "left-handed Moon." Cut your corns or bunions during this time and they won't come back. And the best time to have surgery is during the fourth-quarter waning Moon because your wounds will close more quickly.

Cutting and splitting wood is best done during a waning Moon. Vegetables should be harvested during a waning Moon, and canning and drying produce is best done at this time as well. Pick flowers and herbs during a waning Moon and they will last longer. The waning Moon is a great time to pull weeds.

Plant root crops, biennials, and perennials during this time. Always plant trees and saplings in the third-quarter waning Moon. The rule of thumb is that if your plants remain in the ground longer than one growing season, plant them during a waning Moon. This encourages good root growth. Strawberries do best when planted during the third quarter Moon.

Start your compost heap during a waning Moon and it will decompose more rapidly. Divide perennials, thin plants, and prune during a waning Moon.

Follow the rhythms of the waxing and waning Moon and make a point of observing its beauty as often as you can. I guarantee your life will be richer and will unfold with a grace that seems truly magical.